The Status of the Translation Profession in the European Union

Anthem European Studies

The **Anthem European Studies** series publishes rigorous and thorough works of scholarship and research on the subjects of European culture, history and politics. This series investigates Europe in its entirety, from European integration and public policy to European history, literature and culture. The series aims to broaden informed discussion and debate on European affairs by publishing texts with great intellectual resonance for both scholars and students.

Related Series
The Anthem-European Union Series
Anthem Studies in European Ideas and Identities
Anthem Series on Russian, East European and Eurasian Studies
Anthem Irish Studies

The Status of the Translation Profession in the European Union

Anthony Pym, François Grin, Claudio Sfreddo
and Andy L. J. Chan

Supplementary website:
http://isg.urv.es/publicity/isg/projects/2011_DGT/tst.html

Disclaimer: This report was funded by the European Commission's
Directorate-General for Translation. It nevertheless reflects the views of the
authors only, and the Commission cannot be held responsible for
the nature of use of the information contained herein.

ANTHEM PRESS
LONDON · NEW YORK · DELHI

Anthem Press
An imprint of Wimbledon Publishing Company
www.anthempress.com

This edition first published in UK and USA 2014
by ANTHEM PRESS
75–76 Blackfriars Road, London SE1 8HA, UK
or PO Box 9779, London SW19 7ZG, UK
and
244 Madison Ave #116, New York, NY 10016, USA

First published in hardback by Anthem Press in 2013

Source: European Commission, DG Translation, © European Union, 2014

The information and views set out in this book are those of the authors and do not necessarily reflect those of the European Commission.

All rights reserved. Without limiting the rights under copyright reserved above, no part of this publication may be reproduced, stored or introduced into a retrieval system, or transmitted, in any form or by any means (electronic, mechanical, photocopying, recording or otherwise), without the prior written permission of both the copyright owner and the above publisher of this book.

British Library Cataloguing-in-Publication Data
A catalogue record for this book is available from the British Library.

Library of Congress Cataloging-in-Publication Data
The Library of Congress has catalogued the hardcover edition as follows:
The status of the translation profession in the European Union / Anthony Pym, Francois Grin, Claudio Sfreddo and Andy L. J. Chan.
pages cm.
Includes bibliographical references.
ISBN 978-0-85728-126-5 (hardcover : alk. paper)
1. Translating services–European Union countries. 2. Translating and interpreting–European Union countries. I. Pym, Anthony, 1956– II. Grin, Francois. III. Sfreddo, Claudio. IV. Chan, Andy L. J.
P306.8.E85S73 2013
418'.02094–dc23
2013027443

ISBN-13: 978 1 78308 347 3 (Pbk)
ISBN-10: 1 78308 347 6 (Pbk)

European Union

EU ISBN: 978-92-79-28067-2
European Union catalogue number: HC-31-13-398-EN-C
Digital object identifier (DOI): 10.2782/64819

This title is also available as an ebook.

CONTENTS

GENERAL INTRODUCTION	vii
1. METHODOLOGICAL ISSUES	1
1.1. What Do We Mean by Status?	1
1.2. What Do We Mean by "Signalling" and "Asymmetric Information"?	5
1.3. What Do We Mean by "Certification", "Accreditation", and "Authorisation"?	5
1.4. Data-Gathering Methodology	6
2. RESULTS	9
2.1. What is the Status of Translators in Official Categorisations?	9
2.2. What is the Relative Status of Educational Qualifications and Training?	11
2.3. The Status of Translators of Official Documents	15
2.4. The Role of Translator Associations	24
3. CASE STUDIES	33
3.1. Germany	33
3.2. Romania	38
3.3. Slovenia	42
3.4. United Kingdom	45
3.5. Spain	49
3.6. United States	53
3.7. Canada	59
3.8. Australia	62
4. SOCIOLOGICAL MODELLING	69
4.1. Models of Professionalisation	69
4.2. The Changing Role of Translator Associations	74
4.3. A Majority of Women – So What?	75
4.4. A Profession of Part-Timers and Freelancers?	76
4.5. The Role of Employer Groups	80
4.6. Comparison between Translators and Computer Engineers as Emerging Professions	83

5. ECONOMIC MODELLING	89
5.1. Information on Rates of Pay	89
5.2. Estimations of Earning Equations	92
5.3. Asymmetric Information, Signalling, and Equilibrium on the Market for Translations	102
6. POLICY OPTIONS FOR ENHANCED SIGNALLING	109
6.1. Free Market or Controlled Entry?	109
6.2. One Signal or Many?	110
6.3. Signalling as a Commodity or a Service?	111
6.4. Modes of Possible Intervention	112
7. RECOMMENDATIONS	121
APPENDIX A. Translator Associations: Years of Foundation and Numbers of Members	123
APPENDIX B. Why There Are About 333,000 Professional Translators and Interpreters in the World	132
APPENDIX C. Online Translator–Client Contact Services: New Modes of Signalling Status	136
APPENDIX D. Types and Use of Economic Perspectives on Translation	139
APPENDIX E. Equilibrium on the Translation Market	150
NOTES	153
REFERENCES	169
ACKNOWLEDGEMENTS	177
NOTES ON THE RESEARCH TEAM	181

GENERAL INTRODUCTION

The status of translators is not to be confused with how well anyone translates. It concerns the *perception* of a translator's value – what people *think* a particular translator can do, and how well or badly the translator is assumed to do it.

Seen as such, the question of status is extremely important because, almost by definition, someone who needs a translator cannot judge objectively how well that translator performs. Translations are among the products and services, perhaps along with used cars and legal services, where the buyer does not have direct knowledge of what they are buying – they have to rely on what people say, or on what the translator looks like, or on the translator's academic qualifications, or their membership of professional associations, or their official certification. That is, status is created by a set of social signals, which come in many shapes and sizes. Without those signals, the users of translations would be involved in an endless process of trial-and-error, as can indeed happen when buying a used car or trusting a lawyer.

These days the question of status is of particular importance because, with a website and business model, virtually anyone can start certifying translators. It is not excessively hard to supply novice translators with the external trappings of a profession: an official stamp, a place in an official-looking list, perhaps letterhead paper or a corporate email address. In this report we give examples of how this is being done and how the process of status creation is entering a new online sphere. As some simple economic modelling will show, in a world where everyone can signal status, there is no longer any relative status to signal.

The bulk of this study then considers the more traditional signals of status. How much weight is put on academic qualifications? To what extent does membership of a professional association count? What happens in the field of sworn or authorised translation? What professional certification systems are in place? Which ones have a clear market value?

Our general finding is that most of the traditional status signals are failing, and that there is a general need for strengthened certification systems. At the same time, each country has a different approach to status, as does each segment of the profession, so there are many nuances to describe, and numerous stories to tell.

Chapter 1

METHODOLOGICAL ISSUES

1.1. What Do We Mean by Status?

The signalling of qualifications can be seen in the following recent developments, cited here as mere examples:

- The Global Translation Institute[1] is managed by Adriana Tassini from an office in Portland, Oregon (although it seems not to be registered with the Portland Revenue Bureau, which does not list it at the address given). It sponsors a Certified Translation Professional (CTP) Designation Program[2], managed by Adriana Tassini with a telephone number in Massachusetts. It links to free information on the translation industry and how to become a translator[3], all of which comprises some 40 short online articles by Adriana Tassini. Adriana Tassini describes herself as a "Harvard University Alumni Member with a background in international relations and translation work in São Paulo, Brazil and Boston, Massachusetts (USA)". She names no completed degrees. Her declared training team comprises 12 people, none of them with any formal training in translation. To become a Certified Translation Professional, you pay US$227 per language pair, study the learning materials (none of which is language-specific) and sit the online exam. It is not clear to what extent the exam tests language skills, but the programme offers certification in 22 language pairs, of which the training faculty are presented as being experts in five.
- The International Association of Professional Translators and Interpreters[4] was founded in Buenos Aires in 2009. It accepts members who 1) have a degree or diploma from "a recognized institution", or 2) have at least four years' experience as a translator or interpreter. No list of "recognized institutions" is offered. You can become a member for US$60 a year, which entitles you to use the association's logo and an email address with the association's domain, and benefit from discounts on industry publications, and inclusion in the association's online directory. The association lists its "Honorary members" as including Noam Chomsky, who has no professional training in translation but nevertheless retains considerable academic standing.

Such cases indicate how status can be given to translators. It seems that virtually anyone can pay US$227 to gain certification as a Translation Professional. A practising translator with four years' experience can become a member of the International Association and gain the other trappings of status: a logo, a professional email address, a public listing, and some apparent academic backing. Of course, you may not be able to translate very well, but neither of these organisations appears to be testing that.

Status, as seen in these examples, is not competence, expertise, the ability to render a service, the exercise of visibility or power, or a question of fair recompense. Status is here taken to be the set of social signals that create, first, the *presumption* of some kind of expertise, and second, the *presumed value* of that expertise. In an ideal world, we would be able to test the objective expertise of all translators, then rank and reward them accordingly. In the world we live in, however, most employers and users of translations have to rely on the various signals of status. They do so individually, when assessing the value of a particular translator, and also socially, when making assumptions about the relative value of translators as a professional group.[5]

From the perspective of the individual translator, status is something that must be acquired, in addition to actual translation skills. You should be able to translate, but you also need some way of signalling your skills to your clients or employers. In this sense, a degree or a certification becomes a commodity, something that can be bought, something that you need in order to set up shop as a professional translator. It should perhaps not be surprising to find "Certification" listed alongside Computer Aided Translation tools and a Database of Agencies as one of the things a translator might want to purchase online (Figure 1).

From the collective perspective, status concerns the various signals that rank a social group or profession with respect to others. This concerns several related kinds of value, beyond questions of objective competence or expertise:

– *Trustworthiness*: Since translating always concerns communication with another culture, and thus with people we do not know so well, the translators themselves are always open to mistrust: since they presumably speak the language of the other side, and they purport to know the culture of the other side, they could always be working in the interests of the other side. This millennial problem is partly handled by claims to fidelity or its technocratic surrogate equivalence: translators will always signal their loyalty to the cause of their client. In particularly closed cultures, trustworthiness is only properly signalled by the translator being born into one social group rather than the other, or even by the translator belonging to a family of hereditary professional translators (as in the case of the *Oranda tsuji* in Japan). In constitutionally regulated societies, translators may come from external or hybrid positions but might require authorisation by educational or judicial institutions. The translator's trustworthiness is thus ultimately signalled not by their birth, nor by their claims to neutral expertise, but by their having been accepted by state institutions.
– *Professional exclusion*: If some translators are to be trusted, then there must be others who are somehow less trustworthy. A profession is partly a discourse of concepts and values that signal precisely this exclusion: some translators are to be considered "professional", and others are not. This exclusion is particularly

Figure 1. The "L Store" webpage, showing Certification as a commodity (one is not surprised to find that all the links lead back to the "Global Translation Institute" and its certification product).[6]

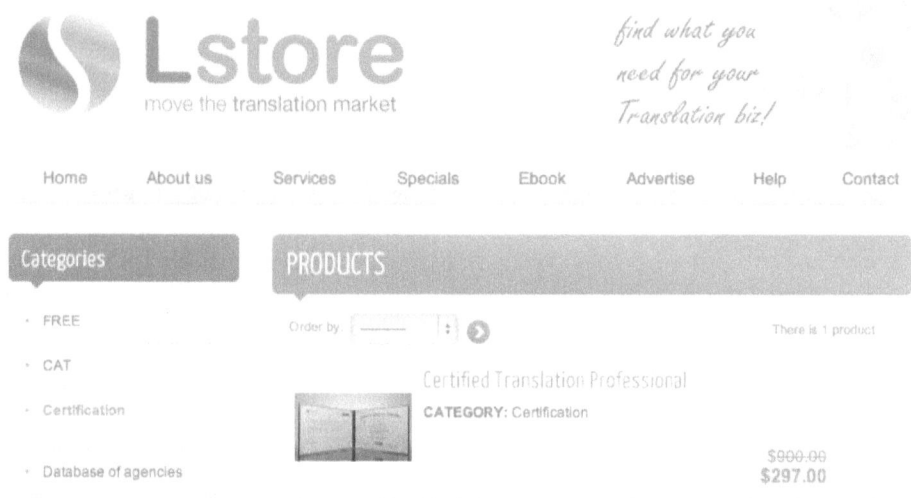

problematic in the field of translation because, as we have seen, virtually anyone can purchase the signals of a certain professional status. At the same time, there is a growing practice of volunteer translation, where people translate for fun or for "the good of the cause", without financial reward. The study of status must thus account for cases where some translators are accepted and others are excluded or are regarded as having status of a different kind. The mechanisms of this exclusion include professional examinations, certification systems, and membership of professional associations and societies.

– *Rates of pay*: In some societies, high social status normally correlates with high rates of pay for services rendered. A survey of pay scales must thus be an essential part of any survey of status. In this case, however, we seek to go beyond relative pay scales. This is partly because reliable information is hard to come by (see 5.1 below). But it is also because the financial economy is not always the one that counts most. For example, we know that literary translators are paid at below the minimum wage in most countries in Europe (Fock et al. 2008), yet many very intelligent and gifted people continue to translate literature. In many cases, the reason is that the activity brings them status in neighbouring fields, often as academics, in publishing institutions or as writers of literature. In other cases, literary translation ranks with the volunteer translating by activists, done for the "good of the cause". The status in such cases is cultural, symbolic and social, rather than strictly financial. But it is a socially valuable status nevertheless.

– *Recognition and prestige*: A general signal of status is the appearance of the translation profession in official documents like listings of economic activities, census records, and taxation systems. These constitute signals of recognised identity, not necessarily of prestige and rates of pay. Such recognition is the first step towards prestige, and the relative rankings can make a difference. For example, the category "Secretarial and translation activities" is reported as appearing in the "General Industrial Classification of Economic Activities within the European Communities" (2008),[7] whereas the current version lists "Translation and Interpretation" as a category in its own right.[8] This difference is seen as an improvement, not because it brings anyone more money, but because the recognition is more exclusive and official.

– *Authority*: When status is signalled, much depends on who has the authority to send the signal. Translators themselves generally do not have that authority, even when operating collectively in associations and the like. Individual or collective authority may be accrued from experience or longevity (if a translator or association has existed for a long time, they have presumably been able to earn trust on the market) and possibly from size (if there are many translators in an organisation, it might be a strong organisation). Alternatively, it can come from integration into state structures (which in turn offer both longevity and a certain size), as when translators are certified by legal institutions or various government ministries. This authorisation has the benefit of ensuring that trustworthiness is more on one side than the other – the translators are presumed to work in the interests of the instance that is authorising them. Increasingly, though, authorisation comes from educational institutions, which may be private or state. We thus recognise three broad sources of authority: experience (presumed to be survival on the market), state authorisation, and academic qualifications. The study of status must track the ways these three interact.[9]

If we now return to the "Global Translation Institute" and the Argentine "International Association of Professional Translators and Interpreters", we see that both work as remarkably efficient signallers of status. We have no evidence that the translators benefiting from these signals are in any way incompetent. However, it is not hard to see why the signals might not be wholly convincing. Neither organisation has more than three years of experience, so they have had little time to build up their own trustworthiness or prestige. Neither has any link to state structures, leaving them in an area where self-proclaimed "global" or "international" status might not carry much weight. In the absence of other authorities, both are thus forced to rely on academic qualifications of some kind: one makes a point of being a Harvard alumna (but lists no completed degree) and has a string of Internet publications, and the other accepts members on the basis of a degree or diploma from "a recognized institution" (naming no criteria for recognition) and lists leading academics as honorary members. In short, their main source of authority is a set of vague appeals to educational institutions and to the suggestion of academic status.

Of course, these two start-up signallers are tilting at significant alternative sources of authority. The "Global Translation Institute" is selling something that is also offered (much more expensively) by training programmes in about 300 university-level institutions worldwide, some with more than 50 years of experience, whereas the Argentine international association is proposing an alternative to the Fédération Internationale des Traducteurs, which was founded in 1954 by a French ministerial order, represents more than 100 professional associations (many with state status) and claims to speak for 88,103 translators.[10] In fact, in 2010 three of the founding members of the Argentine international organisation were expelled from the Argentine Association of Translators and Interpreters, ostensibly for founding an association with competing aims.[11]

The traditional granters of status are thus being challenged by new, parallel modes of signalling, and some of the traditional systems are responding to the challenge.

1.2. What Do We Mean by "Signalling" and "Asymmetric Information"?

The various signals of status will be modelled here in terms of sociology, information economics, education economics, and labour economics.

"Asymmetric information" describes the situation in which one party (the principal) has more or better information than the other (the agent). This concept was first applied to the labour and education markets (Spence 1973). In a job market, firms usually know less than workers do about workers' innate productivity. Some workers may wish to signal their ability to potential employers, and do so by choosing a level of education that distinguishes them from workers with lower productivity. Therefore, education is sometimes considered a "signal".

The concepts of "asymmetric information" and "signalling" can be applied to the translation market. Due to regionalisation and globalisation, an increasing number of clients need translation services. However, because of asymmetric information, translation service buyers cannot effectively determine the quality of a translator. This means that some good translators may not be paid what they deserve. When this happens, good translators will logically leave the translation market and take up other forms of academic activity, in a process known as "adverse selection". That may be what is happening in the translation market, particularly in segments where the signalling mechanisms are weak or outdated.

As discussed above, there are a number of signalling mechanisms in the translation market. They may concern the value of a translation, a company, an educational institution or an association. Here, though, our main focus will be on signals that represent the value of translators.

1.3. What Do We Mean by "Certification", "Accreditation", and "Authorisation"?

The many different kinds of signalling mechanisms go by many different names. Here we will adopt the terms established in this field by Jiri Stejskal, who carried out a series of studies on translator certification from 2001 to 2005.

For Stejskal (2003h), the general field of professional signals is known as "credentialing". Within this field, Stejskal distinguishes between the following (working from Knapp and Knapp 2002):

- Certification: A voluntary process by which an organisation grants recognition to an individual who has met certain predetermined qualification standards.
- Accreditation: A process by which an entity grants public recognition to an organisation such as a school, institute, college, programme, facility, or company that has met predetermined standards.
- Registration: A process by which the possession of specific credentials relevant to performing tasks and responsibilities within a given field is verified.
- Licensure: A mandatory credentialing process by which a government agency grants permission to persons to engage in a given occupation or profession by attesting that those licenced have attained the minimum degree of knowledge and skills required.

Here we are thus mostly concerned with certification and only occasionally with accreditation. As for "registration" and "licensure", the only field in which they concern our study is that of sworn translators. Here we shall also use two further terms:

- Authorisation: A mode of certification that grants not just recognition but also the power to act on behalf of the certifying institution. Translators who are "sworn" in the sense that they can say a translation is legally valid have thus been "authorised" to say this by a government agency.
- Revalidation: The procedure by which authorisation (or licensure) is reaffirmed after a given period, usually by a process of "registration" (in the sense given above).

These concepts are discussed further in 2.3.1 below.

1.4. Data-Gathering Methodology

Because of the ideological nature of status, which concerns beliefs more than objective skills, most of our methodology is more qualitative than quantitative. The main research methods used in this study are as follows:

- *Literature review*: Many of the data on status are available in surveys conducted in recent years. Our work has been to make those data speak to each other in such a way that they answer our questions about status.
- *Initial questionnaire*: In October 2011 a short initial questionnaire[12] was sent to all European translator associations affiliated with the Fédération Internationale des Traducteurs, as well as to translators and/or translation scholars in the countries covered by the project (most of whom are members of the European Society for Translation Studies). The questionnaire was designed to function as a first

contact only: it covers basic information on the status of government translators, sworn/authorised translators and translator associations. The questionnaire also has three "opinion" questions designed to help us position the informant with respect to the relative values of experience, professional associations, and academic qualifications. The responses to those questions have not been analysed in any quantitative way.
- *Follow-up exchanges*: For most cases, the initial questionnaire indicated the informants who were the most knowledgeable and open to further discussion. Further details were thus sought through follow-up email exchanges and online interviews. These exchanges concerned points where the various informants disagreed, or where the particular situation was not clear. In cases where the information was still contradictory or lacking in clarity, we have chosen to reproduce the statements presented to us.
- *Country factsheets*: The basic information from the questionnaire and follow-ups has been compiled in short factsheets on each country, which are available on the project website.[13]

The present report has been written on the basis of the literature review and the country factsheets, where the latter are regarded as checks and updates of the former. The data gathered from these sources are then fed into our sociological and economic models.

It should be noted that the field we are working on is changing even as the research progresses. This particularly concerns debates in the United Kingdom about a private company being employed to handle certification for the justice system, moves within the American Translators Association to enhance their certification programme, a new certification system on ProZ (see Appendix C), and discussions within TISAC[14] to set up a global body to accredit translation certification programmes. Our data-gathering, and indeed our analyses, have had to pay close attention to these changes.

Chapter 2
RESULTS

Here we summarise the results corresponding to the following questions: 1) the status of translators in the various census, taxation and job-description systems, 2) the relative status of academic qualifications and training, 3) the status of sworn or authorised translators, and 4) the role of professional associations.

These results are followed by a series of case studies, where the four questions are answered in terms of more or less unified national signalling systems.

2.1. What is the Status of Translators in Official Categorisations?

2.1.1. General classifications of economic activities

In the "Statistical Classification of Economic Activities in the European Community" (NACE)[1] we find "Translation and Interpretation" listed as a separate category (74.3), alongside "Specialised design activities", "Photographic activities" and "Other professional, scientific and technical activities".[2] This classification is picked up in some of the national listings (in Croatia, Poland, Portugal and the United Kingdom, for example) and in principle should apply throughout the European Union.

The International Labour Organization has an International Standard Classification of Occupations (ISCO-88)[3] in which translators and interpreters are categorised in major group 2 "professionals", sub-major group 24 "other professionals", minor group 244 "social science and related professionals" and unit group 2444 "philologists, translators and interpreters". This classification has been reported as being used in Austria.

There are, however, reports of other classification systems being used alongside the international ones. In Portugal, for example, the National Statistics Office uses the Código de Actividades Económicas (Code of Economic Activities), which corresponds to the NACE (category 74.3). At the same time, there is a Classificação Portuguesa das Profissões (2010), where translators are in Group 2643: "Philologists, translators, interpreters, and other linguists" (Ferreira-Alves 2011: 259). The Spanish public administration includes translators and interpreters in the category of "Técnico Superior de Gestión y Servicios Comunes" (Advanced Technician for Management and Common Services).[4]

Translators occasionally appear as a category in other kinds of lists. For example, in Norway, translators (along with authors) are mentioned in the regulations describing various types of employment contracts.[5] In the United Kingdom, we are told that "translator" appears in the drop-down menu when you search online for a house insurance quote.[6]

We have no reports of other major official categorisations of translators, other than those used for taxation purposes and social security systems, mentioned below.

2.1.2. Census categories and national statistics

Very few countries report a separate census category for translators. In fact, we have only found census data on translators in Canada and the United States, with reports on census data in Australia (these are three of the cases used in Appendix B to estimate the number of professional translators in the world). Inclusion in census data might nevertheless be a growing trend. In the United Kingdom, for example, translators and interpreters were first recognised in the national census in 2011.

Several countries report a specific category appearing in national statistics, primarily based on taxation data. In Norway, the national statistics distinguish between two categories: "Oversetter" ("Translator") and Fagoversetter ("Professional Translator"), where the latter appears to refer to graduates of a four-year degree programme that no longer exists.[7] In Portugal, the Ministério das Finanças (Ministry of Finance) has data on how many translators and interpreters are registered with the corresponding "Código de Actividades Económicas" ("Economic Activity Code", which corresponds to the NACE), but informants doubt that this represents the true extent of professional translation activity in the country.[8]

In Germany, translators are generally part of the *freie Berufe* (liberal professions). In the order regarding judicial fees, they are mentioned under *Sachverständige* (area experts).

More detailed information on the various categories can be found in the country factsheets on our project website.

2.1.3. Status in taxation systems

Most informants report that there is no special category for translators in the national taxation system. In most cases, translators must list themselves either in the general category of salaried workers or as "self-employed workers", where the latter group includes translators who receive royalty payments.

In Spain there is a special tax regime for self-employed workers, which explicitly includes "Translators and Interpreters" (Group 774 of the Régimen de Trabajadores Autónomos). This system enables freelancers to be covered by the social security system (for which they have to pay each month).

Greek taxation law considers translators and interpreters as service-providers, similar to doctors, lawyers, poets, writers, and artists. There is a specific "tax code" for translators, interpreters and editors but it is up to the freelancer to include one or all three professions when they register.

2.1.4. Status in social security systems

The status of translators in the various social security systems tends to derive directly from their categorisation (or non-categorisation) in the taxation systems.

In general, freelancers are categorised along with all other self-employed workers; salaried translators have coverage corresponding to the nature of their contract and terms of employment (not specifically as translators). In Greece, for example, the Social Insurance Institute (IKA) groups in-house translators along with desk clerks and administrative personnel, without a specific mention. Freelancers have to register with the Insurance Organisation for the Self-Employed (OAEE).

2.1.5. Special status for literary translators

In most countries, translators who receive royalty payments are included in the category of "self-employed worker" for tax purposes, alongside all freelancers. In some countries, however, translators who are copyright holders (and are thus mostly literary translators) enjoy certain tax benefits.

In Austria, literary translators are eligible for health insurance support, provided by Literar Mechana, the Austrian association of copyright holders. They have a special fund to support copyright holders with low earnings.[9]

In Lithuania, the social security system for authors (including literary translators) is such that,

> freelancers pay the health and social security contributions on 50% of income (in total about 35%). For those who have official artist status (registered in the Ministry of Culture), literary translators included, the state will cover the other 50%. It also will provide minimal social and health insurance for freelance artists whose health and social security contributions do not cover the required minimum – if their income per month is less than 800 Lt (232 euros).[10]

In Poland, authors of published translations are entitled to deduct 50 per cent of their royalties before taxes.[11]

In Slovenia, translators who have the status of "self-employed workers in culture" have all social insurance paid by the state if they can prove that they have limited income (e.g. they can have this status in 2011 if they earned less than 21,605 euros gross in 2010).[12]

In Spain, literary translations are exempt from VAT.

2.2. What is the Relative Status of Educational Qualifications and Training?

What is the specific legal status of educational qualifications when translators are recruited or hired? Here we are not concerned with the broader question of how much subjective value various people attach to educational qualifications – our concern is whether such qualifications are strictly necessary.

2.2.1. Qualifications required to work as a translator

In no country that we have surveyed is any academic qualification – or indeed any kind of formal qualification at all – required in order to use the term "translator" or its equivalent *generic* terms. Almost anyone at all can be called a "translator". More technically, the general title of "translator" is virtually unprotected.

There are, however, some exceptions. In Denmark, a distinction is made between the generic term *oversætter*, the traditional translator, and *translatør*, the authorised translator, denoting a status that is indeed officially protected. Similar terms and distinctions are found in Norway and Sweden.

A more generalised exception, without the use of two separate terms, is in the field of sworn or authorised translation, where different countries have different ways of protecting who can translate. We will explore this in more detail below. We should note, however, that even in this sub-field there is no complete protection of the title; the age of immigration has created a demand for many language combinations for which no training or certification is available, and in those particular combinations, virtually anyone can still translate.

A more concerted exception would appear to be Slovakia, where Appendix 2 of the Trades Licensing Act No. 455/1991 was amended in 2007 so that translation, interpreting and teaching became licenced trades. This means that in order to present an invoice for a translation, the translator needs to be professionally qualified as a translator, with a degree either in Translation and Interpreting or in the languages concerned. There are, however, several ways of getting around this, and we would hesitate to claim that this constitutes complete protection of a professional title.[13]

Other moves have been made to protect the title of "translator". In 2009 the *Ordre des traducteurs, terminologues et interprètes agréés du Québec* made an attempt to ensure that only members of the Ordre could call themselves translators in Québec.[14] The move did not meet with success, but the existence of such an attempt is of interest in itself. Why should the Ordre, which was founded in 1940, have waited 59 years to seek protection? The timing would appear to indicate recent discontent among professionals, possibly related to electronic translation aids and new ways of signalling status.

2.2.2. Recruitment of translators by intergovernmental institutions

Even if there is no general protection of the title of translator, is some kind of implicit protection operative in the way official institutions find and employ translators?

To become a translator within the European Commission's Directorate-General for Translation, the candidate has to be successful in an open competition that can last between five and nine months. Candidates must have two foreign languages and "a university degree, not necessarily in languages".[15] Candidates do not require a degree or diploma in translation.[16]

Non-requirement of a degree or diploma in translation seems to be the accepted practice for most intergovernmental organisations. A study conducted among IAMLADP[17] member organisations in 2008–09, with replies from the European

Commission DGT, IAEA, ICC, ICRC, ILO, ITU, OECD, UN (ESCWA, UNHQ, UNOG and UNOV), World Bank, WIPO and WTO, reports as follows:

> The findings on admission criteria for examinations and tests show a universal requirement for a first-level university degree but not for a specific translation qualification, which is required by relatively few organizations but seen by many as an asset. Experience appears to be a lesser requirement for the larger organizations, where admission at entry level depends on success in the examination, experience being recognized in the grade or step awarded. All organizations test for translation into and not out of the mother tongue (or main language), and testing précis-writing in an examination appears to be confined to the UN in this respondent group. Most organizations test ability to translate out of at least two languages and other expertise is occasionally an alternative to a second source language. (IAMLADP 2009: 79)[18,19]

With respect to academic qualifications, the only clear exception seems to be the OECD, for which "candidates are required to hold a first degree in either languages or other specialization and a masters' degree/diploma in translation" (88).

The IAMLADP documents indicate that there is support for trying to recruit translators from among students in other fields (law, economics, and international relations). According to Lafeber, "many heads of service believe, based on experience [with recruits who have passed demanding entrance exams], that people with degrees in subjects other than languages often make better translators." However, "only students on Master's courses in translation or interpreting get internships or work experience, which can be a passport into a job at many organizations."[20]

Surprisingly, the eligibility requirements for employment as a translator at the International Criminal Court (Court Interpretation and Translation Section and Office of the Prosecutor, Language Services Unit) do not make any reference to the need to be a sworn, authorised or otherwise certified translator (IAMLADP 2009: 85).

2.2.3. Recruitment of translators by national governments

Few national governments indicate special *sine qua non* requirements for the employment of government translators, at least outside of the various justice systems for which sworn translators or certified translations are required.[21]

In many cases, a university degree in translation is reported as being required, but further research suggests that this is not the case in a strictly legal sense. For example, the German government is reported as requiring the degree of *Diplom-Übersetzer* (and more recently a Master's in Translation) as a minimum requirement, but this is a question of standard practice, not of any law. Or again, a Master's degree in Translation is said to be necessary in Hungary, but there is doubt as to whether this requirement is always respected by the various ministries and it is clear that the requirement is not respected for some of the smaller or exotic languages for which there are few translators available. In Spain, a detailed survey of 136 translators in the public administration shows that they work at many different administrative levels, and with different entry requirements, often a four-year or five-year university degree (*Licenciatura*) but not necessarily in translation.[22]

A notable exception is Greece, where there have been changes in this respect. Until recently, calls for translator posts in the public sector, published in the National Gazette, asked for candidates with a degree from secondary-level education (ΔΕ), i.e. an "Apolytirion" from a Lyceum. Following legal action from members of the Panhellenic Association of Professional Translators Graduates of the Ionian University (ΠΕΕΜΠΙΠ), recent calls ask for candidates with tertiary-level education (ΠΕ). This description includes 1) graduates of the School for Modern Languages, Translation and Interpreting, Ionian University at Corfu, and 2) graduates from universities abroad who hold a university degree in translation recognised by the National Academic Recognition Information Centre (Hellenic NARIC, ΔΟΑΤΑΠ). This is a case where an association attached to a particular translation school has been able to ensure that a translation degree is required in order to work as a translator for the government. Nevertheless, the Hellenic Armed Forces require a university degree in translation *or foreign languages* from candidates for their permanent translation posts (Law 2913/2011, Presidential Decree 300/2002).[23]

Outside of Greece, we have found no situation where government translators strictly require a university degree in translation. And even in Greece, the current situation seems to be a result of direct pressure from the Panhellenic Association of Professional Translators Graduates of the Ionian University, rather than a requirement enshrined in law.

2.2.4. Recruitment of translators by translation companies

Quality Standard EN15038 (2006) applies to translation companies, not to translators as such. It basically seeks to regulate the quality of translations by stipulating the workflow by which translations are produced. With respect to ensuring quality by controlling the status of translators, here is what it says:

> The above competences should be acquired through one or more of the following: 1) a formal higher education in translation (recognised degree); 2) an equivalent qualification in any other subject plus a minimum of two years of documented experience in translating; 3) at least five years of documented professional experience in translating. (2006: 7)

A degree in translation might thus be seen as the rough equivalent of five years of professional experience. It is perhaps gratifying to see that study is considered to have the same status as work in industry. However, this trade-off might be cold comfort to people who have spent five years paying to study for a BA then a Master's degree, when they could have been working and earning money for the same period of time.[24]

2.3. The Status of Translators of Official Documents

The translation of "official documents" (to borrow the general term used in Mayoral 2003) constitutes the one field where translators generally do require a strong official signal of their status. It is thus worthy of particular attention here.

This field involves two activities, which are frequently mixed. On the one hand, "certified translations" are official documents that are in some way accompanied by signals of the authority of the translator; they may be required by any official institution, for whatever reason (academic enrolments, applications for visa, passports, etc.); the translator may be a "sworn" or "authorised" translator. On the other hand, translators are sometimes required to work for the various justice systems, where they may be called "legal translators", since they deal with documents of a legal nature.

Since legal translators are usually qualified in the same way as the sworn or authorised translators who produce certified translations, here we shall regard "legal translator" as a specific instance of the wider category of "sworn translator".

Here our focus must be on the wider category, i.e. the general question of who has the authority to certify translations of official documents. It is nevertheless within the various justice systems, where legal translators work, that the issues have received most attention in recent years. The new attention is largely due to the important issue of equal access to justice, which becomes problematic in immigrant societies where non-traditional languages have to be translated.

We will thus briefly consider the status of legal translators, and then look at the wider question of how status is constructed for sworn or authorised translators.

2.3.1. Previous research on legal translators

Directive 2010/64/EU[25] seeks to ensure access to quality translation and interpreting in criminal proceedings. However, it has very little to say about who is qualified to translate: "In order to promote the adequacy of interpretation and translation and efficient access thereto, Member States shall endeavour to establish a register or registers of independent translators and interpreters who are appropriately qualified" (5/2). The directive does not refer to any signal of what "appropriately qualified" may mean, although it would appear to explain why some countries have been paying attention to their lists of translators.

Information on translation and interpreting in the justice systems can be found in the various research projects led by Professor Erik Hertog in Antwerp (see Hertog ed. 2001, 2003; Keijzer-Lambooy and Gasille, eds 2005; Hertog and van Gucht eds 2008). Reports on those projects are now available through EULITA (the European Legal Interpreters and Translators Association), founded in 2009.[26] For all specific questions on legal translators and access to justice, we refer to EULITA.

Within this frame, a major survey reported as *Status Quaestionis* (Hertog and van Gucht eds 2008) was carried out in all EU countries except Luxembourg. It asked a wide range of questions concerning the use of translators and interpreters in criminal proceedings. Information came from 194 respondents, of which 18 were from government sources. The report intriguingly maps the differences between responses by "government sources" and those by "professional sources" – official claims often do not correspond to lived realities, and the professionals are sometimes not aware of the official regulations and instruments. The report also gives scores to the various countries for how well they are reported as performing on the many points involved.

Some of the questions asked are of direct interest for the present study:

1. Is the title of legal translator protected?
2. Is the profession of legal translator regulated?
3. Is there an official body for the accreditation of legal translators?
4. Is there a national register of legal translators?
5. If there is a national register, what data is provided in the register?
6. Is there a national or regional Code of Conduct for legal translators in your country?
7. Is there a disciplinary procedures system in relation to legal translators in your country?

An overview of the way these questions were answered is reproduced in Figure 2, which shows scores based on responses by professionals (government sources were missing for many countries in this case). The map basically indicates a central body of countries that score average or above average for the way they regulate the profession of legal translator, with a periphery of countries (Ireland, Portugal, Greece, but also Belgium) that have below-average scores.

We note that the *Status Quaestionis* survey did not ask what qualifications are required to become a "legal translator", and that the concept of "legal translator" does not correspond to the concept of "sworn or authorised translator", which is what we are mainly interested in investigating here. The report is nevertheless a valuable point of reference.

2.3.2. What is the difference between "sworn", "authorised", and "legal" translation?

When translators put their stamp or signature on a translation, they are in fact taking an oath that the translation is true, as indeed may be indicated in a text added to the actual translation. Anyone at all can make such an oath. Status, however, requires that some signal be given about who has the authority to back up the oath.

There are at least three basic forms that the signal can take:

1. *Certified translations*: In some countries, the justice system does not require translations to be done by a specially qualified person; instead, it requires that the translations, as documents, be certified (stamped and signed as being true) by a notary or similarly qualified legal professional. The notary may require to see the qualifications of the translator, and the translator's status may be signalled in some way on the translation (via a stamp, mention of academic qualifications

Figure 2. Degree of regulation of the profession of legal translator in EU Member States, according to professional sources (adapted from Hertog and van Gucht eds 2008: 142). Colour codes represent the degree to which the highest standards are found (30 per cent as lowest in sample, 70 per cent as highest).

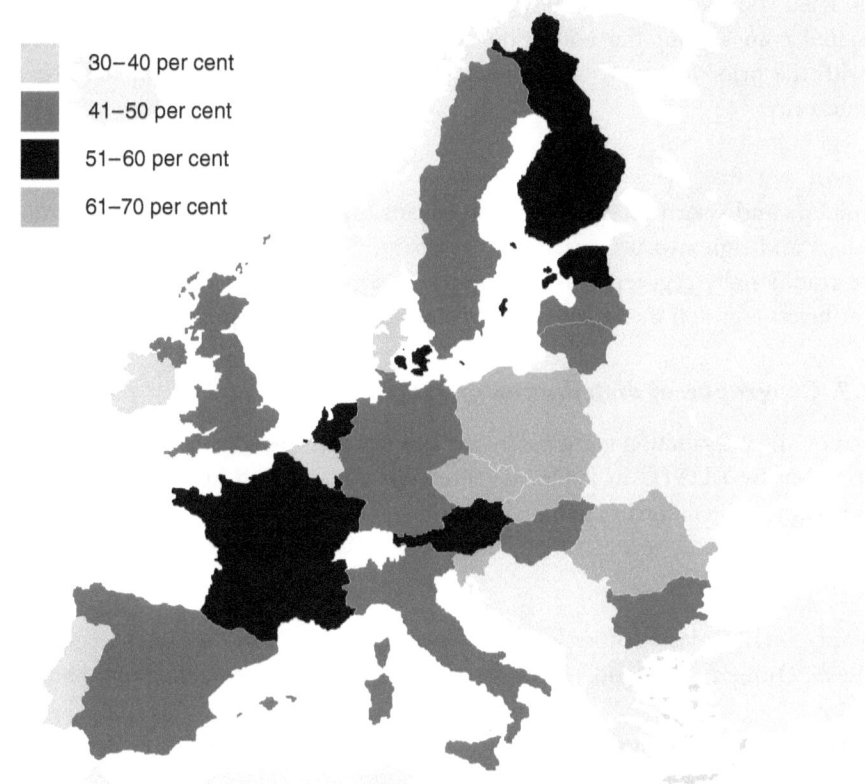

or membership of an association), but the only formal requirement is that the translation be certified by a notary or a qualified official.[27] In some cases (e.g. Turkey) translators swear to the notary that their translations are true, and they thus technically become "sworn translators". In all these cases, the authority behind the oath is that of the legal official, not the translator.

2. *Sworn or state authorised sworn translators*: In other systems, the state administrative institutions, at one level or another, test translators in some way, qualify the successful candidates as "sworn" or "authorised" translators in some way, and ideally maintain an official register of the sworn translators, as required by Directive 2010/64/EU. Only those translators may produce legally valid ("sworn") translations, without any intervention by a notary. In Europe we find the terms "sworn" and "state authorised" being used in much the same way, so here we will adopt them as synonyms describing this general category. In this system, the authority of the signal derives from the government institution (usually the Ministry of Justice or of Foreign Affairs) that administers the selection process. The authority is that of the state.

3. *Academically authorised sworn translators*: In some systems, translators can become "sworn" or "authorised", and recognised by the state as such, on the basis of their educational qualifications, without further tests or exams. This is usually on condition that the candidate's degree is in translation and includes courses in legal translation and/or legal systems. In this case, the authority behind the signal comes from the education system in the first instance, usually acting with the prior approval of the justice system (and thus exercising a delegated authority).

In most systems, there is no functionally operative distinction between sworn translators and sworn interpreters. This means that sworn interpreters can usually produce and sign sworn translations. In Spain, for example, all sworn translators were traditionally registered as interpreters (*intérpretes jurados*) until 2009. We shall nevertheless focus on the act of written translation wherever possible.

2.3.3. Geographical distribution of systems

Based on the information gathered in our country factsheets and on a similar survey carried out by EUATC in 2009, the three systems outlined above would seem to correspond to the following national situations:

2.3.3.1. Certified translations

Reliance on notaries or other legal professionals is basically the system in Cyprus, Greece, Hungary, Ireland, Italy, Latvia, Lithuania, Portugal, Romania, and Turkey.

In Ireland, there are no sworn translators as such, but the authorities nevertheless insist that translations carry the translator's stamp.

In Hungary, the only institution able to certify translations is a government agency, the National Office for Translation and Attestation (OFFI).

In the United Kingdom, there is traditionally no body of sworn translators as such, but translators can certify that their translation is true.[28] However, the situation is currently in flux. In 2011, the Ministry of Justice contracted the private company Applied Language Solutions for language services, and "linguists" are invited to register with the Ministry through the company (see 3.4.5 below).[29]

2.3.3.2. Sworn or state-authorised translators

In some countries, the granting of "sworn" or "authorised" status to translators is carried out by local or regional courts (as in Austria, Belgium, Croatia, Czech Republic, France, and Germany), although there may also be a national register of sworn translators (as in Austria).

In Germany, the system (and the nomenclature) is determined within each *Land*.

In Switzerland, the conditions under which sworn translators are required appear to depend on each canton.

In other countries, authorisation is by the Ministry of Justice (Czech Republic, Estonia, Poland, Slovakia, Slovenia, Romania), the Ministry of Foreign Affairs (Malta, Spain) or a specialised government agency (Denmark, Sweden).

In Finland, one can become an authorised translator ("auktorisoitu kääntäjä") either by passing an exam organised by the Authorised Translators' Board or by completing a degree in Translation and Interpreting with specific courses in authorised translation. The exam is organised by the Authorised Translators' Board under the auspices of the National Board of Education.

In Norway, the Norwegian School of Economics (NHH) organises the exam to become a *statsautorisert translator*.

In Bulgaria, the translation *companies* must be accredited by the Ministry of Foreign Affairs, and when doing this they have to present a list of their translators and their qualifications. The companies then certify the translations (EUATC 2009).

2.3.3.3. Academically authorised sworn translators

In Luxembourg, anyone can be registered as a sworn translator if they have a degree in languages and at least five years' professional experience as a translator/interpreter or language teacher.[30]

In Romania, anyone with a degree in languages can be registered as a "traduc tor autorizat", as can even secondary-education graduates of bilingual high schools (especially applicable for minority languages).

In Spain, one can become a sworn translator/interpreter (*traductor/intérprete jurado*) either by passing an exam organised by the Ministry of Foreign Affairs or by completing a degree in translation and interpreting with specific courses in legal translation. The justice system may nevertheless use translators who have no training at all.[31]

In Austria, a degree in translation reduces the amount of experience one has to have in order to be accepted as a Certified Court Interpreter.[32]

In Poland prior to 2004, sworn translators/interpreters (the one person is required to carry out both functions) were registered at regional courts. Since 2004, they are certified by the Ministry of Justice on the basis of an examination. Candidates for the examination must have a Master's degree in any area. Prior to 2011, the Master's degree had to be in languages, or combined with a postgraduate degree in translation.[33]

We have contradictory information from Greece. On the one hand, we are told that the 2008 Kassimis law is designed to set up a body of sworn translators and interpreters, but that the law remains inactive. On the other hand, the website of the Association of Professional Translators Graduates of the Ionian University states: "In accordance with the Presidential Decree 169 of 17.06.2002 (Official Gazette 156/2.7.02), the graduate translators of the Ionian University are considered certified translators having the right to make official translations for the public and private authorities in Greece and abroad."[34] It is not entirely clear what the term "certified" means here.

Figure 3. Geographic distribution of systems for certified translations, sworn or authorised translators, and the possibility of becoming an authorised/sworn translator on the basis of academic qualifications (with other options being available). None of these systems seems entirely operative in the United Kingdom.

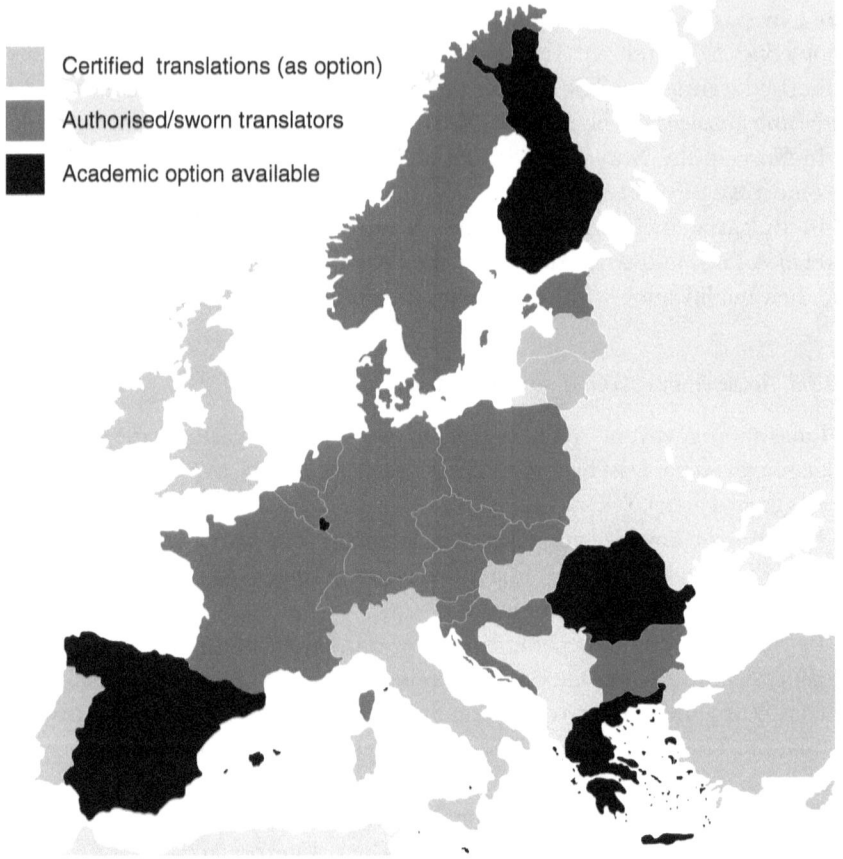

We have found no case where the only way to become a sworn translator is on the basis of academic degrees alone. The closest situation appears to be Denmark, where candidates require a Master's in Translation from Aarhus University or Copenhagen Business School, but candidates for language pairs not taught at those institutions can still sit the exam without having a degree in translation.[35]

The geographical distribution of these three systems is indicated in Figure 3.

When this map is compared with the map for "regulation of the profession of legal translator" (Figure 2), a similar pattern appears: the core system of sworn or state authorised translators corresponds to fairly good regulation of legal translators, and that core is surrounded by a periphery of countries where the certified translations system corresponds to weaker regulation of legal translators.

Note that these distinctions do not correspond exactly to the general distinction between Common Law and Statutory Law countries. This should suggest that the differences are not necessarily embedded in immutable cultural preferences.

The above comparison should raise questions with respect to cases like Romania, where the Ministry of Justice lists 32,856 "certified translators and interpreters" (since anyone with a degree in languages can qualify), in a country where the main translator association has just 112 members, and yet the "protection of the profession of legal translator" is apparently above average.[36] Part of the problem in such cases could be that we are accepting the information given by the people who have obtained protection, of whatever kind, thanks to the system they are reporting on.

2.3.4. Revalidation of authorisation

The status of sworn or state-authorised translator is usually for life, although some countries (Croatia, Sweden and Finland) require periodical revalidation on the basis of work done or continuing education.

There is a growing tendency towards revalidation systems, which goes hand in hand with the growing awareness of the need for life-long learning.

2.3.5. Numbers of authorised or sworn translators

In Romania, as mentioned, the Ministry of Justice lists 32,856 "certified translators and interpreters". At first blush, this high figure does not appear entirely exceptional. In Germany, for instance, there are 21,516 names listed in the national registry of sworn translators and interpreters;[37] in Poland the Ministry of Justice lists about 10,500 sworn translators; in Spain the registry of the Ministry of Foreign Affairs and Cooperation includes at least 4,164 sworn translators; in the Czech Republic there are 3,386 translators and interpreters registered with the Ministry of Justice.[38]

However, when these numbers are calculated as percentages of the potential demand for professional translators and interpreters for each country (Table 1), the figure for Spain means that the number of sworn translator/interpreters there could be about 60 per cent of the potential number of professional translators in all fields, whereas the number for Romania is about 25 times the potential for professionals, and in several other countries the number of authorisations similarly exceeds the

Table 1. Sample of numbers of sworn translators/interpreters, numbers of potential professional translators/interpreters, and the percentage of the actual supply with respect to the potential demand.[39]

Country	Sworn T/Is	Potential demand for T/Is	Percentage of sworn T/Is
Romania	32,856	1,299	2529
Germany	21,516	14,219	151
Poland	10,500	3,330	315
Czech Republic	3,385	1,299	260
Spain	4,164	6,960	60

potential for professionals. This should raise serious questions about our estimates of potential demand, which are at best rough rules of thumb (see Appendix B). There are, however, reasons why the lists of translators could exceed the market demand.

In particular, we should note that the concept of "potential demand" depends very much on language combinations. In Poland, for example, where the figure of 10,500 authorised translators seems more than three times the total demand, there are very few sworn translators for Chinese (only 10 are listed), Greek (8), Finnish (6), Korean (5), Latvian (4), Hindi (2), Albanian (3), Armenian (1), or Georgian (1), and none for Estonian, Mongolian, Azerbaijani and Somali.[40] For as long as Poland maintains an eastern border of the European Union, its security force and legal services have to handle the numerous languages involved in cases of illegal border crossing, illegal stay, absence of work permits, or smuggling. So the demands cannot be calculated in terms of an abstract global figure.

2.3.6. Cross-country recognition

There is little consistency with respect to cross-country recognition of these signalling systems. In Spain, for example, translators who are qualified as sworn translators in another EU country are recognised as having the same status for work in Spain (so all those qualified for Spanish on the very long Romanian list can theoretically work as sworn translators in Spain).[41] In Germany, on the other hand, qualification as a sworn translator in one *Land* may not be automatically recognised in another,[42] although the sworn *translations* are indeed recognised.

From ongoing research by Josep Peñarroja i Fa (2012) it seems that Spain is the only European country that recognises the professional qualifications of sworn translators and interpreters from other European countries.[43] Peñarroja's case was brought to the Cour de cassation in France and received a preliminary ruling by the European Court on 17 March 2011. According to this preliminary ruling, among other reasons, "[t]he duties of court expert translators, as discharged by experts enrolled in a register such as the national register of court experts maintained by the Cour de cassation, are not covered by the definition of 'regulated profession' set out in Article 3(1)(a) of Directive 2005/36/EC of the European Parliament and of the Council of 7 September 2005 on the recognition of professional qualifications."[44] This ruling in effect means that sworn translators, who would seem to be the most legally protected segment of the translation profession, cannot benefit from European legislation on the cross-country recognition of professional qualifications. As it happens, Peñarroja's case has been successful with respect to the Cour de cassation (personal communication, 20 April 2012), so a small window may have been opened for European recognition of the status of sworn translator (see 3.5.5 and 6.4.2 below).

The situation is a little more complicated with respect to the circulation of *translations*, rather than translators. In Germany, as we noted, sworn translations done in one *Land* are considered valid in all. However, serious problems can arise when official documents cross national boundaries and have to be translated. Most embassies keep lists of translators who are authorised in accordance with their country's system and who are available for work in the foreign country. Note that the authorisation has to be according to the system used in the country that is *receiving* the translation, since they are the ones who have to recognise the authority. So the Bulgarian embassy in London, for example, keeps a list of translators "authorised to perform translations on its behalf",[45] but they are theoretically for translations that are going to be used in Bulgaria. Then again, since the British system is based on certified translations, those translators also have the right to produce translations in the United Kingdom, with whatever affidavit might be necessary.

The difficulties are exemplified by a query posted to ProZ:

> I have done a translation (FR>EN) of a diploma from a Belgium university and now the client asks for it to be sworn. I am English and live in England, client is Belgian living in Belgium (I guess), and I got the work via a Swedish agency. Needless to say I do not know the client.[46]

The answer is probably that the translator should have been registered as a sworn translator by the court in the Belgian city where the diploma was issued. But the important point is that, at present, neither the translator nor the client has any idea of the answer – the cross-country signalling mechanism is very weak.

In a world of professional mobility, the absence of cross-country recognition can effectively counter the establishment of protected titles in particular countries. Dam and Zethsen (2010: 201) cite the view that the Danish authorisation process is "undermined by the fact that the title of translator (*translatør*) is an unprotected title abroad". It is no longer sufficient to seek status on the national level alone.

2.3.7. The value of educational qualifications for sworn translators

In none of the countries covered by this survey is an academic degree in translation strictly required in order to work as a translator into all languages, not even in the fields of sworn translation and legal translation. In Germany it would be very hard to get a government job as a translator without a university degree in translation, but it is legally possible. In many other countries, academic degrees make it easier to become a sworn or authorised translator, but in all the cases we have studied there is at least one way to attain that status without a degree in translation.[47]

This situation might be seen as an indication that the degrees in translation are not seen as meeting professional standards. One should nevertheless bear in mind the following:

– Certified translations and sworn translations are needed for many more language pairs than are currently taught in European translator training programmes. This is particularly true in the case of many of the languages of recent immigrants. For language pairs where there are no academically qualified translators, the various justice systems must call on translators whose status is signalled by little more than experience.[48]

– The rates of pay for many translators working for the various legal systems are sometimes so low that a long-term academic education programme cannot be justified: no one will invest in the training in order to receive the fees.

These two factors might constitute a double-bind situation: for many extra-European languages, sworn or legal translators (and especially interpreters) are not trained because they are underpaid (it is not a profession one would pay to study for), and they are underpaid because they are not trained.

The way out of this double bind must be to enact policy able to modify the market, probably through short-term training and certification programmes that are accessible to those who need them.

2.4. The Role of Translator Associations

Membership of a professional association, society, or union is one of the clearest ways in which a translator can signal professional status. An overview of these organisations must be an essential part of any study of the status of translators.

Any association constructs its authority from a number of factors, over and above the actual expertise of its members. In the field of translation, the key factors tend to be admission criteria, longevity, size (number of members), inclusion in wider or parent associations, specialisation, and in some cases the number and quality of services to members and public interventions. Here we review each of these factors in turn.

2.4.1. Admission criteria

All of the translator associations included in our survey admit new members on the basis of experience and/or academic qualifications. Only in a few cases do we find that a degree in translation is absolutely necessary: the Panhellenic Association of Professional Translators Graduates of the Ionian University clearly defends the interests of a very particular group of graduates (it is reported as having 140 members in 2011), and the Pan Cyprian Union of Graduate Translators and Interpreters adopts similar criteria in Cyprus (it is reported as having 66 members in 2011). Further cases are the Association of Danish Authorised Translators (Translatørforeningen), which states that all its members have a degree in translation or business languages (*erhvervssprog*),[49] and Danish Authorised Translators and Interpreters (Danske Translatører), which specifies that all its members "are active professional translators and interpreters who have received a Master's degree in translation and interpreting in Danish and one or more other languages from an accredited Danish business school."[50] All the other associations mix experience with admission criteria based on recommendations and/or academic qualifications.

2.4.2. Longevity and size

Figure 4 shows the years of foundation and numbers of members of the main translator associations in the countries covered in this study (including the comparison countries).

Figure 4. Numbers of members and years of foundation of translator associations (data from Appendix A).

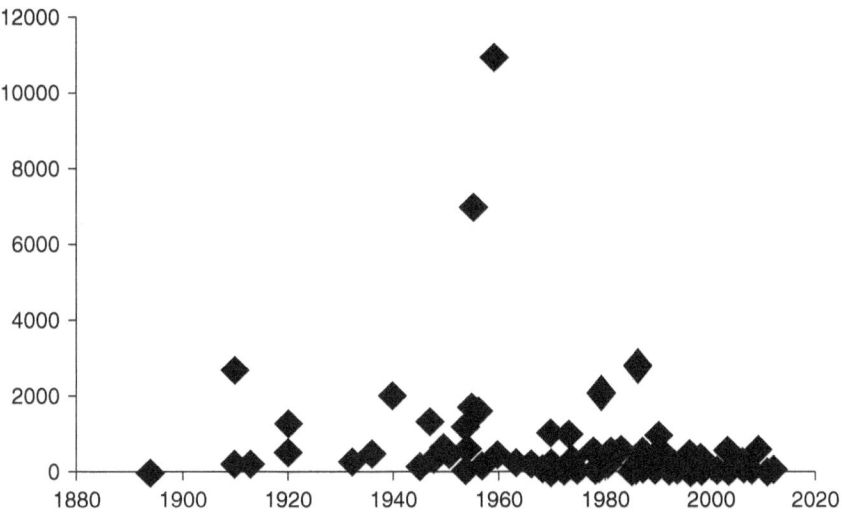

There are clearly several different types of associations:

1. A few associations are surprisingly old: the Society of Greek Playwrights, Musicians and Translators dates from 1894; The Danish Translatørforeningen was established in 1910; the Norwegian Statsautoriserte Translatørers Forening (Association of State Authorised Translators) was created in 1913; the Swedish Federation of Authorised Translators was founded in 1932. The British Chartered Institute of Linguists dates from 1910, although its widely respected Diploma in Translation was not introduced until 1989.[51]
2. The two giants of the field are the Bundesverband der Dolmetscher und Übersetzer (BDÜ), with about 7,000 members, and the American Translators Association (ATA), with about 11,000 members in "more than 90 countries."[52,53] Both were founded in the 1950s (in 1954 and 1959 respectively), in the heroic age of the translation profession in the West – the same years also saw the founding of the CIUTI, the FIT, and the first major professional translation schools in the university systems. These associations actively represent the profession in dealings with governments and administrative bodies; they reach their members through publications (*MDÜ Fachzeitschrift für Dolmetscher und Übersetzer* and the *ATA Chronicle*); they give their members considerable professional standing. In our questionnaire survey, ATA membership is reported as having a clear market value (i.e. translators can attract better clients and receive better payment), whereas BDÜ membership is reported as having a strong market value but at a level slightly less than academic qualifications (the traditional *Diplom-Übersetzer*). ATA organises stringent certification exams, whereas the BDÜ, as a federation of associations, receives members through the member organisations. Some associations within the BDÜ offer healthcare plans and insurance benefits.

Mention should also be made here of the Chartered Institute of Linguists (CIOL) in the United Kingdom, which has "around 6,300 Fellows, Members and Associate Members", of which 2,700 are in the Translation Division. The CIOL is involved with far more than just translation, but its overall size enables it to represent the translation profession with respect to government policy (for example with regard to the justice system) and its translator certification system (the Diploma in Translation) has a definite market value. On these points, the CIOL uses its size in ways similar to ATA and the BDÜ.

Of similar size to the 2,700-member Translation Division of the CIOL is the Institute of Translation and Interpreting (ITI), also in the United Kingdom, which has 2,800 members. The two memberships partly overlap, as do the functions of the two associations. Both have considerable weight, and their membership has a positive market value.

3. Further national associations were also founded in the heroic age of the 1950s and 1960s. There are two distinct groups here. Some associations, in France (1947), Italy (1950), Finland (1955), and the Netherlands (1956), now have between 700 and 1700 members, making them large enough to speak with some authority on behalf of a profession. These are generalist associations, bringing together technical translators, interpreters, sworn translators/interpreters, and often literary translators as well. However, other associations founded in the same years have remained quite small, now representing between 200 and 600 members. This has been the case in Norway (1948), Austria (1954), Spain (1954), Sweden (1954), Belgium (1955), Croatia (1957), Greece (1963), and Switzerland (1966). These are also generalist associations. Their limited size may in some cases be due to the reduced dimensions of the market (although the Finnish association has 1726 members, in a population of some 5m. people, and the Netherlands Society has 1625 members in a country of 16 m.). These smaller associations might appear to have somehow stagnated, or have failed to speak for a profession. In some cases they have been rivalled by younger associations.

4. Perhaps the most surprising aspect of Figure 4 is that, as can be seen, the creation of new associations has been fairly constant. Some impetus might be due to the enhanced importance of translation associated with the various waves of EU accession. The constant founding of small associations throughout the 1990s and into the 2000s might nevertheless be considered symptomatic of a different kind of association, with different functions. In these cases, longevity and size are clearly not what translators are looking for.

The most recent association that we have found was in the process of being set up in November 2011: the Deutscher Verband der Übersetzer und Dolmetscher (DVÜD) describes itself as "eight translators and a lawyer".[54] It does not set out to oppose the 7,000-strong BÜD; it simply "wants to get things moving". The new association appears to stem from a very active Internet discussion group;[55] it might aspire to a degree of involvement and interactivity that the large traditional organisations cannot offer.

Table 2. Associations for translators and/or interpreters: number per country; total membership; membership as percentage of potential demand for translators. Data from FIT Treasurer, 17/11/2011 and from country factsheets.[56]

EUROPEAN UNION	Associations	Members	Potential T/I	Percentage of potential
Austria	5	1,415	1,631	87
Belgium	1	380	1,898	20
Bulgaria	2	359	466	77
Croatia	8	726	366	198
Cyprus	1	66	100	66
Czech Republic	5	978	1,299	75
Denmark	4	1,440	999	144
Estonia	2	291	166	175
Finland	3	4,342	966	449
France	5	2,615	10,256	24
Germany	5	8,878	14,219	62
Greece	6	729	1,665	44
Hungary	2	257	966	27
Ireland	1	118	966	12
Italy	5	1,363	8,924	15
Lithuania	2	121	333	37
Luxembourg	1	48	200	24
Netherlands	4	2,340	3,263	72
Poland	5	1,839	3,330	55
Portugal	4	772	1,165	66
Romania	3	380	1,299	31
Slovakia	3	611	599	102
Slovenia	4	809	300	269
Spain	12	2,571	6,960	37
Sweden	3	1,651	1,698	97
United Kingdom	8	6,998	10,822	64
Total	103	41,286	74,856	55
NEIGHBOURING COUNTRIES				
Norway	4	1,183	1,332	89
Switzerland	6	1,021	1,498	68
Turkey	3	521	3,463	15
COMPARISON CASES				
Australia	4	1,082	3,929	28
Canada	11	4,438	6,394	69
United States[57]	31	16,560	69,130	24

2.4.3. Specialisation and fragmentation

Many of the newer associations (and a few of the older ones) aim to represent just part of the overall translation profession. This mainly concerns associations that are specifically for sworn or authorised translators (especially in northern Europe) or conference interpreters (the AIIC and various national associations), others that are specifically for literary translation, and still others that correspond to languages that have gained official status (in Spain). A further development is the creation of associations specifically for audiovisual translators (in Norway in 1997, now with a respectable total of 152 members, and more recently in France in 2006, Poland in 2007, Spain in 2010, and Croatia in 2012).

In some cases, the specialised association existed prior to the general ones (as in Greece and Norway). In most cases, however, the specialisation has come later, either as a split from the generalist association or as a parallel development.

By counting the number of associations in each country, we obtain a rough index of the degree of fragmentation within the translation profession. Table 2 shows approximate numbers for the countries covered in this survey. The actual number of associations is likely to be larger, since translators are also represented within the various societies or associations for writers. The fragmentation would appear to be significant for countries like Spain, the United Kingdom, Norway and Greece, and rather surprising in the cases of Denmark and Sweden.

In some cases, the apparent fragmentation is countered by the creation of an "association of associations" of some kind. This has happened in Canada[58] and Portugal,[59] and the large associations in China, Germany and the United States are groupings of mostly regional associations.[60] The Fédération Internationale des Traducteurs, with 83 full members and 31 associate members, successfully manages to bring together many of the associations that would otherwise appear to be rivals at the national level. For example, four of the associations listed for the United Kingdom are members of the FIT.

Table 2 also offers a rough comparison of the percentages of translators and interpreters who are members of an association. The "potential T/I" is the possible number of professional translators and interpreters who could be employed in accordance with the macroeconomic indicator of the country, taking the percentage for each country from Parker's (2008) calculations for 2011, then multiplying by the estimate of 333,000 professional translators and interpreters (see Appendix B).[61] These numbers are to be taken with many grains of salt – most significantly, they do not include the translation work associated with membership of the European Union. We have then calculated the association memberships as percentages of the potential number of translators and interpreters. The resulting percentages are mapped in Figure 5.

In some cases, the membership numbers are worryingly low: Malta, Latvia, Ireland, Italy and Turkey are all under 20 per cent.

In other cases, our calculations suggest that there are *more* association members than the macroeconomic data can account for. This is the case in Denmark,

Figure 5. Membership of all T/I associations in country as a percentage of potential professional translators and interpreters in country (data from Table 2).

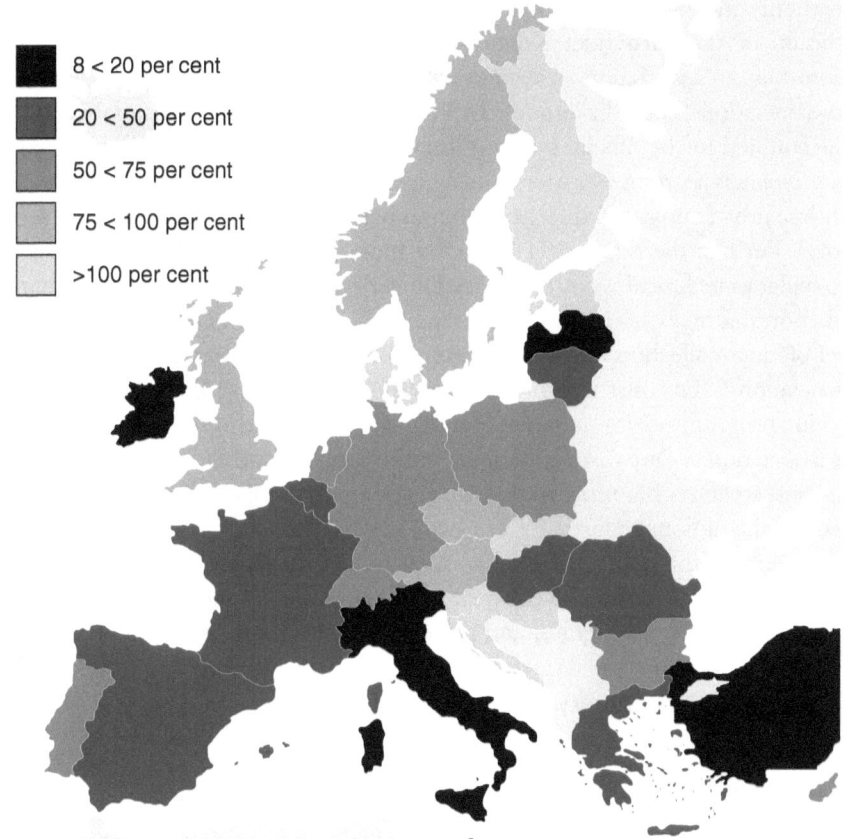

Finland, Croatia, Slovakia, Estonia and Slovenia – all countries with relatively small populations where the effect of having an official EU language is relatively great and trumps the macroeconomic projection.[62] For countries of recent accession, a possible tendency (admittedly except for Estonia) is that the smaller the population (and the smaller the potential number of translators and interpreters), the more the association membership exceeds macroeconomic prediction (see Table 3). The way this logic plays out in the case of Slovenia is dealt with in some detail below (3.3).

Table 3. Association membership as percentage of potential, in relation to population, for EU Member States of recent accession.

	Accession	Population (m)	Potential T/I	% membership
Estonia	2004	1.3	166	175
Slovenia	2004	2.1	300	269
Croatia	2012	4.4	366	198
Slovakia	2004	5.4	599	102

In Denmark, the apparent excess of association members may also be a result of translators and interpreters who are members of more than one association (as is certainly the case in the United Kingdom as well[63]), particularly in view of our inclusion of the Forbundet Kommunikation og Sprog (KS), which is more of a union than an association as such (a translator might thus be a member of one or two associations, plus the union). In Finland, the apparent oversupply might also be accounted for by official bilingualism (Finnish/Swedish), extensive international work (Nokia is a strong exporter), and a high number of members who are not active full-time professionals (cf. the also high number of "authorised translators", see 2.3.5 above). Further, the Finnish "Translation Industry Professionals" (KAJ) association also includes technical writers, localisation experts, terminologists, project managers and coordinators, who could not be separated out from our data. Similarly on the level of data-collection effects, the figures for Croatia appear to be skewed by five "associations" for court interpreters, which appear to have been set up to provide training programmes for a market that might need around 100 court interpreters (20 per association?). One suspects that the enthusiasm behind these five associations, all of recent creation, has more to do with accession to the EU than with the long-term needs of the national courts.

The important point to be made with respect to the memberships is that the associations with less than 20 per cent of the potential market may be too marginal to emit strong effective signals, and associations with more than 100 per cent might similarly compromise their capacity to separate wheat from chaff, unless there are good reasons to the contrary.

2.4.4. Services offered by translator associations

There is a great deal of variety in the services offered by the associations. In all cases they fulfil the minimal function of giving members some added prestige. In many cases the associations maintain publicly accessible lists of members, and thus may help clients locate translators for work. That function, however, has increasingly been taken over by online communities like ProZ (see Appendix C).

The range of possible activities might be illustrated by the following list of services offered by the ITI in the United Kingdom:[64]

– A bi-monthly journal
– Web-based job posting by members for members
– Promoting services in the online directory of members
– 15 Regional and 19 Special Interest Network groups supporting members and a dedicated group supporting new members
– Online Membership listing
– Discounted Professional Indemnity Insurance
– Job advertisements through the ITI bulletin and website
– A legal helpline offering free advice on a wide range of legal matters
– Technology reviews published in the ITI bulletin

- Private discussion forum
- Help and advice on marketing, setting up business and model terms of business
- Annual events including Weekend Workshops, Conferences and Professional Development Courses – reduced rates for members
- Representation on FIT, Fédération Internationale des Traducteurs
- Representation on various National Language Bodies
- Special offers for members, such as discounted software, weekend breaks, hotel reservations, vintage wine tours, etc.

The Chartered Institute of Linguists (CIOL) in the United Kingdom offers similar services, albeit with more emphasis on the signals of status: their members can use official letters after their names (MCIL, FCIL or ACIL), have the right to use the Institute's centenary logo, and are offered a range of discounts on anything from insurance to t-shirts.[65] The BDÜ in Germany offers a similar range of activities, albeit devoid of T-shirts.

The tendency in recent years is for the well-established associations to offer more online services and training initiatives, as can be seen in the above lists. The list we have presented would appear to be near the maximum of what an association can do: almost all other associations offer fewer services.

It is nevertheless instructive to follow the advice given to a beginner translator in a discussion group on ProZ. The beginner wants to know whether he should join the ITI or the CIOL.[66] The answers generally agree that both are good and he could join both, as many people seem to. Other answers, though, point out that he will probably be getting more work through ProZ, and that he might better invest his money and time in improving his status in the online community.

2.4.5. *The relative market value of association membership*

What gives a translator more status: academic qualifications or being a member of a professional association? The answer should probably be: both. Increasingly, translators seek to benefit both from a specialised academic degree and from a professional association of some kind.

Our analysis of data from the Société Française des Traducteurs (SFT 2010) does indicate that, in this case, association members tend to enjoy higher pay than non-members (see 5.2.5 below). The finding nevertheless has to be interpreted: it could be because clients recognise the SFT label and are prepared to pay more (because the association signals status), but it could also be because the translators who earn more money are more likely to join the association, satisfying the membership criteria and in this case investing resources in the 195 euros annual membership fee.

What is changing is the dynamic relation between training and associations as signals of status. The large national associations were established in the 1950s and 1960s, when there were only a handful of translator training programmes in Europe and the function of professional associations was more or less limited to excluding outsiders. These days, when there are about 300 translator training programmes in the world, vast numbers of trained translators are seeking more than an exclusive club: they demand interactive peer-to-peer formats, up-to-date information, continuous training opportunities, and direct access to clients.

Some of the larger associations have been able to adapt to these new demands; others have not. The cases of non-adaptation might explain why translators have kept forming new associations, even while they turn to the online communities that are predominantly international and non-exclusive.

Chapter 3
CASE STUDIES

Here we sketch out case studies of the way the various signalling mechanisms interact in Germany, Romania, Slovenia, the United Kingdom, and Spain, as well as the external comparison countries the United States, Canada, and Australia.

The case studies broadly address the following questions:

- What is the relationship between academic training and professional certification with respect to the recruitment of translators?
- What has been the historical development of these signalling mechanisms in the field of translator qualifications?

We look at the general language policy of each country, the main features of academic qualifications, the professional associations, and the specific systems in place for sworn or authorised translators. In each case, we propose some tentative conclusions about the ways academic and professional signals are working, especially in relation to the size of each potential market.

The United States, Canada, and Australia have been selected as comparison bases because they have all seen close critical attention to accreditation and certification systems in very recent years.

3.1. Germany[1]

Germany is a significant case study because of the specific weight of the German economy within Europe, its successful export orientation, its high levels of foreign-language competence, the presence of immigrant languages, and a well-established and generally successful system of translator training and associative representation.

3.1.1. Language policy

The official status of the German language (*Hochdeutsch*) is not only juridical but also deeply cultural. Deprived of a unified state until 1871, German culture was identified with language more than with institutions. Further, at least since Goethe and Schleiermacher, the development of the German language was to happen through relations with other languages, notably through translation as a way of enriching German. The result has been a body of highly influential translation theory, based on substantial respect for the difference of foreign languages, and a very dynamic translation culture.

3.1.2. Translator training

The contemporary system for training translators in Germany took impetus from the immediate aftermath of the Second World War: university-based institutes in Heidelberg (actually from 1930), Germersheim (1947), and Saarbrücken (1948) now have large numbers of translation students, and the system has grown to include at least 22 tertiary institutions across Germany, offering a wide range of BA and specialised MA programmes.[2] We estimate the number of students in these programmes to total about 6,850,[3] which could mean that about 1,000 graduates are entering the market each year.

The traditional model in this system is to train translators through a full first-cycle and second-cycle curriculum (i.e. what is nowadays called a Bachelor's plus a Master's), as opposed to the second-cycle model developed in France, for example. The system was designed to produce a fully trained translator (and/or interpreter), rather than an area expert who can also translate.

The German federal government was interested in the development of the institutes, ostensibly because of its role as an employer of graduates. In 1965 it expressed "detailed views on the entry qualifications, academic objectives and courses of the university institutes" (Wilss 1999: 152).

From the early 1980s, this university system, from within the traditional centres at Heidelberg, Germersheim and elsewhere, produced a radical rethinking of the professional role of the translator, and consequently of translator training. There was a change from philological studies to practical training. What became known as *Skopos* theory posited that the translator's aim was not to produce an equivalent text, but to satisfy the client's communicative purpose. This opened the way to a more situational and industry-relevant mode of training, although the new theories were for many years the object of considerable academic debate.

3.1.3. Translator associations

Germany has the following translator associations, presented here in the chronological order of their founding:

VdÜ: The Verband deutschsprachiger Übersetzer literarischer und wissenschaftlicher Werke (Association of German-language Translators of Literary and Scientific Works) was founded in 1954. In 1974 it joined forces with the Verband deutscher Schriftsteller (VS) (Association of German Writers), so that its members also became members of the writer's association. In 2011 the VdÜ claimed to have "more 1200 members".[4] It offers its members information, development courses, advice, and legal support, and it sees its ongoing struggle as being to improve the financial position of translators with regard to publishers.

BDÜ: The Bundesverband der Dolmetscher und Übersetzer e.V. (the Federation of Interpreters and Translators) was created in 1955 through the unification of two existing federations: the Deutsche Dolmetscherbund (DDB, 1952) in the south and the Bund Deutscher Dolmetscher-Verbände (BDDV, 1953) in the north. (Note that both the previous associations named their identity as Dolmetscher, "interpreters", and that the BDÜ puts "Dolmetscher" first in its name.) The BDÜ is now an umbrella organisation comprising 14 regional associations. An individual translator cannot be a general member of BDÜ, but only of a regional association. On its website the BDÜ claims to speak for 7,000 or so translators and interpreters, including members of Assoziierte Dolmetscher und Übersetzer in Norddeutschland (DÜ Nord), Fachverband der Berufsübersetzer und Berufsdolmetscher (ATICOM), Verband der allgemein beeidigten Verhandlungsdolmetscher und der öffentlich bestellten und beeidigten Urkundenübersetzer in Baden-Württemberg (VVU), Verein öffentlich bestellter und beeidigter Dolmetscher und Übersetzer Bayern (VbDÜ), and the Verein beeidigter Dolmetscher und Übersetzer Leipzig e.V., Leipzig. It is a member of the FIT (as indeed are some of the other associations it is allied with) and of national organisations that share its interests.[5] It is a parliament-registered lobby organisation. The BDÜ publishes an important bulletin (*MDÜ*), organises regular courses in further training, offers legal advice and insurance, and publishes books on various aspects of translation and interpreting. The regional associations also organise seminars, and on the local level they have group meetings and do networking.

ADÜ Nord: Assoziierte Dolmetscher und Übersetzer in Norddeutschland (Associated Interpreters and Translators in Northern Germany) was founded in 1997 from the former regional associations in Hamburg and Schleswig-Holstein. It is affiliated with the BDÜ but is an independent member of the FIT. It was reported as having 348 members in 2011 (FIT). Its services include continued education seminars and advice on financial planning, translation tools, legal matters, tax, and marketing. The ADÜ Nord website gives a breakdown of its membership in 2007: about 70 per cent women; about 92 per cent self-employed; most between 40 and 50 years old (only 2.7 per cent are under 30).[6]

ATICOM: The Fachverband der Berufsübersetzer und Berufsdolmetscher (Union of Professional Translators and Professional Interpreters) is affiliated with the BDÜ but is an independent member of the FIT. It is reported as having 180 members (FIT). According to its website,[7] it provides group insurance, legal assistance, and discussion groups.

VÜD: The Verband der Übersetzer und Dolmetscher (Association of Translators and Interpreters) was founded in 1990 and is an independent member of the FIT. In 2011 it was reported as having 150 members (FIT). It offers its members an information bulletin, an intranet discussion forum, as well as job postings (surprisingly not restricted to the intranet) and a searchable database of translators and interpreters.[8]

QSD: Qualitätssprachendienste Deutschlands is an association of translation companies, founded in 1998. A member of the EUATC, in 2011 it had some 24 member companies. One of its main initiatives is to offer internships for graduates of translation and interpreting programmes.[9]

There are also the various regional associations that are brought together within the BDÜ.

The general situation is one where the main federation, the BDÜ, claims to speak for 7,000 members and thus has a strong voice. At the same time, a string of regional and more specialised associations, each with fewer than 600 members, are presumably able to promote more active involvement from its members and offer more specialised services.

In between these two levels we find the VdÜ, which focuses on literary translation and is affiliated with the Association of German Writers.[10]

The large associations were founded in the 1950s; others date from the 1990s. If we can judge from the profile of members of the ADÜ Nord, the membership is largely over the age of 40, and may constitute a body of established professionals. This might explain why we find initiatives to set up younger, more interactive associations such as the Deutscher Verband der Übersetzer und Dolmetscher (DVÜD), "eight translators and a lawyer",[11] set up in 2011 and visibly in tune with virtual technologies.

3.1.4. Census, taxation, and social security

There appear to be no special categories for translators in the census or taxation system. Translators are generally considered part of the "freie Berufe" (liberal professions).

Bundesagentur für Arbeit statistics nevertheless indicate that in March 2011 there were 6,814 actively employed translators and interpreters registered with the social security system as having fixed employment.[12] This represented a 9.3 per cent increase since 2005.

The only federal law that directly governs translators is the order regarding judicial fees, which determines how much legal translators and interpreters receive. In this categorisation, translators are mentioned under "Sachverständige" (area experts).

3.1.5. Sworn and authorised translators

Although the translation profession is not defined or delimited by any law, the field of sworn and legal translation is indeed defined and delimited, in several different ways.[13]

The designation and certification of sworn interpreters is organised differently within each of Germany's 16 *Länder*, where 135 *Landgerichte* (regional courts) appoint and swear in translators. This involves a variety of legal concepts: translators may be "bestellt" (appointed), "ermächtigt" (authorised, empowered), "beeidigt" (sworn, or sworn in), "vereidigt" (put under oath), and more.[14] This diversity should not, in itself, have any bearing on the status of translators. It does nevertheless have a negative effect when the differences prohibit certification in one *Land* being automatically recognised in another. For example, in order to be certified in Hamburg, candidates must pass a stringent exam. This is not the case in other *Länder*, so translators who are certified in those other *Länder* may not enjoy the same status in Hamburg (Stejskal 2003a). One solution to this problem might be for the Hamburg model to be adopted everywhere else;[15] another solution would be for all courts to recognise only academic qualifications (although academic training is not available for all the foreign languages required).

That said, the actual sworn *translations* done in one *Land* are recognised in all others, and there is an online registry of sworn translators and interpreters for the whole of Germany,[16] which has 21,516 entries in 2012.

The regime by which legal translators and interpreters are paid is stipulated by federal law. The Justizvergütungs- und -entschädigungsgesetz (JVEG) has been operative since 2004, but it has been the object of debate and criticism by the main translator associations, basically because of the low rates of pay.[17] There are regional laws that also govern the status and professional activities of sworn translators.[18]

One of the fundamental problems with such laws is that the government is both providing status to the translator (through certification or authorisation) and establishing the corresponding rate of pay, when the same institution is also the client of the translator. In short, the government decrees how much it wants to pay to the people it employs.

In most *Länder* there are no continuing education requirements for sworn or authorised translators and no fixed revalidation procedures.

3.1.6. Summary of the status of translators in Germany

The situation in Germany seems superficially secure: the training institutions are solid; the associations operate at two different levels, allowing both powerful representation and local interaction; the translation companies are interested in professional training; and if the different regimes for sworn translators pose problems for mobility and remuneration, the main translator associations are still large enough to raise a collective voice in protest.

One might nevertheless doubt the extent to which these various features represent the one phenomenon. The training programmes in major languages, like the association of translation companies, seem oriented toward the use of translation for export and for European relations, whereas many of the needs in the courts and for sworn translators in general concern immigrant languages in which professionals are not always being trained. At the same time, the large established associations have generally adapted poorly to new communication media, and younger translators may seek new ways of constructing status.

Attention should also be paid to some of the quantities involved. According to Parker's very abstract calculation (2008), the potential translation market in Germany is 4.27 per cent of the world total, which might represent some 14,219 professional translators and interpreters. If the BDÜ speaks for about 7,000 professionals, and we add 1,200 from the VdÜ, we estimate some 8,200 actual professionals who are members of associations. This would mean that about 57.6 per cent of all professionals are members of associations, which is a very healthy situation.

At the same time, the university training institutions would seem to be producing about 1,000 new translation graduates each year, into a market that would not appear to be growing at a similar rate. This is partly confirmed by an internal BDÜ survey conducted in 2010, where 39 per cent of BDÜ members, mostly self-employed, report an annual turnover of below 17,500 euros, and 42 per cent say that in the year 2009 their volume of work was below their capacity. A majority of the latter group had fewer than five years of activity in the profession.[19]

Indeed, the BDÜ estimates that there are some 40,000 translators and interpreters in Germany, of which the overwhelming majority are self-employed[20] and many of them would appear to be under-employed or engaged in translation on a part-time basis.

There are 21,516 people listed in the German registry of sworn translators and interpreters,[21] a number that is considerably higher than our estimate of 14,219 as the potential number of *professional* translators and interpreters. One can only assume that many of the sworn translators and interpreters are also engaged in other professional activities.

According to one informant speaking in 2003, "Germany boasts some 10,000 sworn translators and interpreters. This is 10 times more than are needed" (Zänker, cit. Stejskal 2003a: 17). The signs of status need not correspond to a substantial livelihood for all.

3.2. Romania[22]

Romania is selected as a case study here because it is a recent member of the European Union (since 2007). The accession process was associated with a relative boom in the Romanian translation industry (Greere and Tătaru 2008: 96) and with increasing attention to the modes of connecting training with industry. At the same time, however, the specific developments associated with the accession would seem to have conflicted with the established system for the public certification of translators, which appears to come from the previous regime.

3.2.1. Language policy

The only official language of Romania is Romanian, although there are minorities speaking Hungarian (6.7 per cent) and Vlax Romani (1.1 per cent). The linguistic demands of the Hungarian minority led to violence in 1990. The 1991 law on public administration allows that a minority language can be used in public administration, alongside Romanian, in localities where the minority makes up more than 20 per cent of the population.[23] Although this should create a certain demand for translation, functional bilingualism in diglossic regions means that it is not a major professional demand. Hungarian and Roma appear not to be taught in the main translator-training programmes.

3.2.2. Translator training

According to Greere (2008: 80), translator and interpreter training is mainly carried out by departments of Applied Modern Languages, set up from 1991 on the model of the French *Langues Étrangères Appliquées*, in which translation and interpreting are second-cycle higher education specialisations. This happened in universities including Universitatea Babeş-Bolyai in Cluj-Napoca, Universitatea Bucureşti in Bucharest, Universitatea Al. I. Cuza in Iasi, Universitatea de Vest in Timişoara, Universitatea Transilvania in Braşov, and Universitatea Lucian Blaga in Sibiu.

A European Master's in Translation Studies and Terminology, in accordance with EMT guidelines, is offered at Universitatea Babeş Bolyai in Cluj-Napoca, with Romanian as an A language and English, French, German, and Spanish as B or C languages. To date this is the only programme member of the EMT Network, following the 2009 selection procedure conducted by the DGT.

The Master's at Universitatea Babeş-Bolyai has 10–18 students per cohort for all language combinations;[24] the Degree in Applied Languages with Specialisation in Translation and Interpreting at Iaşi has about 66 students; the two-year Master's in Translation and Terminology also at Iaşi has about 25 students every year; at Universitatea Bucureşti the numbers of regular places offered are 50 for the Master's in Translation of Contemporary Literary Texts, 30 for the Master's in Translation and Specialised Terminology, and 15 for the European Master's in Conference Interpreting.[25] We do not have information on the size of the other programmes.

3.2.3. Translator associations

Romania has a relatively small general association, an association of unspecified dimensions for authorised translators, and a recently unified association of translation companies. All were founded in years close to Romania's EU accession.

ATR: The Asociaţia Traducătorilor din România (Romanian Translators Association) was founded in 2004 and is a full member of the FIT and a full member of EULITA. In 2011 it is reported as having 112 members, although its website indicates that its newsletter has 1,938 subscribers.[26] A full member (*membru titular*) must have previously joined ATR as an associate or student member. The procedure for becoming full member is based on professional qualification requirements (education) as well as proof of sufficient experience. An associate member (*membru aderent*) must have a BA degree in translation and interpreting or show proof of being authorised or certified as a translator/interpreter by the Romanian authorities. A student member (*membru debutant*) must be enrolled in a higher education training programme in translation and interpreting (BA, MA, or PhD) and may not comply on application with the requirements for associate member.

UNTAR: The Uniunea Naţională a Traducătorilor Autorizaţi din România (Certified Translators' National Union) was founded in 2008.[27] There is no regulation that authorised translators must be members. The union is reported as having about 40 members, mostly authorised translators and interpreters,[28] although its interactive forum appears to have some 500 subscribers. The union offers reduced rates for professional insurance.

AFIT: The Romanian Association of Translation and Interpreting Companies, a EUATC member, was founded in 2005 and in 2010 merged with the Association of Romanian Translation Agencies (ABTR), also founded in 2005.

3.2.4. Census, taxation, and social security

At the 2011 census, Romanian translators were able to declare their occupation specifically as "translator and interpreter". The ATR issued instructions to translators wishing to report their occupation during the census.

Authorised translators and interpreters are considered members of a liberal profession and specific instructions for fiscal registration apply. Registration requirements for other freelance translators and literary translators are different (a different law applies).

Translators can work as freelance translators, can set up companies or they can be employed (in some cases, a mixture of the three).

3.2.5. Authorised and certified translators

The Romanian system does not have permanently "sworn translators" per se (court interpreters are sworn with each distinct case). However, translators can be authorised (the Romanian term is *autorizat*) by the Ministry of Justice. To do this, they require a Bachelor's degree (or equivalent) from a higher education institution in the fields of a foreign language, applied modern languages, or translation and interpreting, or proof of a bilingual high school graduation diploma with teaching in the language for which authorisation is applied for; candidates do not require special training in translation. They are then listed in the national register as translators and interpreters and can be called to serve in the judicial system. According to Romanian Law 178/1997, this means they can support the activities of the Ministry of Justice and related institutions such as notaries public, attorneys-at-law, and courts.

Candidates for the status of authorised translator must be citizens of "an EU Member State, a member of the European Economic Area, or Switzerland". Non-Romanian candidates nevertheless have their knowledge of Romanian certified in Romania.[29]

By 2011, a total of 32,856 people had been authorised as translators and interpreters. The authorisation issued by the Ministry of Justice covers both translation and interpreting, as it is considered that both modalities are required by the institutions concerned.[30]

According to Law 178/1997, the Romanian Ministry of Justice is the only institution able to authorise and maintain a list of translators and interpreters qualified to produce translations for the Romanian legal system, including the Ministry itself, the courts, public notaries, lawyers, and legal executors. For translations to be used by other people or institutions, the translator does not need to the authorised by the Ministry – it is enough to have an "atestatul de traducator" (translator's licence) issued by the Ministry of Culture and National Heritage.[31]

The Ministry of Culture and National Heritage "licences" translators through its Centre for Professional Training in Culture (Centrul de pregătire profesională în cultură), where candidates must pass a written translation test, which is organised regularly. The test focuses on specific domains and consists of translating a 2000-character specialised text to be rendered with bilingual dictionaries.

This means that higher academic qualifications are not required; candidates need only high school graduation. This certification procedure is appealing to candidates who do not have a foreign-language degree. Such certification in specific domains and for specific translation direction (*from* or *into* the foreign language) will allow them to work on the market, especially as freelance translators ("traducător persoană fizică autorizată"). In order to be certified in "legal sciences" the candidate must nevertheless take two further tests. The Centre for Professional Training in Culture does not administer any testing procedure for interpreters; the certificate covers written translation only.

Documents translated by authorised translators are certified (using a specific certification text stipulated by law where the translator vouches for the validity and accuracy of the translation, accompanied by the translator's signature and stamp) and may subsequently be legalised by a notary public, thus becoming *traduceri legalizate*. The legalisation by the notary public acknowledges conformity of the signature of the translator as being that of a translator authorised by the Ministry of Justice. Not all documents translated by authorised translators require legalisation by a notary public.

Law 178/1995 regarding the authorisation of translators and interpreters by the Ministry of Justice does not include provisions regarding continuous professional development. The authorisation can be withdrawn in the following situations (according to Law 281/2004 Art. No. 6): the translator or interpreter has been convicted for an offence committed with intent; for lack of professional skills, as notified in writing by the beneficiary; in the case of court translators or interpreters, for consistent and unmotivated refusal to offer the services required.

If translators authorised by the Ministry of Justice or certified by the Ministry of Culture opt for a freelance career, they must register as *persoană fizică autorizată* (sole traders), apply for a Code of Fiscal Identification from the local administration and keep invoice books and different registers. The fiscal registration in itself does not give them "authorised" status. Alternatively, translators may set up companies, in which case private limited liability companies (SRL *Societate cu Răspundere limitată*) are generally favoured.

3.2.6. Rates of pay

In 2009 the Ministry of Justice (Ordinul 772/2009)[32] set the prices for court interpreters and translators as: 23.15 RON (5.31 euros) per hour for interpreting, and 33.56 RON (7.69 euros) per page for written translation (A4, font Arial 12, 1.5 lines, and 2.5 cm borders). The fees are supposed to be indexed annually by agreement between the Ministry and professional organisations.

At the same time, Government Decision 1291/2002 on the authorisation and payment of translators and interpreters working for institutions with judicial authority indicates fees of 41 RON for translations into Romanian and 56 RON for translations into the foreign language. These fees are per page (defined as "format A4 double spacing").

Both laws appear to be in force, even though they specify different rates and different definitions of what a page is.[33]

Fees on the market for common languages fluctuate from 8–10 RON per page (translations by students or people who do not have a certified professional status) up to 50–60 RON for highly specialised translations performed by established translation service providers. Rare languages will be charged at higher rates, as are translations commissioned by foreign clients. In these cases, fees will compete with those on the European and international market (7–15 eurocents per word) (see Greere 2010).

3.2.7. Summary of the status of translators in Romania

Romania has a developing system of specialised translator training at the Master's level, and a public system of translator authorisation/certification that seems to be taking little account of the specialised training. The training system has developed since 1991, whereas the public certification system more properly belongs to an earlier era when there was no specialised training of translators.

The first result of this is an unfortunate mixing of signals: "Clients often consider the authorisation [by the Ministry of Justice] a sign of professionalism and seek out authorised translators for any task, regardless if the task they are commissioning involves a legal/official text-genre" (Greere and Tătaru 2008: 97).

A second result is that, since Romania keeps a very complete list of certified translators and has a set of legal regulations, as recommended by Directive 2010/64/EU, it scores quite well in the *Status Quaestionis* survey (Hertog and van Gucht eds 2008) (see 2.3.1 above). On paper, the system should be allowing access to justice.

One might hope that publicly authorised translators will realise that they need more training and will then turn to the university Master's programmes (as envisaged in Greere and Tătaru 2008). However, it is equally possible that younger translators will enter the newer sectors of the translation and localisation industry and will pick up their skills there.

Based on Parker (2008) we estimate that the potential market for professional translation and interpreting in Romania requires 1,267 people (0.39 per cent of the world potential). This would mean that only a small percentage of the 32,856 "authorisations" correspond to active professional translators and interpreters. Further, if the main translator association has 112 full members (this is the number they have reported to the FIT), that particular signal of status would appear to be of interest to just 8.8 per cent of the potential population of professional translators and interpreters.

3.3. Slovenia[34]

Slovenia is of interest here because it is a relatively new member of the EU (since 2004) and its official language, Slovene, is protected and promoted by national policies: it is spoken by about 2.5 million people.

As is the case with most languages of limited diffusion, the proportion of translations in published books in Slovene is quite high: 25 per cent overall, rising to 42 per cent of literary works (Fock et al. 2008). One would thus expect translators to be of considerable importance not just in enhancing the status of Slovene as a European Union language, but more especially as builders of a Slovene written culture.

3.3.1. Language policy

The official language in Slovenia is Slovene. The Slovenian Constitution nevertheless recognises three minorities: Hungarians (0.32 per cent), Italians (0.11 per cent), and Roma (0.17 per cent). Hungarian and Italian are also official languages in the localities where those communities live.

Slovene is promoted through the Public Use of the Slovene Language Act (2004) and the National Programme for Language Policy (2007).

3.3.2. Translator training

The Department of Translation at the University of Ljubljana began teaching in 1997. It now offers a three-year Bachelor's course in Interlinguistic Communication (BA), an MA in Interpreting, and an MA in Translation. It is a member of the CIUTI, the consortium for the European Master's in Conference Interpreting, and the European Master's in Translation. It offers courses in Slovene with English, German, French, and Italian (Hungarian and Romani are not offered). It currently has some 540 students.[35]

The University of Maribor has a Translation Studies department that offers first-cycle programmes in "Interlingual Studies" with English, German, and Hungarian.[36]

The Slovenian Armed Forces have a School of Foreign Languages that "provides translation, interpreting and proofreading services for the needs of the Slovenian Armed Forces and the Ministry of Defence".[37] The school appears not to teach translation, interpreting, or proofreading.

3.3.3. Translator associations

A Slovenian Translators Association was founded in 1953. It later split into two parallel associations, although the literary association claims to have inherited the mantle of longevity:

DSKP: Društvo slovenskih književnih prevajalcev (Association of Literary Translators of Slovenia). Its website lists 241 members.[38] It is a member of the Conseil Européen des Associations de Traducteurs Littéraires.

DZTPS: Društvo znanstvenih in tehniških prevajalcev Slovenije (Association of Scientific and Technical Translators of Slovenia) has 476 members (FIT), is a member of the FIT, and its website claims it has 50 years of history.[39] It is one of the few associations that published recommended rates of pay for translations.

We should also note the existence of the Slovenian Association of Conference Interpreters (KTS), founded in 1972 and now with 48 members,[40] and the Association of Interpreters for the Slovene Sign Language (ZTSZJ), founded in 2004, whose website lists some 44 interpreters.[41]

Osolnik-Kunc (2009), affiliated with the Judicial Training Centre of the Ministry of Justice, has proposed the creation of a Slovene Association of Court Interpreters and Sworn Translators.

The Slovenian Association of Translation Companies (SATC) was founded in 2008 and has 27 member companies.[42] It has applied to become a member of EUATC.

3.3.4. Census, taxation, and social security

We have no information on special categories for translators in the census, taxation system, or social security system.

We note, though, that translators who have the status of "self-employed workers in culture" have all social insurance paid by the state if they can prove that they have limited income (e.g. they had this status in 2011 if they earned less than 21,605 euros gross in 2010).[43]

3.3.5. Sworn and authorised translators

Sworn translators are certified and authorised by the Ministry of Justice on the basis of an exam. The certification is normally for life. They may work in the justice system at all levels.

According to Osolnik-Kunc (2009),[44] 90 per cent of all court interpreters actually work as legal translators. Osolnik-Kunc also mentions there are 871 court interpreters, so there must be about 784 people doing translations for the justice system.

3.3.6. Summary of the status of translators in Slovenia

Looking at the association memberships, we might suppose that about 809 people belong to a translator or interpreter association in Slovenia (give or take double or triple memberships). Using Parker's rule of thumb (2008), the potential market might require 292 translators and interpreters (0.09 per cent of the world potential), and yet we find far more than twice that number joining the associations, not to mention the more than 700 people apparently doing translations (or certified to do them) in and around the courts, plus more than 60 or so new translation graduates entering the market each year.

One might surmise that the function of translators in Slovenia extends well beyond the country's economic needs. Many must be working for love, culture ("self-employed workers in culture"), subsidies, or the role of Slovene as an official language of the European Union.

The limited presence of Hungarian in the training programmes, and indeed in the statistics on the court interpreters, suggests that Slovenia's internal multilingualism policy is not a major generator of translations.

3.4. United Kingdom

The United Kingdom merits inclusion as a case study because of the apparent success of its translator certification systems, notably through the Chartered Institute of Linguists, the development of several large active associations, and the recent challenge to those systems in the field of legal translation and interpreting.

3.4.1. Language policy

The *de facto* official language of the United Kingdom is English. Welsh is spoken by some 582,000 people (20 per cent of the population of Wales); about 110,000 people speak Irish in Northern Ireland; Scottish Gaelic is spoken by some 65,000 people (1.3 per cent of the Scottish population).[45] Internal translation services are thus required for at least English–Welsh.

More significant internal translating is nevertheless required for the many documents and services associated with immigration. According to the 2001 Census, some 4.9 million people (8.3 per cent of the population) were born outside of the United Kingdom. Since 2004 there has been significant immigration from central and eastern Europe, due to the free movement of labour within the European Union.

3.4.2. Translator training

Translator training in the United Kingdom began with postgraduate programmes, mainly for interpreters, at Westminster in London (1963) and Bath University (1966). A four-year Bachelor's programme was established at Heriot-Watt University in 1976. The predominant model is nevertheless for translators to be trained in one-year or two-year postgraduate programmes, as has been the case in Surrey (1985), Bristol (1994), Middlesex in London (1994), Leeds (1996), Edinburgh (1992), Salford (1992), Aston in Birmingham (1997), Swansea (2000), Imperial College London (2001), Hull (2002), and Roehampton in London (2003). A programme in literary translation has been offered at the University of Essex since 1966.

Many further programmes have been opened since 2005, mainly with a one-year Master's structure. Many of these programmes cater especially to overseas students, who pay considerable fees to study in the United Kingdom. In some cases the programmes emphasise translation theory and courses on general practice, with minimal training in specific language pairs. It would be misleading to suppose that all these training programmes were supplying the internal translation market in the United Kingdom. They are responding more to the global market for English-language education.

In 2011 the University of Westminster closed its MA in Conference Interpreting due to financial constraints.[46]

3.4.3. Translator associations

CIOL: The Chartered Institute of Linguists was founded in 1910 and "serves the interests of professional linguists throughout the world and acts as a respected language assessment and recognised awarding organisation delivering Ofqual (Office of Qualifications and Examinations Regulator) accredited qualifications". In 2011 its Translating Division had 2,700 members.[47]

The admission criteria for full membership are quite subtle but might be summarised as follows: candidates require the IOL Diploma in Translation or "a recognised postgraduate degree of a British or overseas University in a modern language or languages, or in bi-lingual translation/translation studies". Alternatively, candidates may be admitted if they have at least three years' professional experience and one of the following: the CIOL Diploma, the Ministry of Defence examination in interpreting, or a First or Second Class Honours degree in Modern Languages from "a recognised British or overseas University or awarded by the Council for National Academic Awards".[48] Admission for associate membership is similar but at a less demanding level. There is thus a balance of academic qualifications, the CIOL's own exams, and experience.

The Institute of Linguists Educational Trust (IOLET) Diploma in Translation was introduced in 1989 and is widely respected. Some universities offer short-term training courses in preparation for the public examinations for the Diploma.[49]

The CIOL also offers "Chartered Linguist" status, for which candidates require:

> the Diploma in Translation awarded by the Chartered Institute of Linguists, or an equivalent qualification in translation at Masters level (NQF Level 7), in the relevant language combination(s). An MA used in support of an application must have contained an assessed practical translation module, completed in the language in which the applicant wishes to register. It should be noted that, depending on content and skills assessed, some Masters degrees in translation may not be acceptable; potential applicants requiring guidance are advised to contact the CIOL. Qualified Members of ITI must satisfy the ITI requirements for translation membership in the relevant language combination(s). In exceptional circumstances qualifications other than those indicated above, supported by appropriate demonstrated experience, may be accepted.[50]

This appears to mean that not all Master's programmes in Translation are recognised as being equivalent to the CIOL's Diploma in Translation. The CIOL nevertheless has not compiled a list of Master's programmes that might be considered unacceptable.[51]

ITI: The Institute of Translation and Interpreting (ITI) was founded in 1986 as a breakaway from the CIOL. It is a member of the FIT. "Qualified" members require "a first degree or postgraduate qualification in a relevant subject or a corresponding qualification accepted by ITI"; "associate" membership requires "evidence of professional interest in translation or interpreting".[52] In 2007 there were 2,642 members.[53] The institution is organised in terms of 13 regional groups, and specific networks in accordance with languages and modalities (translation, interpreting, subject matter, new members, etc.).

The ITI and CIOL offer a wide range of services, including a free legal helpline, reduced-rate Professional Indemnity Insurance, discounts on things like hotels and stationery purchases, and (CIOL only) a health insurance plan (see 2.4.4 above).

TASA: The Translators Association of the Society of Authors was established in 1958. It is a member of the FIT and the Conseil Européen des Associations de Traducteurs Littéraires and lists 330 members. Membership is based on publications.

NUPIT: The National Union of Professional Interpreters and Translators was founded in 2001 as a part of Unite, Britain's largest trade union.[54] It is reported as having about 100 members.[55] Its website states: "Most of our members are public service interpreters; many are involved in court and police work, others work with agencies or for health authorities. We have a small but growing membership among business and conference interpreters. All are self-employed and freelance."

APCI: The Association of Police and Court Interpreters was founded in 1974 and had 350 members in 2011.

ATC: The Association of Translation Companies was founded in 1976. Its website lists 173 member companies.[56]

Further associations have been founded in very recent years, apparently in the wake of the Ministry of Justice outsourcing its interpreting and translation services to the private company Applied Language Solutions (see 3.4.5 below):

PIA: The Professional Interpreters' Alliance was formed in 2009: "It will fight against exploitation of the profession by commercial intermediaries and the outsourcing of interpreting services within the public sector".[57] Membership is open to public service interpreters registered with the National Register of Public Service Interpreters (NRPSI). It is reported as having 400 members and appears to have had some success in boycotting Applied Language Solutions.[58]

SPSI: The Society for Public Service Interpreting was formed in 2011 to represent interpreters listed with the National Register of Public Service Interpreters (NRPSI): "As with all professions, interpreters need to be listed by the regulatory body as well as by the membership body of their choice."[59]

The significant fragmentation of the field since 2001 is mostly due to movements within public service interpreting, which is the segment closest to the politics of immigration. With respect to written translation, the two large associations (the Chartered Institute of Linguists and the Institute of Translation and Interpreting) appear to remain strong stable voices.

3.4.4. Census, taxation, and social security

The category "translator" was listed in the United Kingdom Census for the first time in 2011.

We have no information on any special category for translators in the registration system for national insurance and taxation.

The 2003 Standard Industrial Classification (SIC) listed "translation" under "74.83 Secretarial and translation activities", alongside "Call Centre Activities".[60] The 2007 SIC lists "translation" under "74.3 Translation and interpretation activities".[61]

"Translation and Interpretation Services" are included in the Office for National Statistics data. Their Services Producer Price Index (2011) indicates that the value of these services grew by just 3 per cent between 2005 and 2010.[62]

3.4.5. Sworn translators

The United Kingdom has no system of sworn translators as such.

In practice, legal documents (writs, statements) are accompanied by a certification stating the qualifications of the translator, but this is not required.

The Institute of Translation and Interpreting (ITI) qualifies some members as "Police and Court Interpreter Members" but this has no official standing with the police or courts.

The Chartered Institute of Linguists, in conjunction with the Metropolitan Police Service, created a test that led to a public service interpreting qualification relating to the police service within the UK and which is reported as being recognised by the National Register of Public Service Interpreters (NRPSI).

Interpreters registered in accordance with the above systems may be required to complete some translation tasks.

On 1 April 2011 the National Register of Public Service Interpreters (NRPSI) was detached from the Chartered Institute of Linguists and became a not-for-profit company. The Register lists "over 2,350 interpreters in 101 languages".[63]

As noted above, in 2011 the Ministry of Justice contracted the private company Applied Language Solutions for language services, and "linguists" were invited to register with the Ministry through the company.[64]

According to the Chartered Institute of Linguists, this means that the commercial supplier of services is now also responsible for recognising the qualifications of translators and interpreters, which could constitute a conflict of interests.[65] An online petition against the outsourcing had collected 2,374 signatures by 15 November 2011.[66] In December 2011 the CIOL claimed that "there is a large number of NRPSI-registered interpreters who have stated that they will not work for the Ministry of Justice through ALS – a survey over the last few weeks listed 1,167, out of the total registration on NRPSI of approximately 2,300."[67] On 19 December 2011, the of the NRPSI recognised that it would be difficult to maintain standards "if so many qualified and quality vetted interpreters refuse to make their services available".[68]

In March 2012 it was reported that 90 per cent of interpreters were boycotting Applied Language Solutions,[69] suggesting that outsourcing may not be the best applied solution.

In 2011, Applied Language Solutions argued that registered interpreters must complete 30 hours of Continued Professional Development per year in order to stay registered.[70] This appears to apply to translators as well.

3.4.6. Summary of the status of translators in the United Kingdom

If the United Kingdom has 3.25 per cent of the world potential market, it might have 10,420 professional translators and interpreters.

The combined membership of the 10 associations and registries is 9,289 translators and interpreters (assuming the members of the public service interpreters' associations are already counted in the corresponding national registry). Even if the figure is brought down to 8,000 in order to compensate for dual memberships,[71] the percentage of association membership is still a very high 76.7 per cent.

We thus find that the professional associations are performing the main signalling function. Academic qualifications, on the other hand, are increasingly catering for an international market and are not always recognised as professionally valid.[72]

The move to outsource government translation and interpreting services to a private company should be considered in all its ramifications. There can be little doubt that it upsets many of those whose status was constructed on the basis of previous systems.

3.5. Spain

Spain is of interest here because of the rapid expansion of translator training programmes in the 1990s and the relative fragmentation of the translator associations, due in part to the system of co-official languages.

3.5.1. Language policy

The Spanish Constitution of 1978 stipulates that Spanish is the official language of Spain and that Basque, Catalan, and Galician are co-official in their corresponding *comunidades autónomas* (regional administrative communities).

This creates a certain internal demand for translation between the official and co-official languages, although the co-official languages are rarely in evidence in the justice system.

Spain's accession to the European Community in 1986 enhanced the importance of translation between Spanish and other European languages. It also led to increased trade and investment, which has created further demands for translation.

Although the Spanish tourism industry represents about 11 per cent of the country's GDP, it would not seem to employ the corresponding percentage of professional translators.

3.5.2. Translator training

University-level translator training began in 1959 with the Centro Universitario Cluny in Madrid, which was an extension of the ISIT in Paris. This was followed in 1972 by a three-year first-cycle programme at the Universitat Autònoma in Barcelona, and in 1974 by the postgraduate programme at the Universidad Complutense in Madrid. The three-year model was repeated in Granada in 1979 and in Las Palmas in the Canary Islands in 1988.

In 1991 a law was passed allowing a new four-year undergraduate structure, which was adopted by programmes in Málaga (1990), Alacant (1990), Universitat Pompeu Fabra in Barcelona (1992), Vic (1993), Salamanca (1992), Vigo (1992), Comillas in Madrid (1993), Jaume I in Castelló (1994), Alfonso X in Madrid (1994),

Universidad Europea in Madrid (1995), Universidad de Valladolid in Soria (1995), and Fundación Felipe II in Aranjuez (1999).

To this should be added various short-cycle Master's programmes at the universities of Deusto (1990), Vitoria-Gasteiz (1990), Santander (1991), Valencia (1993), and Valladolid (1995), together with a Master's in conference interpreting at the Universidad de La Laguna in the Canary Islands (1988), and courses in Spanish–English translation have been taught at the Spanish open university UNED since 1988.

With the entry into the European Higher Education Area, Spain adopted a general structure where a four-year Bachelor's programme is followed by a one-year Master's. This has led to maintenance of the existing undergraduate programmes and a profusion of one-year Master's programmes, with varying degrees of specialisation.

In all, there might be some 27 Spanish universities that have specialised translator-training institutions. In 2000 it was estimated that they were teaching some 6,909 students at any given moment (Pym 2000: 232), and we might want to extend that some 10,000 now. Even when we allow for the high drop-out rates in Spanish universities, these institutions could still be producing at least 1,200 academically qualified translators – also qualified as 'interpreters' – a year.

3.5.3. Translator associations

The first translator association was the Asociación Profesional Española de Traductores e Intérpretes (APETI), founded in 1954. We do not know how many members it has, and it does not respond to repeated requests for information.

The Asociación española de traductores, correctores e intérpretes (ASETRAD) dates from 2003 and claims to have 601 members. It would appear to be in direct competition with APETI.

Newer associations have been founded in the regions with co-official languages: in the Basque Country (1987, with 185 members), Catalonia (2003, with 598 members), and Galicia (2001, with 98 members). There are also regional associations in Aragon (2002) and Valencia (2003).

Specialised associations include the Asociación de Intérpretes de Conferencia de España (1968, with 70 members), the Associació de Traductors i Intèrprets Jurats de Catalunya (1992, with 166 members), the Asociación Profesional de Traductores e Intérpretes Judiciales y Jurados, and the Asociación de traducción y adaptación audiovisual de España (2010).

Literary translators are also often members of the various societies and associations of authors.

In 2011 the Agrupación de Centros Especializados en Traducción changed its name to the Asociación de Empresas Certificadas en Traducción e Interpretación de España (ACT CALIDAD). It has 24 companies as members.[73]

For the size of the market, there is considerable fragmentation, only part of which can be explained in terms of co-official languages. It may be that the traditional association APETI, has stagnated and is unable to represent the complexity of what is happening on the market.

Some of these associations have been associated with calls for a Colegio de Traductores, which would be an official organisation comprising only those who are qualified to work as translators, presumably through academic qualifications or some degree of experience. That is, there have been calls for a "protected title", similar to the calls in Québec.

3.5.4. Census, taxation, and social security

In the Special Regime for Self-Employed Workers (Régimen de Trabajadores Autónomos) there is a specific recognition for translators and interpreters (more precisely, epigraph 774 / section 2). Freelance translators can thus issue invoices and have specific obligations to the Spanish tax system (besides paying the VAT every three months they also have to pay a monthly fee in order to be registered with the Social Security system).

3.5.5. Sworn translators

Sworn translators (from 2009 officially called "Traductores/as-Intérpretes Jurados/as")[74] are authorised by the Spanish Ministry of Foreign Affairs and Cooperation. Candidates have to pass a written and oral exam that is organised once a year. They must have a nationality of the European Union.

Candidates who have a degree in Translation and Interpreting may be automatically recognised as sworn translators, without passing the exam, if they have passed courses in legal translation.[75]

Further, applicants who have been recognised as sworn translators in another EU country are also recognised as sworn translators in Spain for the corresponding language pair. According to ongoing research by Josep Peñarroja i Fa, President of the Asociación de Traductores e Intérpretes Jurados de Cataluña (2012), Spain is "the only country in Europe that officially allows recognition of our European colleagues, whereas there is no reciprocity in any of the other European countries."[76] Since writing those lines, Peñarroja has nevertheless been recognised as "traducteur agréé par la Cour de cassation" in France (personal communication, 20 April 2012), suggesting that the asymmetry might not be complete.

In Catalonia, Galicia, and the Basque Country the regional administration can appoint sworn translators who work with the corresponding language (Catalan, Galician, and Basque).

Authorisation as a sworn translator is for life.

The current list of sworn translators is available on the website of the Ministry of Foreign Affairs and Cooperation. The list is 1,252 pages long and includes 4,164 translators who list email addresses.

The system of sworn translators is relatively distinct from what happens in the Spanish courts. Section 231.5 of the Spanish Judiciary Act (Ley Orgánica del Poder Judicial) reads: "In oral hearings, the Judge or Court may appoint any person who knows the required language to act as the interpreter and he/she shall take a prior oath or promise to that effect."[77]

In 2008 the Ministry of the Interior contracted its translation and interpreting services to the private company SeproTec.[78] Numerous scandalous situations have been reported, where interpreters hired by the company have been engaged in non-professional conduct.[79] The outsourcing has also been criticised by a magistrate as contributing to low professional standards.[80] It is not entirely clear, however, whether the lack of professional status is caused by the private company, or whether the outsourcing is simply an inadequate response to a more fundamental problem of inadequate availability of translation and interpreting services. Immigration in Spain has created a demand for interpreters in more than a hundred languages of limited diffusion; no academic training is offered for translators and interpreters in those languages; the recruitment of interpreters is thus necessarily from among non-professionals, and often from the same communities as the people requiring translation services. At the same time, budget cuts mean that there is pressure to reduce the numbers of in-house translators. A report in January 2012 claims that the Madrid courts are planning to eliminate translation services for 114 minority languages.[81] Such a measure would contravene European legislation, but neither the legislation nor the outsourcing can guarantee justice.

3.5.6. Summary of the status of translators in Spain

If Spain has 2.09 per cent of the world potential demand (Parker 2008), it could have some 6,960 professional translators and interpreters. This suggests that the 10,000 or so students in the various training programmes are finding it very hard to enter the professional market, and that the 4,000 or so sworn translators/interpreters are not all working professionally.

When production of academic certification exceeds market demands, the strength of the signal is logically diminished – a degree in translation will not have a great market value. FIT Europe (2010) reports that the average payment for translations in Spain is 0.07 euros per word, which is significantly lower than in France, Finland, or the United Kingdom.[82]

We might find a similar overproduction of graduates in Germany, for example. In that case, however, the overproduction is to some extent compensated for by a strong and relatively unified system of associations, which can represent the profession and to some extent fight for reasonable rates of pay. In Spain, on the other hand, the system of associations is highly fragmented and no unified voice is in evidence.

Spain has been progressive in recognising the professional qualifications of sworn translators and interpreters from other EU countries. However, this move appears not to have been reciprocated by any other country in Europe.

Spain has also been innovative in outsourcing the translation and interpreting services of its Ministry of the Interior, prior to a similar move in the United Kingdom. The result, however, would not appear to have solved the problem of providing access to justice for immigrants who do not speak Spain's official languages.

3.6. United States

The United States is of interest here as a comparison country because the size of its economy is similar to that of Europe, its degree of subsidiarity is in some cases comparable to Europe, and the American Translators Association operates a certification system that appears to be successful in terms of impact on the market.

Although accused by one of its own translation scholars as being "imperialistic abroad and xenophobic at home" (Venuti 1995: 17), the United States is very largely a country of immigrants, and translation and interpreting thus serve important internal functions, in addition to its importance for globalising capitalism and national security.

3.6.1. Language policy

The United States has no official language, although 31 states have some form of law recognising English as an official language. Even in those states there are "commonsense exceptions permitting the use of languages other than English for such things as public health and safety services, judicial proceedings, foreign language instruction and the promotion of tourism".[83]

In the 2007 census, some 55 million people reported speaking a language other than English at home, and of them 34.5 million spoke Spanish or Spanish creoles at home.[84] This would make the United States the world's fifth largest Spanish-speaking population.

3.6.2. Translator training

Translator and interpreter training in the United States may be dated from the foundation of the programme at Georgetown University in 1949, as a direct follow-up from the end of the Second World War at the Nuremberg trials. This was followed by the international programme at Monterey from 1965, then the creation of programmes at Brigham Young in 1976, Florida International University in 1978, Delaware in 1979, San Diego State in 1980, Kent State in 1988, and Hawaii in 1988. Programmes in literary translation were established at Binghamton in 1971, Arkansas in 1974, and Iowa in 1977.

These years are similar to those of the main translator training institutions in Europe, although the student numbers would seem to be significantly lower. Perhaps because of the high fees charged for university-level education, there has been little development of the model of the large school offering specialised three-year or four-year training in translation and interpreting. The programme at Georgetown was reported as having closed in 2001, and the programmes at Monterey largely survive because of the significant student intake from China.

There has nevertheless been a significant expansion of training in recent years. The TISAC website lists 103 programmes offered at a total of 45 institutions (2011).[85] Many of these are short-term certificate programmes or summer schools.

3.6.3. Translator associations

Civil society in the United States is highly developed, and there are numerous non-government associations for translators and interpreters. The field is dominated by the American Translators Association, but there are many further associations at the state and regional levels. The many associations for medical interpreting are under the umbrella of the National Council on Interpreting in Health Care, while court interpreting is represented at national level by the National Association of Judiciary Interpreters and Translators.

A remarkable feature of the field is the way in which many associations, including the two umbrella organisations for medical and court interpreting, expressly include employers, interest groups, academics, administrators, and sometimes government agencies, alongside practising language professionals.

No association that we have seen requires its members to have academic certification in translation or interpreting.

ATA: The American Translators Association was founded in 1959; in 2011 it stated it had "over 11,000 members in 90 countries".[86] It is organised in terms of 13 chapters in various regions of the United States, and it lists a further nine "affiliated groups", also in the United States. ATA organises a certification programme that has a positive market value.

TAALS: The American Association of Language Specialists, founded in Washington in 1957 mentioned having some 150 members in 2001 (Phelan 2001: 169). New members must be approved by a two-thirds majority at the General Assembly.[87] The statutes specify that admission is based on sponsorship and experience, not on academic qualifications.

NAJIT: The National Association of Judiciary Interpreters and Translators was incorporated as the Court Interpreters and Translators Association Inc. (CITA) in 1978,[88] although its current by-laws date from 2005. Its website claims it has "over 1200 professionals" in 2011.[89] Its members include "practicing spoken language judiciary interpreters and translators, as well as those who interpret or translate in other settings, judges, Ph.D. linguists, educators, researchers, students, administrators, and managers of non-profit community language bureaus and for-profit language agencies". It also includes interpreters who work between English and American Sign Language.

NCIHC: The National Council on Interpreting in Health Care was founded in 1998 and is a multidisciplinary organization whose mission is to promote and enhance language access in health care in the United States. It comprises "leaders from around the country who work as medical interpreters, interpreter service coordinators and trainers, clinicians, policymakers, advocates and researchers".[90] Its values include "the empowerment of limited-English-proficient communities" and "the evolution of culturally appropriate practices in health care interpreter training".

NETA: The New England Translators Association was founded in 2004 and has about 150 members. "There are no certification prerequisites for membership."[91]

ACIA: The Arizona Court Interpreters Association[92] was founded in 1980. Its 2011 directory lists 120 members.

CHIA: The California Healthcare Interpreting Association is a public charity dedicated to improving the quality and availability of language services in the delivery of healthcare. The organization was founded as the California Healthcare Interpreters Association in 1996 by group of interpreters and programme managers. The name was changed in 2003 to the California Healthcare Interpreting Association to better reflect the mission of serving the public interest and interests of LEP patients, rather than serving as a strictly professional association of interpreters. The association publishes the California Standards for Healthcare Interpreters. It offers low-cost liability insurance, financial services, training, and professional resources.

CAPI: The Colorado Association of Professional Interpreters was founded in 2001 to promote "all facets of interpreting in our community".[93]

IITA: The Iowa Interpreters and Translators Association was founded in 2004. It is affiliated with ATA and is an organisational member of the NAJIT and the Registry of Interpreters for the Deaf (RID).[94] Its 2011 directory lists about 60 members.

NATI: The Nebraska Association for Translators and Interpreters was established in 1998. In 2011 it states it has "over 200 independent contractors, NGOs, government employees, businesses, volunteer language access activists, ESL instructors and healthcare providers".[95] In 2011 it became an affiliate of ATA.

TAPIT: The Tennessee Association of Professional Interpreters and Translators has 259 members in its directory in 2011.[96]

AATIA: The Austin Area Translators and Interpreters Association was founded in 1985.[97]

HITA: The Houston Interpreters and Translators Association was founded in 1993. Its online members directory offers special filter options for ATA Certified Translators, Texas Licensed Court Interpreters, and Federally Certified Court Interpreters.[98] It is an affiliate of ATA, but not an ATA chapter.

ALC: The Association of Language Companies is "a national trade association representing businesses that provide translation, interpretation, localization, and language training services".[99]

TISAC: The Translation and Interpreting Summit Advisory Council was founded in 1991 and aims to "provide a vehicle for cooperation among organization concerned with language translation and interpreting".[100] Its members include United States and Canadian associations and representatives of translators, interpreters, employers, researchers, and government agencies.

The website of the National Council on Interpreting in Health Care (NCIHC) lists a further 10 regional associations specifically for medical interpreters, in addition to several of the regional chapters of ATA.

3.6.4. Census, taxation, and social security

The United States Department of Labor has a code for translators, and that is used for statistics as well as contracts to provide services for the government. The taxation code number is 541930 ("Translation and Interpretation Services").

The Bureau of Labor Statistics classifies translators and interpreters under "Media and Communication Workers". It gives the following information on salaries:

> The median annual wage of interpreters and translators was $43,300 in May 2010. [...] The lowest 10 percent earned less than $22,950, and the top 10 percent earned more than $86,410.[101]

By comparison, the median wage for all "Media and Communication Workers" was US$49.060, about 13 per cent higher.

Note that, although the government provides these data, the civil-society associations are not allowed to recommend or otherwise influence fees charged by translators and interpreters. In 1994 the Federal Trade Commission prohibited the "Professional Association of Interpreters", registered in Washington, from "fixing or otherwise interfering with any form of price or fee competition among language specialists in the future; from maintaining any agreement or plan to limit or restrict the specialists working time or condition; for ten years, from making statements at an association meeting concerning fees; and, for three years, from compiling and distributing aggregate information concerning fees already charged".[102]

3.6.5. Sworn translators

There is no system of sworn translators as such. Court interpreters, on the other hand, are certified by entities acting for the federal or state governments.

Certified translations are generally not required except for documents submitted to courts, which often require certification as a court interpreter. Holly Mikkelson, author of textbooks on court interpreting, comments:[103]

> The courts still haven't figured out that not all interpreters can translate, and that the court interpreter certification exams don't test translation ability. The requirement to be a certified court interpreter to provide translation for a court is not universal, and since certification is only offered in a few languages, there is no requirement at all for non-tested languages.

3.6.6. Translator certification (ATA)

No professional or academic certification is required on order to work for the United States government as a translator or interpreter. Holly Mikkelson reports:[104]

> The sophisticated clients (State Department and other agencies that use a lot of translators for important transactions) look at CVs and give priority to translators with relevant degrees, credentials, and experience. A lot of government translations are contracted out to private agencies, some of which are fairly demanding. Since it's a public tender system, the contract goes to the lowest bidder, so standards are compromised for the sake of price. In the calls

for tender, the government often states that one of the requirements is that all contract linguists be tested or certified, but they don't know what that means and the requirement isn't really enforced.

The American Translators Association and the National Association of Judiciary Interpreters and Translators certify translators (although the NAJIT translation test is a minor component of the interpreting test). Private language service companies sometimes test their contractors, and some of them use the term "certification" for that process.

The ATA certification system is based on a set of public exams, intended for "experienced translators with a high level of education". Candidates for the exams must provide prior proof of "a combination of education and work experience". A postgraduate degree is considered sufficient evidence to take the exam, but "the advanced degree need not be in translating or interpreting".[105] People with no professional experience are allowed to sit the exam but are advised against doing so.[106] The exam fee is currently US$300 and the current overall pass rate is "below 20%".[107]

Certified translators "may refer to their certification and are entitled to use the designation CT after their names in their résumés, business stationery, cards, and other related materials, provided they specify the language pair(s) and direction(s)."[108]

As such, the ATA examination system would appear to accord great value to experience and relatively little value to academic certification of translators (since no such certification is considered necessary prior to taking the ATA exam). At the same time, however, ATA maintains a worldwide list of "approved translation and interpretation schools". This list is not used to exclude anyone from the certification system.

The Translation and Interpreting Summit Advisory Council (TISAC) meeting on 25 October 2011 discussed the various certification programmes in the United States. The following are excerpts from their unofficial minutes:[109]

> Legal interpreting: NAJIT certification became superfluous with the state and federal court certifications of interpreters. NAJIT is now looking at revamping its certification program. NAJIT is looking at the ASL model which has a general exam and specialized exams (medical, legal).
>
> Healthcare interpreting: the current focus on certification might be misplaced. Standards for training should be given priority.
>
> ATA translator certification: new project identified five key points based on ISO 17024 (which is not specific to T&I industry but rather is designed for evaluation of any certification program): (1) perform job task analysis; (2) create advisory council representing all stakeholders; (3) involve the advisory council, job task analysis results and the certification committee; (4) document the workings of the certification system; and (5) establish psychometric validity, reliability and fairness.
>
> Glenn Nordin's[110] personal vision of the future of translator certification in the US [...]: Government at all levels need to seek a national certification

program and process. A tiered approach with context domains seems to be needed (apprentice – journeyman – professional – expert) in terms of competency within contextual usage domain. ATA certification could be the first step. Funding will be needed and a consortium of language associations (ACTFL, MLA, AAAL, ATA, NAJIT, JNCL, AMTA) plus state agencies can bring the political pressure to make that happen. (These are Glenn's views and do not represent USG or DoD position).

Fundamental question: Does the market want a national (or any other) certification program? With the exception of state and federal courts, there is currently no certification requirement in the T&I industry.

3.6.7. *Summary of the status of translators in the United States*

If the translation profession in the United States is compared to that in European Union, several differences are striking:

– The United States has a system of national civil-society umbrella organisations (ATA, NAJIT, TISAC, NCIHC, TISAC) that find few or no equivalents in the European system, give or take the umbrella role of the BDÜ in Germany, the fledgling CNT in Portugal, and the EUATC, which might roughly correspond to the American Association of Language Companies (ALC).
– This degree of supra-regional organisation allows ATA certification to have a market value, being recognised (although not required) by employers in both government and industry.
– The larger organisations include more than just translators and interpreters. They bring in a wide range of professionals, who might be broadly labelled stakeholders in the language industry. The European organisations, on the other hand, tend to separate translation from the wider questions of language training and use.
– The United States has just a handful of very large companies providing language services (translation, interpreting, localisation, technical writing). This means that the large US companies have a global reach that directly affects the European market. Translators involved in those sectors are more likely to seek status in terms of international organisations and employers rather than on the national level.
– Labor Department Statistics suggest that the rate of self-employment among translators and interpreters is just 26 per cent in the United States.[111] If this figure is exact, it would be much lower than the estimates for Europe.[112]
– Labor Department statistics predict that the employment market for translators and interpreters should increase by 42 per cent between 2010 and 2020.[113] This is comparable to the Bundesagentur für Arbeit statistics that show a 9.3 per cent increase in the German market from 2005 to 2011.[114] (A similar growth is predicted for Canada, although for reasons that have more to do with the retirement of the first generation of government translators.)[115]

3.7. Canada

Canada is of importance as a comparison case because it is a large country with official bilingualism, a highly developed language policy, and extensive use of translation. It is also of interest because of recent public discussion following the release of extensive reports on the costs and benefits of the language policies (Vaillancourt and Coche 2009; Vaillancourt et al. 2012), where the reported total cost (including language learning and transition) for 2006/07 was Can$2.4 billion, or Can$85 (65 euros) per capita (2012: xii).[116]

3.7.1. Language policy

Canada has two official languages, English and French. Both languages are given equal status through The Official Languages Act of 1969,[117] which makes Canada officially a bilingual country for its entire territory. The English-speaking community is distributed fairly evenly across Canada, but French-speaking Canadians are concentrated in Québec, New Brunswick, Ontario, and parts of Manitoba.

The federal Translation Bureau, founded in 1934, plays "a lead role in terminology standardization within the Government of Canada, standardizing the vocabulary used in various areas of government activity"[118] as well as providing all necessary translations for parliament. They also provide services to all Canadians in the official language of their choice.

Although many non-official languages are also spoken, there is no clear policy concerning them. In addition to non-official languages, there are over 50 different indigenous groups throughout the country.[119]

3.7.2. Translator training

Most Canadian translators, interpreters and terminologists have studied at universities or community colleges to receive training in their respective fields. In 1999 it was reported that more than 87 per cent of students registered in translation-related programmes pursue their studies in the Québec-Montréal or Ottawa areas.[120]

There are ten institutions that offer a certificate or BA with a minor in translation. Eleven institutions offer a BA Honours programme. Four institutions offer a Master's degree, however only two universities (the Université de Montréal and the University of Ottawa) offer a PhD programme in Translation Studies. The universities of Concordia and Ottawa offer a "co-op" (work-study) while Ottawa University also offers a one-year programme in conference interpretation at postgraduate level. Only those holding a BA or higher degree are eligible to apply for the reserved titles of Certified Translator (C.Tran./C.Tr.), Certified Terminologist (C.Term.), and Certified Interpreter (C.Int.), which are granted by the provincial associations. Applicants with equivalent training and experience may be eligible if certain conditions are met.[121]

3.7.3. Translator associations

Translator and interpreter associations in Canada are divided on a provincial basis and most come under an umbrella organisation, the Canadian Translators Terminologists and Interpreters Council (CTTIC), which describes itself as being "generally recognized as the national body representing professional translators, interpreters and terminologists."[122] Here we list the various organisations:

CTTIC: The Canadian Translators, Terminologists and Interpreters Council was founded in 1970 and is the legal successor of the Society of Translators and Interpreters of Canada (STIC), which was incorporated in 1956. It represents Canada in the International Federation of Translators (FIT). CTTIC "seeks to promote professional certification as a guarantee of quality and competence, thereby contributing to the advancement of the profession and the protection of the public".[123]

ATIA: The Association of Translators and Interpreters of Alberta was founded in 1979 and is an association of 151 certified translators, court interpreters and conference interpreters; it is a member of the CTTIC.

ATIM: The Association of Translators, Terminologists and Interpreters of Manitoba is a non-profit organisation founded in 1989 made up of 50 members from the private and public sectors. They are also affiliated with the CTTIC.

ATINS: The Association of Translators and Interpreters of Nova Scotia is a provincial association founded in 1990. It has 15 associate members and 48 certified members. When it was founded, ATINS became a member of the CTTIC.

ATIO: The Association of Translators and Interpreters of Ontario is the oldest organisation of translators, conference interpreters, court interpreters, and terminologists in Canada. It was founded in 1920 as the Association technologique de langue française d'Ottawa. The association adopted its current name in 1962. ATIO has 1225 members. It was the first translator association in the world whose members were legally recognised as certified professionals: in February 1989 the Province of Ontario granted a reserved title for certified members of ATIO through the Association of Translators and Interpreters Act. However, section 14 point 10 states: "This Act does not affect or interfere with the right of any person who is not a member of the association to describe himself or herself as a translator, or interpreter, or to practice as a translator or interpreter."[124]

ATIS: The Association of Translators and Interpreters of Saskatchewan was incorporated in 1980 with the aim of fostering and promoting translation and interpretation in the province. It is a non-profit professional association and an affiliate of the CTTIC. It has 65 members.

ATTTLC: The Literary Translators' Association of Canada was founded in 1975 and has literary translators working in some 30 languages. They have 150 members.

CTINB: The Corporation of Translators, Terminologists and Interpreters of New Brunswick was founded in 1970 and has 206 members. It became a member of the CTTIC in 1972.

Nunattinni Katujjiqatigiit Tusaajinut: the Nunavut Interpreter/Translator Society was incorporated under the Societies Act of the Northwest Territories in 1994.

It has 56 associate members and 20 certified members. It is affiliated with the CTTIC.

OTTIAQ: The Ordre des traducteurs, terminologues et interprètes agréés du Québec was founded in 1940 and has gone through several name changes. The OTTIAQ has close to 2000 members, all of whom are certified. On 11 June 2012 it withdrew from the CTTIC.[125]

STIBC: The Society of Translators and Interpreters of British Columbia, incorporated in 1981, is a non-profit professional association and an affiliate of the CTTIC. It has 12 founding members, approximately 300 certified translators and interpreters, and 140 associate members.

The combined membership of the ten associations is 4,438.

3.7.4. Census, taxation, and social security

Service Canada (2012) cites Canadian census figures when indicating the statistical breakdown of translators in Canada, the latest numbers being available for 2006.[126]

The National Occupational Classification is 5125 "Translators, Terminologists and Interpreters", along with sign-language interpreters.

3.7.5. Sworn translators

Canada does not have a system that involves becoming a sworn translator; instead, translators are "certified".

In order to become a certified translator, the first step is to pass the exam to become a member of an association affiliated with CTTIC. Following that, there is an exam for the CTTIC itself. Should you wish to work as a translator for the government, additional exams are involved. As part of the job requirements to work as a translator in Canada, Human Resources and Skills Development Canada states: "Certification on dossier or by examination from the Canadian Translators, Terminologists and Interpreters Council may be required for translators, terminologists and interpreters. Sign language interpreters may require a certificate or certification evaluation in LSQ or ASL."[127]

According to the CTTIC, "[t]he titles of certified translator, certified conference interpreter, certified court interpreter and certified terminologist are now protected by law in New Brunswick, Ontario, Québec and British Columbia, where ATIO, CTINB, OTTIAQ and STIBC have gained legal professional recognition by their provincial governments, bringing to fruition years of work by the leaders of those bodies."[128] The reserved title of Translator for certified members was granted by the respective provincial governments of Ontario and New Brunswick in 1989, Québec in 1992, and British Columbia in 2004.

3.7.6. Summary of the status of translators in Canada

Canada would seem exceptional in that a series of laws have made the professional associations the effective instruments of certification, rather than academic qualifications or a government institution. As explained above, this does not mean that all members of all associations are certified, it does not mean that academic qualifications have no value (they give you access to the certification process), and it does not prevent anyone from calling themselves a translator or interpreter.

Bowker (2005: 19) reports that, on the basis of her survey of 151 job advertisements for translation positions in the Ontario region, "while translators themselves appear to value professional recognition, certified status is not a qualification that is highly sought after by employers". Employers are reported as giving greater weight to candidates' experience and university degrees.

Attempts have been made to achieve a stronger form of certification, in which only members of an association have the right to call themselves translators. In 2009 the Ordre des traducteurs, terminologues et interprètes agréés du Québec (OTTIAQ) presented a *Demande de modification de statut et de réserve d'actes professionnels* to the Office des professions du Québec.[129] According to Johanne Boucher, executive director of OTTIAQ (personal communication, 2 April 2012), the request was denied, apparently because of the legislative complications involved.[130]

According to Service Canada (2012) "[o]ver the past few years the number of translators, terminologists and interpreters has increased significantly. Growing demand for information explains this increase. Since this trend should be maintained, it is expected that their numbers will continue to increase significantly over the coming years. The proportion of those who are aged 55 and over in 2006 was much higher than that of all occupations (22% compared with 15%, according to census data)."[131]

There is also expected growth in the market due to many current active translators seeking other career opportunities in journalism, writing, or teaching. Some of these positions are being filled by immigrants. In 2006, "the percentage of immigrants in this occupation was twice as high as in all occupations (22% compared with 12%)."[132]

3.8. Australia

Australia merits inclusion as a comparison country because it possibly has the world's most complex and evolved system of translator accreditation, embodied in the National Accreditation Authority for Translators and Interpreters (NAATI).

3.8.1. Language policy

In principle, Australia requires translators for trade, immigration-based multiculturalism, and relations with indigenous communities. Its current national language policy, developed from the late 1980s (cf. Lo Bianco 1987, 1990; Ozolins 1993), recognises English as the one official language but seeks to include and maintain other languages as part of the heritage of a multicultural society.

In theory, the presence of immigrant languages should provide a valuable resource for the enhancement of trade (cf. Valverde 1990). In practice, Australia's trade relations are largely conducted in English, and the official interest in translation has been more in terms of immigration and the resulting internal cross-cultural communication.

3.8.2. Translator training

Training in Australia has traditionally been through the Technical and Further Education (TAFE) system, which involves colleges in all states and mainly trained interpreters. From 1978 there were translation and interpreting courses at RMIT (Royal Melbourne Institute of Technology) in Victoria, SA TAFE (South Australia), Macarthur Institute of Higher Education and the University of New South Wales (NSW), and Canberra College of Advanced Education.[133] A Master's in Japanese Interpreting and Translation was started at the University of Queensland in 1980 and a Bachelor's programme at Deakin University in Melbourne from 1981.

The training system has now expanded to include some 20 institutions that offer programmes of one kind or another, ranging from a BA programme at the University of Western Sydney to the paraprofessional courses run by the Institute for Aboriginal Development in Alice Springs. The vast majority of the programmes are at certificate or postgraduate level. Many of the certificate programmes are short-term and part-time, to cater for the provision of social services within Australia. Some of the postgraduate courses, on the other hand, are designed for overseas students from China and South-East Asia. The Australian Institute of Translation and Interpretation in Melbourne offers only Chinese–English as a language pair and is run by Victor Li;[134] the Sydney Institute of Interpreting and Translating similarly offers only English–Chinese and is run by Qingyang Wei.[135] As in the United Kingdom, part of the translator training market has more to do with the global industry of the English language than with the domestic translation market.

3.8.3. Translator associations

Australia has four associations for translators and interpreters:

AUSIT: The Australian Institute of Interpreters and Translators Inc. was founded in 1987, bringing together existing associations and specialist groups. It has 586 members in 2011 (reported as 750 members on Wikipedia) and is affiliated with the Fédération Internationale des Traducteurs. Full regular membership of AUSIT requires "NAATI accreditation or recognition or equivalent qualifications", and members can advance to "senior practitioner" level after at least five years of "full engagement in the T/I industry".[136] AUSIT members have access to professional indemnity insurance and they benefit from significant social networking. Membership nevertheless appears to have little market value as such, and the market impact of AUSIT would appear to be reduced because, because of NAATI, it is not associated with accreditation.

AALITRA: The Australian Association for Literary Translation was founded in 2005 and had 68 members in 2011.[137]

WAITI: The Western Australian Institute of Translators and Interpreters, Inc. was founded in 1975 and has about 50 members.[138] It was the first organisation in Australia and participated in the discussions leading to the founding of NAATI and AUSIT, the national association. It has nevertheless retained its independent voice.

ASLIA: The Australian Sign Language Interpreters' Association was founded in 1991 and had 378 members in 2011.[139] According to its website, 139 signed interpreters have been accredited by NAATI since 1983, and 797 at paraprofessional level.

In all, about 1,082 people are members of one association or another. This could be about 32 per cent of the potential demand for translators and interpreters (which we estimate at 3,389 people).

None of these associations provide accreditation for their members. All accreditation of translators and interpreters in Australia is done by NAATI.

3.8.4. Census, taxation, and social security

The Australian Bureau of Statistics includes the following in its Australian Standard Classification of Occupations, under "social professions not elsewhere classified": "Translator. 2529-15 Translator. Transcribes text or recorded verbal matter from one language into another. Skill Level: the entry requirement for this unit group is a bachelor degree or higher qualification."

The 2006 Australian Census found 1,219 translators and 2,419 interpreters (main occupation) in the country. It is not clear to what extent the two groups effectively overlap,[140] but the remarkable thing is that the numbers give twice as many interpreters as translators.

3.8.5. Sworn and accredited translators

Official documents for some government uses (immigration, education, social security, driver's licence) must bear the stamp of a NAATI-accredited translator, depending on the department. (Note that the governments are co-owners of NAATI.)

Documents for use in court must be accompanied by an affidavit signed by the translator. "Courts tend to have no regard for NAATI accreditation" (Arnall), although this seems to be changing following a report by Hale (2011) and greater awareness of problems with interpreters. The District Court of Western Australia (2011) requires *interpreters* to be accredited by NAATI or to have a "nationally accredited diploma", but only requires an affidavit for written translations.

3.8.6. Translator accreditation (NAATI)

The National Accreditation Authority for Translators and Interpreters Ltd. (NAATI) has as its aim to "strengthen inclusion and participation in Australian society" by accrediting translators and interpreters; its motto is "The key to language diversity". Its vision is thus directed at the internal functioning of a multilingual society.

NAATI was initially part of what was then the Australian government's Department of Immigration. It was established as an independent government-owned entity in 1977 and it issued its first annual report in 1979, although its incorporation as a company is under a 2001 law. It is now a company owned by the

Commonwealth, State, and Territory governments. Its main business activity is to provide "accreditation and other credentialing services for translators and interpreters and related activities" (NAATI 2011). Its services are available through offices in every State and Territory of Australia and New Zealand, with the National Office being in Canberra. It is the only institution providing these services in Australia.

NAATI accreditation as a translator can be obtained by 1) passing a NAATI accreditation test, 2) completing a NAATI-approved course of studies in translation in Australia, 3) providing evidence of a university-level qualification in translation from an educational institution outside of Australia, 4) under some circumstances, being a member of a recognised translation professional association,[141] or 5) providing "evidence of advanced standing in translating".

NAATI maintains a list of approved courses in Australia. The list for 2011 includes some 38 programmes and indicates the level (Paraprofessional and/or Professional) and languages for which they are recognised. No information is provided on the criteria used to compile the list.

NAATI also accredits candidates on the basis of degrees or diplomas completed outside of Australia. In this case, the assessment is based on the numbers of contact hours in each unit of study.[142] The assessment is not based on the nature of the issuing institution as such.

NAATI currently runs online courses on professional practices and ethics, as well as a workshop on "How to work with interpreters". Its direct training role is nevertheless limited.

NAATI also functions as a directory enabling employers to locate qualified translators (its web portal at http://www.naati.com.au/ splits into two: one section for translators and interpreters, the other for those who want to employ translators and interpreters).

NAATI accreditation by testing is available at three levels: Paraprofessional Translator, Professional Translator, and Advanced Translator (the corresponding levels for interpreters are Paraprofessional and Professional).

NAATI's 2011 information booklet lists 62 languages that can be tested at various levels (none of them are Australian indigenous languages), and 23 cities outside of Australia where tests can be taken.

The general nature of the tests is as follows:

– Testing for the status of *Paraprofessional Translator* requires that candidate first have completed education to Year 10 and have proficiency in both languages. The test comprises 1) translation into English of short, non-technical passages, 2) translation from English of short, non-technical passages, 3) three questions on the ethics of the profession. Only one of the two given passages in each direction is to be translated (two passages in all) and two of the three questions answered.
– Testing for the status of *Professional Translator* requires a university degree or diploma in any field, or NAATI Paraprofessional accreditation, or attested work experience in translation, or evidence of relevant post-secondary studies. Each test is in one language direction only and comprises: 1) translation of two out of

three given passages of approximately 250 words, from different non-specialised areas, 2) three questions on the ethics of the profession, of which two must be answered.
- Testing for the status of *Advanced Translator* requires a university degree or evidence of "equivalent professional knowledge and experience", and NAATI accreditation at the Professional Translator Level, as well of evidence of at least two years of professional experience. The test comprises translations of three passages of about 400 words, drawn from highly technical or "intellectually demanding" fields.

Note that requirements for educational qualifications can be circumvented at all three levels: attested work experience may gain access to the Professional Translator level and then to the Advanced Translator level.

For low-demand languages for which no testing is provided, a translator may apply for NAATI "recognition" of them as a translator, with no indication of any proficiency level. The candidate must provide evidence of 1) proficiency in English, 2) completion of an approved short training course, and 3) referee reports indicating at least three months of translation duties.

Table 4. Numbers of translators or interpreters accredited in 2009–10 (NAATI Annual Report 2009–10).

	Translators/Interpreters
Accreditations by testing	547
Accreditations by assessment of non-Australian qualifications	206
Accreditations by completion of approved Australian programmes	1002
Accreditations at Advanced Translator level	5
Recognitions	75
TOTAL	1856

According to NAATI's annual reports, in 2008–09 a total of 2538 tests were administered and 570 candidates were successful; in 2009–10 a total of 2010 tests produced 547 successful candidates. This gives pass rates of 22.4 per cent in 2008–09 and 27.2 per cent in 2009–10.

NAATI has been considering a "Revalidation of Accreditation" system for some time, which would involve accredited translators having to fulfil certain requirements in order to remain accredited. The system is due to start in July 2012.

In 2011 NAATI launched a project for "Improvement to NAATI Testing", calling for tenders for Phase 1 on the "development of a conceptual overview of a new model for NAATI standards, testing and assessment". The tender was won by a consortium led by Dr Sandra Hale and comprising researchers from the University of New South Wales, the University of Western Sydney, Monash University and RMIT University.[143]

3.8.7. Summary of the status of translators in Australia

According to Parker (2008), Australia has 1.18 per cent of the world's latent demand for translation and interpreting services, which means the country could have about 3,389 professional translators and interpreters.

As mentioned, the 2006 Australian Census found 1,219 translators and 2,419 interpreters (main occupation) in the country. And yet, according to the statistics, some 1,800 translators/interpreters were being accredited per year. This could indicate either that the market was being flooded with accredited translators, or that the accreditations are largely for work in sectors that cannot be quantified in terms of economic demand. However, it seems more likely that in the years in question, the accreditation was being used by prospective immigrants in order to enhance their chances of receiving visas for a skilled occupation "in need". Translation and Interpreting have since been taken off the list of occupations "in need".

NAATI was the authority that fostered the setting up of AUSIT, and NAATI accreditation had to be obtained by AUSIT members until 2005–06. However, NAATI accreditation is no longer required to be a member of AUSIT, and there are signs of tension between the two organisations. As one AUSIT member puts it:

> NAATI's role in our profession is a significant and important one as far as community interpreting and translating is concerned. However, if those of us who aspire to a professional standing and lifestyle wish to achieve our ambitions, we need an independent professional institute where the standards are set by professional peers, rather than by bureaucrats with a vested and contrary interest. (Vorstermans 2010: 9)

The "vested interest" here presumably refers to the fact that the administrations that own NAATI are also the main employers of translators and interpreters in the "community" fields, so they have nothing to gain from higher fees for translators or vigorous unionisation.

In effect, the one authority effectively signalling translator quality in Australia is NAATI.

Australian and European translation policies both seek to maintain language diversity. In the European case, however, the concern has been with official languages, whereas the Australian approach has been to adapt to existing social demands, in whatever language. NAATI therefore operates on the basis of the people *requesting* accreditation (if a significant number of people request testing in a language, they must seek to set up tests). Similarly, the assessment of demands is based, in theory, on consultation with the language communities and service providers:

> The number of potential clients using a particular language is not the only relevant factor when choosing appropriate languages for translation. To ensure that printed materials are useful and culturally appropriate, it is important

to consult with Indigenous and ethnic community organisations, community workers (preferably those that work in the specific field covered by the information material) and/or potential clients. (Office of Multicultural Interests 2008: 3)

The Australian policy, as implemented through NAATI, appears not to have relied directly on university-level training programmes. NAATI accreditation can be achieved without any formal training as a translator. The fact that some 1000 translators/interpreters a year apply for and receive NAATI accreditation as a result of tertiary training programmes should nevertheless indicate the importance of (unstated) NAATI criteria in the design and implementation of the programmes. That said, there appear to be no moves towards a centralised project like the European Master's in Translation.

Looking at EU translation policies from an Australian perspective, Podkalicka (2007) observes "the disjunction between the official EU language policies and lived cultural and linguistic heteroglossia" (249). The EU policies concern national languages, whereas the translation needs at community level increasingly stem from immigration, involving the numerous languages and paraprofessional services that characterise the Australian situation. Podkalicka argues that policies need to operate "at the level of populations rather than political and economic elites" (249), and that EU policy-making thus requires "greater diversity of sources, including voices of 'real' people rather than 'experts'" (253).

Chapter 4
SOCIOLOGICAL MODELLING

The above case studies present the ways the various signalling mechanisms interact in different countries. Behind the synchronic regional variation, it is possible to see translators gaining status in a general historical process, which plays out in different ways in different situations. To understand that general historical process, we turn to the sociology of professions, and more particularly to various models of diachronic professionalisation.

Most of the models have historically been based on professions in the United States, and the most relevant applications to the general field of translation are actually from the greater China region (Tseng 1992, Ju 2009, Chan 2012) and the United States (Witter-Merithew and Johnson 2004), in both cases with reference to interpreters. Here we review the models and the applications, then we attempt to adapt them to the recent history of translators in Europe.

4.1. Models of Professionalisation

Professionalisation can be understood as the process whereby occupations seek to upgrade their status by adopting organisational and occupational attributes and traits (US National Center for Education Statistics 1997). As early as 1928, Carr-Saunders defined professionalism (later more commonly referred to as "professionalisation") as "specialized skill and training, minimum fees or salaries, formation of professional organizations, and code of ethics governing professional practices" (1928: 8). In the 1960s, in an attempt to analyse the "newer and marginal professions", Wilensky (1964) specified a number of steps towards professionalisation that can commonly be found in different occupations:

1. The workers in the occupation "start doing full-time the thing that needs doing";
2. Training schools (usually universities) are established by "enthusiastic leaders" and a sub-group of teachers or trainers is created;
3. A professional association is created, and there are efforts in the "[separation of] the competent from the incompetent, ... further definition of essential professional tasks, the development of internal conflict among practitioners of varying backgrounds, and some competition with outsiders who do similar work" (144);
4. There is "political agitation" to win the legal support for the protection of job territory and its sustaining code of ethics. These may include legal requirements for use of the job title and criminal ramifications for misrepresentation in some professions (e.g. medicine); and

5. There are rules to eliminate the unqualified and unscrupulous, rules to reduce internal competition and rules to protect clients and emphasise the service ideal. These are embodied in a "formal code of ethics".

Reflecting on the status of translators, it is quite clear that the field of translation as a whole is still professionalising, as some of the above criteria have not been met. Many of the other criteria, however, are at stake in the various signalling systems that we have been describing.

In his work on the continuing education for professionals, Houle (1980) states a number of characteristics that can serve as goals for occupations desiring to professionalise. These features may be broadly categorised as follows:

1. Conceptual: the clarification of the occupation's defining functions;
2. Performance: mastery of theoretical knowledge, capacity to solve problems, use of practical knowledge and seeking self-improvement; and
3. Collective identity: usually formed through formal training, certification, creation of a professional subculture, legal reinforcement, public recognition, ethical practice and penalties for incompetence, negligence or misrepresentation, and establishment of relations with other vocations and users of the service.

These early studies of professionalisation have since fed into "trait theory" and the "theory of control".

According to trait theory (e.g. Larson 1977; Hodson and Sullivan 2001), how far an occupation has achieved its status as a profession is determined by a checklist of the attributes it possesses. In Witter-Merithew and Johnson's (2004) discussion of sign-language interpreters in the US, the traits for the occupation in question (and perhaps for the field of translation in general) include:

1. An established body of systemic theory;
2. The extent of influence enjoyed by practitioners over the policy-making that affects their work;
3. The acquisition of academic and professional credentials that satisfy established and recognised professional and government standards;
4. The process of transitioning new practitioners into the profession through mentorship, supervision, and direct guidance;
5. A code of ethics reflecting the profession's commitment to uphold the professional ideals and standards;
6. The existence of a range of salary and benefit options;
7. Availability and degree of participation in continuing professional development;
8. Efforts to gain public recognition for the services defined in the practice standards; and
9. The existence of a culture or a formal network of practitioners designed to promote and perpetuate a shared mission, and these networks are often found in the form of professional associations.

Figure 6. Professional continuum (from Witter-Merithew and Johnson 2004: 19).

Although many occupations have sought professional status, very few have attained all the attributes stated above, and only a small number can be considered fully professionalised. Newer occupations are better characterised as "emerging professions". And some occupations can only be found on the fringe of professionalisation: they lack a significant number of these traits and have been unsuccessful in their attempts to obtain professional status. This is summarised in the continuum shown in Figure 6.

As can be seen in Figure 6, Witter-Merithew and Johnson position US sign-language interpreters as being not yet in the category of "emerging" professions. One might be tempted to place all translators in a similar slot, basically because there are few market segments with effective control over who can translate.

The trait model, however, does not tell us how a profession moves from one position to the next, other than by gaining traits. The theory of control can be of some help here. Basically, the theory expands on the framework of the trait theory by relating the occupation to its place in the labour market and within the wider society: the more control practitioners have over their work and the market in which they operate, the more professionalised they might be.

In his model of the professionalisation of conference interpreters in Taiwan, Tseng (1992) builds on both trait theory and the theory of control and further postulates that a profession is defined by the amount of *power* it obtains and that professionalisation is a *collective* effort rather than an individual one: "Powerful professions are characterized by power associations" (20). A more professionalised occupational group can exert both internal control (over the body of expertise knowledge and professional training required for entry into the field and the code of ethics for the existing practitioners) and external control (e.g. working conditions and relationships with clients). One element of full-fledged professions often mentioned as a means of control is the mystification of the specialised knowledge acquired by practitioners. More importantly, these professions can also define the needs of their clients rather than allowing the clients to set the agenda (Freidson 1986).

Although Tseng's (1992) sociological model of professionalisation was developed with respect to conference interpreters in Taiwan, it is relevant to the development of the translation profession in general. In his model, four phases are identified:

1. Market disorder: There is constant competition among practitioners, and unskilled outsiders cannot be easily excluded from the labour market. Consumers usually do not understand the service very well, and purchase decisions are often made based on price only. Hence, there is little incentive for the existing practitioners to improve their skills and knowledge. There is little consistency in training standards, so there is a "'vicious cycle' of unprofessional behaviour and mistrust of practitioners" (Mikkelson 1996: 81) and the mobility ratio (meaning practitioners entering and leaving the market) is the highest of the four stages.
2. Consensus and commitment: There is a general consolidation in this segment of the labour market. The goals for training and professional development have become clearer, and the educational programmes are of better quality and cater more to the needs of the labour market. The development of professional organisations is also better supported.
3. Formation of formal networks: There is better collaboration among the practitioners in further delineating their job descriptions, regulating the practitioners' conduct and behaviour, controlling admission to the profession and enhancing the recognition of the profession.
4. Professional autonomy: Clear and formal ethical standards are established. There is appropriate control over who is admitted to the profession, and the professional organisations work closely with the various stakeholders to achieve market control and influence legislation and certification.

Tseng (1992) also suggests that professionalisation requires a body of knowledge and a situation where consumers know how to locate qualified practitioners. Witter-Merithew and Johnson (2004), in their study of sign language interpreters in the US, put forward some recommendations for their field to move towards professionalisation, including the development of communities of inquiry and practice, a delineation between paraprofessional and professional practitioner competence, clarification of the educational requirements (e.g. a Bachelor's degree as a minimum requirement to enter the market) and educating the community at large. These suggestions are applicable to interpreters and translators in general.

Ju (2009), writing some 15 years after Tseng, refers again to the context of Taiwan and offers a slightly modified version of Tseng's sociological model, where the four stages are related to interactions between various institutions (Figure 7).

Tseng (1992) does not place much emphasis on certification, but Ju (2009) believes certification is of great importance.[1] Ju also holds the view that professional examinations in conference interpreting have played an important role in the process of professionalisation, with the involvement of the Ministry of Education. She further highlights the importance of professional conference organisers (PCOs) – or the "third client" (Ozolins 2007) – playing a role in the professionalisation of interpreters.

Figure 7. Ju's extension of Tseng's model of professionalisation of conference interpreters, adding Professional Conference Organisers (PCOs) and Ministry of Education (MOE) (from Ju 2009: 120).

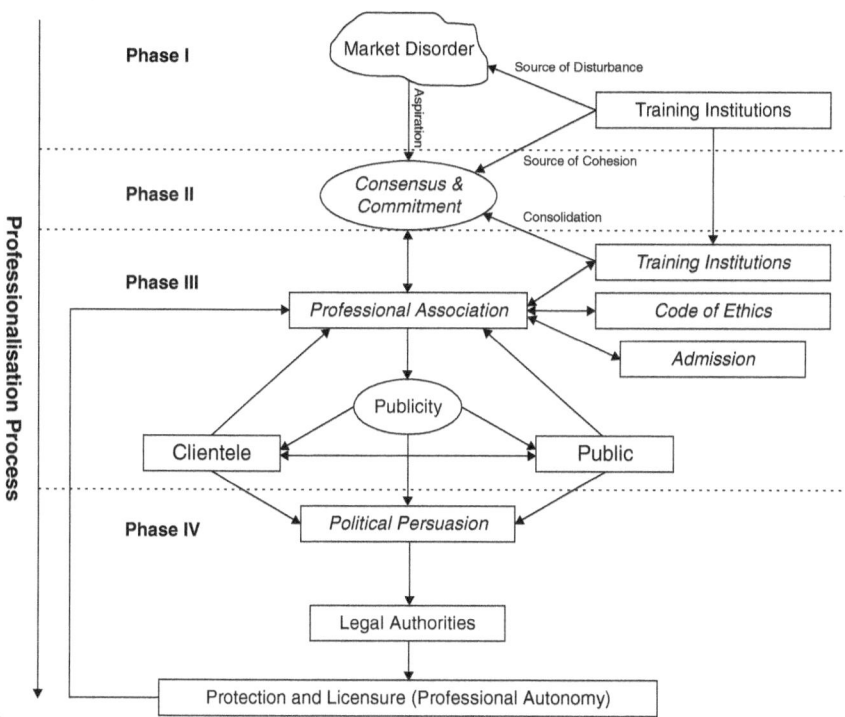

In fact, these organisers can act as intermediaries and reduce the search cost for the end users, thus overcoming one of the obstacles to professionalisation.

In the more general field of translation services, these organisers might correspond to "language service providers" (LSPs) or, more simply, translation companies, and they may have a virtuous effect on the professionalisation process if and when they are able remove the end-client's doubts about the quality of translations. On the other hand, the market for written translations is far wider and more open than the market for conference interpreting, and there are few parallels to the situation where an organisational intermediary can effectively exclude poor practitioners from the market. A bad conference interpreter can be left out in the cold; a bad translator can perhaps always find another client, especially thanks to job-market websites where access is poorly restricted (see Appendix C). In this respect, the models developed for interpreters seem not to apply to the situation of written translators.

If we apply Tseng's four-stage model to the situation of translators in Europe, it is not difficult to qualify many segments as still being in Phase 1 and attempting to move into Phase 2. At this point in the model, most attention is paid to training institutions as a source of consensus and consolidation. This might explain the ideal role of the European Master's in Translation, for example, along with various attempts to make translator training mesh better with market requirements. To move into Phase 3 and Phase 4, however, the models suggest that training institutions are not enough. Development requires active interventions from professional associations, translation companies, legal authorities, and whatever government institutions are pertinent to certification.

The message from the abstract models seems to be that these institutional interventions act together, without any one of them being the key to the rest. The interactions between them generate the energy that then becomes "publicity" and "political persuasion", which are also key elements in the professionalisation process.

Rather than go through a checklist of desirable traits, the theories of control and power invite us to look more closely at the current and potential roles of the professional associations, employer groups, and what can be done on the side of government and intergovernmental institutions. We must also consider some of the factors that might be thought to restrict empowerment: the gender imbalance in the profession, and the proportions of part-time and freelance work.

4.2. The Changing Role of Translator Associations

This history and types of translator associations has been covered in some detail in 2.4 above. Here it should suffice to recall that there are a handful of large associations – TAC (China), ATA (United States), BDÜ (Germany), CIOL (United Kingdom), and ITI (United Kingdom) – that are either directly engaged in certification processes or have the specific weight to influence public policy in the area of translator professionalisation. The Fédération Internationale des Traducteurs is also large enough and sufficiently well established to influence the public dimension of professionalisation.

The numerous other associations, however, appear to address needs that are more indirectly related to professionalisation: information exchange, training courses, legal advice, public listings of translators, surveys of the profession, and so on, bordering on the more social functions and groupings of graduates from specific training institutions.

At the same time, recent years have seen new associations appear in the more specialised fields of translation, particularly sworn/authorised translators, literary translators, and audiovisual translation. This has led to significant indices of fragmentation in some countries (see Table 2, in 2.4.3), creating a potentially confusing plurality of status signals. It may be that the more specialised associations, despite their smaller sizes and mostly fewer years of existence, are able to exercise greater degrees of control and power in their sub-fields. This has been the case of public-service interpreters in the United Kingdom, but we await evidence from other situations.

The role of associations in professionalisation is thus highly variable. On the one hand, the large established associations and federations can become key players in the process of empowerment and public awareness.[2] On the other, the proliferation of smaller associations, while serving valuable social functions, may introduce a degree of fragmentation that creates a confusing plurality of signals.

4.3. A Majority of Women – So What?

The proportion of translators who are women generally seems to be about 70 per cent or over, although this depends very much on the sector concerned.

The CIOL/ITI joint survey of their members in 2011 found that 68 per cent of the respondents were women.[3] In Germany, Bundesagentur für Arbeit statistics for March 2011 indicate that some 70 per cent of the translators and interpreters are women.[4] According to Service Canada (2012), "women held approximately 70% of the jobs in this occupation in 2006, a percentage that has been rising slightly since 1991 (64%)" and "[t]his percentage should continue to increase over the next few years, because between 75% and 85% of the new graduates in translation are women."[5] Statistics Norway data for 2010 put the percentage of women translators and interpreters at 71.6.[6] The membership of the Association International d'Interprètes de Conférence (AIIC) is reported as being 75 per cent women.[7] A survey of 1,140 interpreters in North America (Kelly et al. 2010: 9) found that 76 per cent were women. In a survey of 1,058 translators by the SFT (2010), 77 per cent of the respondents were women.[8] In his survey of professional translation in northern Portugal, Ferreira-Alves (2011: 363–6) finds that 77.3 per cent of translators are women. In Yılmaz Gümüş's survey of 125 translation graduates in Turkey (2012), 84 per cent of the respondents were women. Vigier Moreno's survey of 422 sworn translator-interpreters in Spain found that 86.26 per cent were women (2010: 424). In Dam and Zethsen's survey of 47 in-house authorised translators in Demark, 87 per cent were women (2009a: 3). In Wolf's survey of women's publishing in Germany and Austria, 91 per cent of the translations were done by women (2007: 136).[9] One suspects the percentage of women is lower in the more technical and technological segments of the translation market,[10] but we have found no reliable data on this.

We might accept the rough estimate that the proportion of women translators is 70 per cent or above, and that there are indications that the proportion could be rising (at least according to Service Canada 2012). Does this majority of women act as a boon or an obstacle to professionalisation?

Dam and Zethsen (2010: 214) report the predominance of females being considered a clear "opponent" of professionalisation, with comments such as: "A translator is considered a housewife if she works freelance or a secretary/coffee-maker, with a slightly higher status, if she works in a company." Such views, however, do not seem universal or immutable, and may be merely anecdotal.

One common explanation for the predominance of women is the degree to which part-time and freelance work can fit in with having and bringing up children. Since translation is something that can be done at home and with a flexible schedule, it is thought to be attractive to women at a certain stage of their careers. We note, though, that the consequences for professionalisation concern the variables of part-time work and freelancing (dealt with below), not the predominance of women as such.

One might further imagine that translation and interpreting, like nursing and primary school education, attract a majority of women because they are among the "nurturing professions", where the reward of the activity lies in helping people in addition to accruing social value. Such professions are thus underpaid for their levels of expertise and dedication, and relatively unlikely to go on strike, for example. Further, if women in general tend to be subservient and dominated social agents under patriarchy, as some theories would suggest (see Wolf 2007: 140–41), then they would seem unlikely to assume the degrees of control and power required for any complete professionalisation.

Such simplistic equations are questioned by data in at least three of the surveys we have just mentioned:

- In our detailed breakdown of the SFT data (see 5.3 below), women appear to translate more slowly than men in the freelance market, possibly because of less use of technology, but there is no significant difference between the sexes among salaried translators.
- In Wolf's survey of the role of translators within women's publishing in German, "according to our empirical research, female translators in the female publishing field do not really join in the game of masculine domination" (2007: 141). They are prepared to adopt interventionist translation strategies, and to leave publishers who do not agree with that degree of activism. That is, there is no subservience ontologically attached to the condition of being a woman.
- The survey reported in Dam and Zethsen (2009a) compared translators with the "core employees" of the companies in question – "the employees who carry out the work which defines the company e.g., in a law firm, the lawyers; in a bank, the economists" (2009a: 3), where only 14 per cent were women. One of the many interesting findings was that the women core employees attributed a relatively high status to the translation profession: "we found that the male core employees see translation mainly as a low-status profession, whereas their female counterparts tend to see translator status as high" (2009a: 30). That is, the translation profession may accrue a mode of status that is especially recognised and valued by women, and this may be because it is a largely feminised profession, rather than in spite of it.

These two observations should help raise questions about the kind of status presupposed by the models of professionalisation. It may be that the modes of "power" and "control" associated with the image of a fully autonomous profession are simply not those that are operative in the field of translation.

4.4. A Profession of Part-Timers and Freelancers?

The question of relative or potential power and control leads directly into the proportions of part-time and freelance work, which in turn might be part of the reason why translation seems particularly attractive to women.

4.4.1. Part-time employment

Wolf (2009) considers that translation does not constitute a sociological "field" in Bourdieu's sense of a separate social space where actors are in direct competition for the distribution of value. She argues that translation is not properly a field because, first, it is a *mediation* between constituted fields, such that literary translators are first competing in the field of literature, legal translators first in the field of law, and so on. Wolf's second reason is the high proportion of *part-time contracts*, which means that translators are often professionally active in other occupations as well: if translators can easily move to teaching, writing, or consulting, for example, they have little real need to compete directly against other translators. According to this argument, high levels of mediation and part-time employment would compromise attempts at a complete professionalisation of translators. If translators can and do engage in other activities, why should they need a strong protected profession?

The question of mediation goes beyond our concerns here.[11] The degree of part-time employment, however, has been estimated by various surveys.

In 1999 Allied Business Intelligence estimated that there were 43,222 full-time translators in Europe, and 79,488 part-time translators – about 65 per cent were part-time, and this same proportion holds for their world estimate.

In his survey of professional translation in northern Portugal, Ferreira-Alves (2011: 284–5) reports that 54.7 per cent of his sample had translation as a part-time, secondary, or occasional occupation. Many of these were combining translation with work as teachers, trainers, secretaries, foreign-language correspondents, not only in language-related fields but also in other activities like engineering, software development, economics, law, and authoring.

Katan's survey of over 1000 translators and translation professionals finds a surprising degree of pluri-employment, which implies modes of part-time status:

> In fact, very few in the profession have only one role. Over two thirds (69%) 'also' had a 2nd role, while over half (54%) 'at times' had a third role. This is apart from the 75 (8%) who vaunted a 4th role, which mainly centred around teaching, though also included "painter", "journalist" and "mother". (Katan 2009: 118)

A common form of pluri-employment is found in the number of interpreters who also work as translators. Kelly et al. (2010: 20) report that 72.9 per cent of the 1,140 interpreters they surveyed in North America also work as written translators, 25.1 per cent work in interpreter training, 25.1 per cent in "mentoring", etc. (the one person clearly has multiple occupations).[12] However, this need not indicate a significant degree of part-time work, at least to the extent that interpreting and written translation remain closely related occupations.

In the CIOL/ITI survey (2011: 9) of some 1,350 translators and interpreters, 59 per cent reported that translation was not the only or main source of household income, and the main other activities were teaching (24 per cent), project management (9 per cent), and director of a translation agency or company (9 per cent).

The FIT Europe survey of 1,377 professional translators (2010) found that only 34 per cent were working part-time towards one degree or another. The survey nevertheless explicitly excluded students, retired people, and teachers of translation.

Although it rejoices in the fact that this number "contradicts the widespread image that translation is a secondary activity [*métier accessoire*]", the result is possibly achieved by excluding from the sample precisely the segments where other surveys find significant part-time employment.

The SFT (2010: 15) survey finds that 27 per cent of the 66 salaried translators (*salariés*) who replied work part-time, but does not appear to report data on the general level of part-time employment (see 5.3 below). We also note that the 66 *salariés* are a small proportion of the 1,058 respondents to the general survey.

We might thus surmise that the level of part-time remunerated translation activity is about 60 per cent in general, although this figure can be much lower (or higher) depending on the market segment surveyed or the kinds of questions asked. The estimate of 60 per cent is high enough to be worrying for many models of professionalisation, and could be grist to the mill of Wolf's argument that translation does not constitute a "field" in Bourdieu's sense.

4.4.2. Freelance status

Part-time employment need not involve freelance (or self-employed) status, but there does seem to be considerable overlap between the two. The proportion of freelance translations would generally appear to have grown since the 1990s, when many large companies took to outsourcing their translation demands. The Directorate-General for Translation of the European Commission has been no exception to this trend: 16.4 per cent of its work was done by freelancers in 1997, 23 per cent in 2004, and 26.3 per cent in 2008.[13]

Lagoudaki's 2006 survey of 874 "translation professionals" from 54 countries reports that 73 per cent were freelancers (2006: 32).[14] Of the entire sample,

> the greatest number (48%) were freelancers working independently without an agency, 19% were freelancers working closely with an agency, 6% freelancers working cooperatively with other freelancers, 8% company owners, 9% company employees in translation/localisation companies and 10% company employees in companies/organisations of other sectors. (2006: 9)

Although 90 per cent of the sample comprised translators, Lagoudaki notes that "subtitlers and interpreters are more likely to be freelancers, whereas project managers are normally employees" (2006: 9).

The CIOL/ITI survey (2011: 7) of 1,711 translators, almost all of whom were members of either the CIOL or the ITI, found that 86 per cent were freelance.

Fulford and Granell-Zafra (2005: 8) report that of the 439 professional translators that responded to their survey in the United Kingdom, 89 per cent were freelancers.

In his survey of professional translation in northern Portugal, Ferreira-Alves (2011: 263–6) reports that as many as 84.9 per cent were considered as freelancers, most of whom were officially registered as "one-person companies".

A survey of 125 translation graduates in Turkey (Yılmaz Gümüş 2012: 40–41) found that "about half the respondents defined freelancing as their first or second role", and "about 10% of the graduates mentioned freelancing as the main role, together with in-house translating, language teaching, interpreting or researching".

Setton and Liangliang (2011: 100), in their survey of 62 translators and interpreters in Shanghai and Taiwan, report that 47 per cent were freelancers, and 24 per cent had both staff and freelance work. Liu's online survey of 193 Chinese translators in the greater China region (2011: 111) found that 40.4 per cent were freelance translators.

The weighted average of the above figures suggests that the general proportion of freelancers is around 78.4 per cent. More fairly, however, we might say that the numbers of freelancers range from 50 to 89 per cent, depending on the country and the sector, although there are reports of lower proportions in the greater China region.

There can be little doubt that translators are frequently working on the basis of short-time contracts, part-time contracts and freelancing ("self-employed without employees"), although once again this will very much depend on the particular market segment in question. The traditional career structure of training leading to full-time stable employment would appear to be in the minority. And this may in turn explain why translation seems a relatively attractive occupation for women, since it can be mixed with the tradition of having children and staying at home while they are young.

So is a part-time occupation with a majority of women condemned to never reaching a position of power and control?

In their study of 253 self-employed translators in the United Kingdom, Fraser and Gold (2001: 682) analyse the many shades of "homeworkers" and "teleworkers" but prefer the term "portfolio workers", understood as translators who "charge fees for services and are independent of their clients in employment terms". They find that "freelance translators enjoy higher levels of autonomy and control over their working conditions than other comparable self-employed groups":

> This is largely because the nature of their expertise and their relationship with clients create inelasticities in the supply of their skills. The more successful are then able to use their market position to exert substantial control over areas like pay and deadlines. In addition, the lack of a traditional career structure means that many translators have actively chosen freelance work and that even those who were originally forced into it would not now take an in-house job.

That is, individual translators may find more control and autonomy as freelancers than as in-house salaried workers. Fraser and Gold's current research in the United Kingdom (2011) may also suggest that younger translators are taking on more entrepreneurial professional identities.[15]

These findings should question some of the presuppositions made in the traditional models of professionalisation. A kind of power may indeed come through freelance part-time work at home, and this mode of control might be well suited to a relatively feminised profession. There is little hard evidence that this alternative model of professionalisation necessarily compromises the assumed need for collective action, particularly as concerns associations and relations with employers. In the United Kingdom, the National Union of Professional Interpreters and Translators (NUPIT) states that all its members are self-employed and work freelance; collective boycotting by interpreters, working through various associations, was able to close down parts of the services offered by Applied Language Solutions in parts of the United Kingdom in 2012; and the association Professional Interpreters Alliance, founded in 2009, is reported as having been granted permission to begin a judicial review of the outsourcing.[16]

Such examples should suggest that significant degrees of power and control can be achieved by a profession in which women are in the majority and modes of part-time and freelance work are common. It could also indicate that the existing models of professionalisation should allow space for new, creative ways of enhancing status.

4.5. The Role of Employer Groups

As has been claimed above, employer groups can play a very positive role in the professionalisation process by filtering out inadequate translators. This role is nevertheless not as effective in written translation as it can be in interpreting, basically because the latter involves much smaller and denser social networks. In cases like the outsourcing of police interpreting services in Spain in 2008 and in the United Kingdom in 2011, the filtering process is reported as being ineffective and the end result would appear to be a further de-professionalisation of language services, with negative consequences for the perceived status of translators.

The criteria of commerce may not always work in favour of translators, and the role of employer groups can be quite ambiguous. As is assumed in most economic models (see 5.2), employers have an interest in contracting translators' services as cheaply as possible, while maintaining standards just enough to gain repeat work from end clients. On the other hand, larger companies tend to recognise that it is in their own interest to operate in a stable translation market, with relative certainty about the skills of translators. This has led many companies to set up their own translator certification systems, which can take several forms:

– As we have noted, SDL has developed its own certification for users of its software; Google is known to be interested in setting up its own certification system; when Lionbridge works for Microsoft, its translators need Microsoft certification (see 4.6.3 below) – these are all very big companies with a long-range view of the industry;
– Online translator–client mediators like ProZ (see Appendix C) set up internal certification systems in order to reduce uncertainty;
– Not-for-profit organisations like the Institute of Localisation Professionals have certification systems based on the provision of training;

- A website company like the Global Translation Institute offers translator certification as a clear commodity, again based on the provision of training;
- The NAATI in Australia is a company, owned by the governments that are the main employers of translators and interpreters in Australia.

Beyond these modes, most companies administer a series of tests when recruiting new translators, which might be seen as a type of ad hoc certification. They are also commonly reported as giving more weight to candidates' experience than to prior professional certification (cf. Bowker 2005: 19).

In an ideal world (and in Ju's model of professionalisation), the interests of companies and training institutions should meet in a common translator certification system. In the world we live in, however, many companies seem interested in setting up certification systems that would run parallel to academic degrees, or would accommodate them as only one mode of access to the profession (as in EN15038, see 2.2.4 above).

A key question is thus to what extent employers and trainers can work together in a professionalisation process.

Information on the employers of translators has been gathered by the Optimale project,[17] which presented its findings on 1 December 2011.[18] Their survey covered 772 respondents, most of which were translation companies (mainly "Language Service Providers"), although international organisations and government departments were also included. Asked about the relative importance of professional experience and a university degree, most employers gave slightly more importance to professional experience, although the scores for a university degree are still strong (see Figure 8).[19]

The Optimale survey did not ask about professional certification as such. Further, it seems not to have asked employers if they hire new recruits on the basis of a university degree alone, which would be the question most apt to test the strength of degrees as signals of competence. Although it stands to reason that fresh

Figure 8. Qualifications and experience valued by employers of translators (data from Optimale 2011: 16).[20]

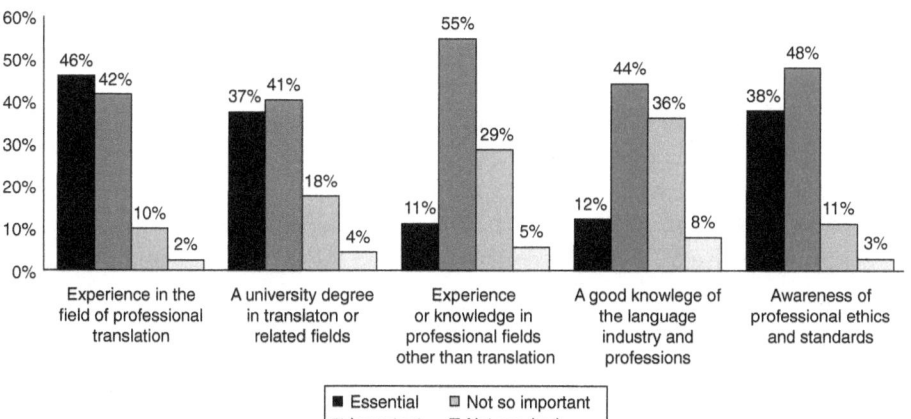

graduates do get hired on the basis of their degrees (otherwise they would never gain experience), there are usually other factors involved: work placements during training give employers first-hand knowledge of candidates; job interviews test language competence; many employers use their own recruitment tests in addition to looking at academic qualifications, and a new translator's first jobs are usually carefully monitored, as a kind of extended entrance test.

At international organisations, new recruits almost universally require a university degree, but not necessarily in translation (see 2.2.2 above), and only as a prerequisite for sitting the organisation's own entrance tests or exams.

The desirability of a university degree seems to be a general trend, although we have found no case in which the degree must absolutely be in the field of translation (the Optimale survey asked about a "degree in translation or related fields"). This latter requirement should in theory depend on how well translator training has developed in different countries. In Germany, *Diplom-Übersetzer* status is generally expected of recruits (see 2.2.3, 3.1.2 above). On the other hand, in Ferreira Alves' (2012) survey of translation companies in the north of Portugal, when asked what was "very important" in order to be a good translator, ten respondents selected "(good) foreign languages", six opted for "software and MT", and only five selected "degree in translation".

From these few indications, one might conclude that employers like recruits to have a university degree but do not generally see it as a unique signal of translator competence; they prefer to make judgements based on a candidate's experience and, in many cases, a specific recruitment test.

This may be because employers do not know enough about university training or are not adequately involved in wider certification systems. We note that ISO/IEC 17024,[21] which seeks to harmonise personnel certification processes, stresses the advantages of including employer groups in a certification process.

From a wide-ranging discussion of these issues at the European Language Industry Association (ELIA) in May 2012,[22] we drew the following tentative conclusions:

- The need for industry certification of translators is a long-term issue that is often beyond the horizon of concern for most of the smaller companies in this field.
- Outsourcing is increasingly company-to-company (seeking synergies in expertise in specific languages and fields), to the extent that issues of trust more commonly arise between language-service-providers rather than with individual translators directly. Hence the practical interest of Quality Standard EN15038, which controls how a company produces translations rather than the quality of translations themselves. Translator certification is thus seen as a secondary issue.
- The relative weight of degrees and certification depends very much on the countries involved. Employers do give weight to the IOL Diploma in the United Kingdom and to *Diplom-Übersetzer* status in Germany, for example.
- Other employers report benefiting from work-placement arrangements with university training institutions, where the qualities of potential recruits are tested "on the job". This would obviate much of the need for industry certification, at least as far as the smaller employers are concerned.

- As the above surveys suggest, the general practice is to recruit translators on the basis of their experience, personal references, and/or performance in each company's tests.
- Thanks to these practices, the relative lack of translator certification does not seem to be a significant cause of market disorder in the general sector of technical translation and localisation.

Despite these points, employer groups are quite willing to discuss these issues, as has been seen by the participation of the European Union of Associations of Translation Companies (EUATC) and Globalization and Localization Association (GALA) in events organised by the Directorate-General for Translation.[23]

4.6. Comparison between Translators and Computer Engineers as Emerging Professions

From a Weberian point of view, "professions" can be defined as occupational groups that have succeeded in controlling and manipulating the labour market in such a way that they can maximise their rewards (Weber 1947). To be more specific, for any group to be qualified as a profession, at least three criteria must be met (Haralambos and Holborn 2008): 1) there is restriction of entry into the profession, which is provided by the profession's control of the training and qualification required for membership; 2) there is an association that controls the conduct of its members in respects that are defined as relevant to the collective interests of the profession; and 3) there is a successful claim that only members are qualified to provide particular services, and this claim is often reinforced by law.

In this sense, translators and computer engineers or information technology (IT) workers,[24] as defined by the National Research Council of the United States (2001), have not yet achieved the status of profession: entry into the profession is generally free and the power of the professional organisations cannot be said to be strong.

The two occupational groups are very different in terms of sex: under 25 per cent of IT workers are women,[25] as opposed to 70 per cent and above for translation (see 4.3 above). The two groups are also vastly different in term of size. We estimate that there is a global market for about 330,000 professional translators and interpreters, whereas in the US alone there were 10.3 million IT workers at the beginning of 2002 (Information Technology Association of America 2003). At the same time, most people in the world are plurilingual and thus engaged in non-professional day-to-day translating of some kind, whereas a much smaller proportion of the global population is using computers. The difference is perhaps not in the size of the occupational groups as such, but in the degree to which the expert stands out against the background of widespread non-professional activity: when your computer hardware breaks down, you look for an expert; when you have a doubt about translation and you think you know the languages, you tend to work on the problem yourself. In both cases, of course, the more serious the problem, the more seriously you look for an expert. The second main difference might be the relative ease with which skills can be assessed: when an IT problem is solved, it is clear that it is solved; when a translation problem is solved, it can often be questioned by another translator or another authority. The user of IT services can see results; the user of translation services might always have doubts.

The two occupational groups may not resemble each other in size, expert image and testable services, but they do share many similarities. Both translation and IT are emerging industries in an information age; both are fledging professions aspiring in recent decades to seek better status and recognition through the introduction or further development of certification programmes.

Our comparative analysis here will focus on educational requirements and industry certification, drawing out implications for the development of translation as a profession.

4.6.1. Educational requirements

Shanahan, Meehan, and Mogge (1994: iii) point out that one of the possible definitions of professionalisation can be "the process of using education and certification to enhance the quality of performance of those within an occupational field".

Nowadays, due to the growth of mass higher education, recruiters in both translation and IT in many countries usually expect potential employees to have a university degree.

In the field of translation, the relative weight of educational qualifications depends very much on how developed the national translator training system is. In Denmark, the translator training system is well developed, to the extent that almost all "authorised translators" are reported as having a Master's degree in Translation and Interpreting (if and when the languages are offered in the training system); in Germany a Master's degree is normally required and respected, even though this is not stipulated by law; in Greece and Cyprus, specific training institutions have been able to ensure enhanced official status for their graduates. In countries where university training in translation is not so developed, the specific weight of a degree appears to be correspondingly less important. In the United States, for example, the training system for translators is relatively undeveloped and fragmented, so the market value of ATA certification is relatively strong.[26]

In the IT industry, according to EduChoice.org (2009), a popular career counselling website in the US, an Associate degree (usually after two years of university training) may suffice for entry-level information technology entry positions. The Bureau of Labor Statistics (2012) nevertheless reports that employers prefer IT professionals (e.g. software developers) with a Bachelor's degree or better. The situation appears similar for translators and other linguists.

For example, 2006 data from Service Canada indicate that nearly two thirds (63 per cent) of translators, terminologists, and interpreters held a degree in humanities and other disciplines that included modern languages and translation (Service Canada 2012): "The translators and interpreters positions are available first to university graduates of translation and sometimes to people who have perfect French, English and a third language with training in a specialized field in demand (law, engineering, computers and so on)."[27] In Germany, Bundesagentur für Arbeit statistics for 2011 indicate that 42 per cent of translators and interpreters have a university-level degree,[28] which seems surprisingly low but is reported as being a 5.2 per cent increase on the number for 2005.

However, a university degree may only be a commonly *necessary* condition for workers seeking entry into the fields of translation and IT, but it is *not sufficient*. In Chan's (2009) survey of translator recruiters, quite a number of respondents pointed out that possessing a university degree is only a basic requirement for translators they intend to hire. As one respondent argued, "experience is the most important thing to a translator" (166). For IT workers, some believe that colleges and universities may play a better role in offering *general* education, and *specialised* training may be provided elsewhere. This is where the certification system comes in.

4.6.2. Plurality of certification systems

The sheer number of designations now operative in the IT field has created a certain confusion among employers and service buyers: some have mocked the certification systems as "alphabet soup" (Stephenson 2002; Dale 1999). Since the first IT certification, Certified Novell Engineer (CNE) appeared around 1989 (reported by Ziob 2003), it is estimated that over 1,000 IT certifications have become available (Rowe 2003). These certifications mostly appear to function as a signal of only basic abilities, however, rather than as absolute criteria for employment:

> Human resource managers have typically used IT certifications as an indicator of an applicant's base-line suitability for a specific IT-related position. Certifications act as a signal to hiring managers that a job candidate has achieved a level of knowledge and skill necessary to perform in a particular IT job role. (Randall and Zirkle 2005: 290)

This reference to "a particular IT job role" would indicate that the plurality of certifications is not necessarily a bad thing, since each certification would ideally correspond to a particular set of skills.

A study of hiring managers from approximately 700 companies both inside and outside the IT industry found that "IT companies viewed certifications as at least as important as a Bachelor's degree while non-IT companies placed certifications slightly below a Bachelor's degree in importance" (Information Technology Association of America 2001). Another study found that over half the Chief Information Officers surveyed would hire a person with a certification, even if they had no work experience. Some even said they would not hire anyone without a certification (Childs 2002).

In the translation market, on the other hand, industry-based certification has not been shown to have such a strong signalling effect, and there are few areas in which a particular certification corresponds to a very specific skill set (ECQA certification of terminology managers would be a possible exception). This might be one of the reasons why recent years have seen many countries revamp their own translator certification systems.

While there are certainly fewer certification systems in translation than in IT, we should recall that the size of the translation industry is considerably smaller. One would hesitate to claim that the various modalities of translator certification are any less confusing or any better recognised than the various IT certifications.

4.6.3. First-party vs. second-party certification

One difference between certification in translation and in IT is that IT certifications are often created by corporate vendors (first-party certification) and to a lesser extent by industry/professional associations (second-party certification). The former includes Microsoft, Cisco, and Adobe Systems; the latter includes the International Information Systems Security Consortium and the National Association of Communications System Engineers.

In the field of translation, there are relatively few first-party systems, and the ones that do exist tend to be in sectors close to the IT industry (in new technologies and localisation): one might mention SDL Certification for the translation memory suite Trados,[29] the Institute of Localisation Professionals[30] based in Ireland, and in the United States project managers will often be certified by the Project Management Institute.[31] In all three examples, the same entity provides both training and certification. In some civil law countries, the examinations for sworn translators might also fall into this category. On the other hand, second-party translation certifications are offered by, for example, ATA in the United States and the CIOL in the United Kingdom, which do not market extensive training programmes as such. Although people from different countries can take these certification tests, the systems remain less international in scope than the IT certification tests.

In the IT industry, certification is normally seen as a product that can be purchased, assuming that one has the required training and/or skills. In the translation field, such overt commercialisation has so far remained marginal, and certification is more often thought of as a community-based service.

4.6.4. Academic vs. industry certification

Some scholars (e.g. Adelam 2000) point out that the traditional and predictable boundaries of colleges and universities can be broken with a certification system, which thus acts as a "parallel postsecondary universe". However, certification and diplomas can play complementary roles of developing multilateral signalling mechanisms, as Chan (2012) suggests. Discussing the benefits and limitations of IT certification, Brookshire (2000) emphasises the strengths of colleges and universities in offering general education and developing "in students a wide variety of less specific abilities: critical thinking, analysis, appreciation of arts and diverse cultures, foreign languages, the scientific method, and the history and politics of their own and other societies" (2). He then adds that a university education "will equip [college graduates] for lifelong success in a dynamic technical field in which a particular technology or vendor product may become useless overnight". For those working in the field of translation, this is even more valid, as the materials that translators need to work on can be constantly changing, and they have to stay abreast of these changes and become lifelong learners.

However, as Adelman (2000: 31) has quite aptly pointed out, "[i]ndustry certifications, whether in information technology or other fields, replace neither experience nor degrees. Nor do they pretend to represent an assessment of the full range and depth of knowledge, skills, or potential contribution to organizational productivity". Instead, we might say, the kind of industry certification prevalent in IT serves to *complement* experience and traditional credentials. Also, certification examinations can be incorporated into university degree programmes to act as a quality check on the effectiveness of the educational services provided by the universities.

4.6.5. Offshoring

Several professions in the developed countries (in particular Europe and the US) are reported as being affected by "offshoring" (Carmel and Tjia 2005). This generally refers to the physical and virtual relocation by a company of a business process from one country to another, typically an operational process. Offshoring has now become rule of the game in IT, as it is for large translation suppliers in the localisation sector.

According to Arora and Gambardella (2004), localisation projects are almost always initiated in North America and Europe but, because of economic considerations, many translation projects are actually carried out in other developing countries with lower labour costs. Strangely, this appears not to have had an impact on the image, nor self-image, of the translation profession, and has not become a topic of debate.

On the other hand, those working in IT, the software industry in particular, appear to have been harder hit by offshoring. According to Bartlett and Steele (2011), Indian software exports totalled a modest US$10 million in 1985; by 2010, they had reached an estimated US$55 billion.

A related phenomenon in IT has been the use of immigrant labour. In 2010, United States Customs and Immigration Service is reported as having approved employer hiring of 90,802 temporary foreign workers in computer-related occupations.[32] While this corresponds to a real demand for skilled labour, it has raised questions about how foreign qualifications are evaluated. This is turn has further stimulated the IT professions to seek better status and recognition.

In summary, as translation and IT have gained importance in an information world, their practitioners are generally desirous of seeking better status and recognition. Although there are important differences regarding the nature and expert standing of their work, both translators and IT professionals are increasingly expected to have a university degree in order to seek entry into the profession. Certification is often regarded as an "add-on" in both occupation groups and the major difference lies in IT certification being more vendor-driven and international in scope. Both occupational groups seem hampered by the plurality of available certification systems. Looking into the future, diplomas and certification can complement with each other more effectively in developing signalling mechanisms in order to achieve better synergy and alignment.

Chapter 5
ECONOMIC MODELLING

5.1. Information on Rates of Pay

Previous surveys have accumulated data on how much translators are paid in various countries. We have access to surveys by FIT Europe (2010),[1] the CEATL (Conseil Européen des Associations de Traducteurs Littéraires) (Fock et al. 2008), the Société Française des Traducteurs (SFT 2010) and a survey carried out jointly by the Chartered Institute of Linguists and the Institute of Translation and Interpreting in the United Kingdom (CIOL/ITI 2011) (see Table 5). This data updates previous surveys carried out by the Canadian Translation Industry Sectoral Committee in 1999, the CIOL in 1999, the ITI in 2001, and the SFT in 2008, as well as reports on individual countries (see case studies).

Table 5. Recent surveys that include information on rates of pay for translators.

Survey	Year of data	Respondents
CEATL (2008)	2005/06	(associations)
FIT Europe (2010)	2008	1,377
SFT (2010)	2009/10	1,058
CIOL/ITI (2011)	2011	1,743

The reports by FIT Europe, SFT, and CIOL/ITI have healthy numbers of respondents, allowing statistical analyses. However, we have only been able to obtain raw data for SFT (2010), thus allowing us to study in depth the possible correlations between earnings and variables including association membership, gender, and type of activity (see 5.3 below). The findings of the other reports will briefly be presented here, before entering the properly economic modelling.

The CEATL report on the earning of literary translators in Europe (Fock et al. 2008) clearly indicates the many difficulties involved in making cross-country comparisons. Not only are translators' outputs calculated in different ways (by the keystroke, word, page, word, hour, or annual salary), but "there are countries (particularly the Nordic countries and the Netherlands) where public lending right or grants account for a significant proportion of income and can double the basic fee" (1). The data in the report appear to come from the various member associations. Some of the numerical data appear rather impressionistic, but the information on the enormous differences in the legal and tax regimes is

Figure 9. Average price per word, from FIT Europe 2010 (analysis limited to the four countries for which there were more than 100 respondents for this question).

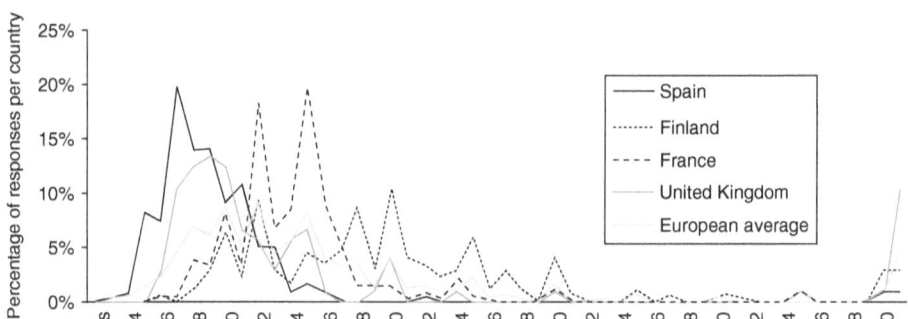

instructive, and the final calculations of literary translators' annual income, related to per capita Purchasing Power Standard (PPS), seem convincing enough. The main finding is that "in 20 out of our 23 countries, literary translators' average purchasing power is less than 60% of PPS" (70), and there are only two countries where maximum earning exceed PPS: the United Kingdom and Ireland, "but in these two cases there are no 'professional' literary translators in the sense that we understand it" (70).[2] That is, literary translators are generally not well paid, and the highest comparative earnings appear to be achieved by literary translators who are not working full-time. If there is any relation between signalling mechanisms and rate of pay, it would seem that literary translation is a field in which high status can be achieved on a part-time basis. As mentioned above (4.4), this should in turn question our assumptions of progress toward a completely autonomous profession.

The FIT Europe report, which refers to 2008, received responses directly from members of the FIT member associations in Europe. Its sample explicitly excluded students, retired translators, and translation teachers, thus gaining an image of a relatively full-time profession. Further, the sample was not weighting in accordance with the size of the various national markets. We thus have 282 respondents from Finland (0.29 per cent of the global market), as opposed to 107 from Germany (4.27 per cent of the global market).

The many findings on rates of pay include a comparison of price-per-word for Spain, Finland, France, and the United Kingdom (Figure 9).[3] Some of the differences are very clear: 0.07 eurocents per word is the most common report from Spain, as opposed to between 12 and 15 eurocents in France and between 25 and 30 eurocents in Finland. These differences are relatively unaffected by purchasing power indices (100 for Spain, 108 for France, 115 for Finland, as percentages of the EU mean).

Also significant are the wide ranges of fees in the United Kingdom and Finland, where there would appear to be quite different market segments represented. Then there is a rise around 50 eurocents per word, which indicates that some translators are quite well paid, although the report does not offer any reasons for this. The prices for certified translations show a similar pattern.

The survey carried out jointly by the Chartered Institute of Linguists and the Institute of Translation and Interpreting (CIOL/ITI 2011) gives information on the annual salaries of 1,110 translators.[4] The most remarkable aspect is the almost even spread of salaries across the categories from under 6,000 euros up to under 60,500 euros (we have converted from sterling), and then a small group who report earning more than 90,000 euros a year. This would seem to correspond to the salary spread described for translators in the United States (see 3.6.4 above), the wide range of prices-per-word in the United Kingdom (see Figure 9), and perhaps the small group of very well paid translations (at the right of Figure 9). The CIOL/ITI report nevertheless posits that the high salaries more probably correspond to translators who subcontracted their work and thus operated as "project managers/intermediaries".

Although the survey by the Société Française des Traducteurs (SFT 2012) will be analysed in some detail below, of immediate interest here is its table of annual net salaries, based on the 66 respondents who had annual salaries and answered the question (of the 1,058 respondents to the survey as such). What is remarkable here is the spread of salaries up to about 42,000 euros, then a small group (10 per cent) at between 70,000 and 90,000 euros (2010: 17). This structure looks similar to the salary spread in the CIOL/ITI survey, as well as the general pattern of the FIT Europe report.

As noted above (4.4.1), the FIT Europe and CIOL/ITI surveys, although overlapping in objects and dealing with comparable sample sizes, present quite different images of the translation profession. This is most succinctly expressed in the fact that the FIT Europe sample includes only 34 per cent part-time translators, as opposed to the 59 per cent of CIOL/ITI sample for whom translation was not the only or main source of income. This difference might ensue from the different sampling criteria (you only find what you go looking for). Even so, the wide range of market segments in the United Kingdom is clear in both surveys, as is the existence of a relatively well-paid top end of the market.

Many in the translation industry say that the prices of translations have been declining in recent years. Service Canada (2012) states that "the rate per word has decreased significantly", and relates this to increased productivity and greater completion from freelancers.[5] The downward trend is marginally reflected in the surveys. SFT (2009: 11) reports 0.16 eurocents per word for English–French in 2008, as opposed to 0.14 in 2009 (SFT 2010: 42), and it reports that the minimum invoicing amount had slightly declined from 2008 to 2009 (2010: 26). CIOL/ITI (2011: 8) finds that 48 per cent of the translators in its sample had the same or lower income as five years previously, whereas 42 per cent had higher incomes (one would generally expect incomes to rise with more experience of the market).

None of the above surveys really help us relate earnings to signalling mechanisms, beyond the fact that most respondents were members of the associations concerned. To look at the effect of signalling, particularly the effect of association membership, we shall attempt to model the data from the SFT survey (2010).

5.2. Estimations of Earning Equations

Here we present a detailed analysis of the report by the Société Française des Traducteurs on their 2009 survey of 1,058 freelance and salaried translators: 78 per cent of the respondents live in France, with an over-representation (33 per cent) of the Île-de-France region (Paris and surrounding areas), while 555 live elsewhere in France and 231 in other countries, mostly in Europe.

5.2.1. Methodological aspects

Our aim here is not to repeat information that can easily be accessed by downloading the report itself.[6] The report provides an account of the situation of translators, based on several key features of their profile (education, age, sex, etc.) and activity (in what language combinations they work, if they are affiliated to a professional association, whether they use computer-assisted translation software, etc.). Here we use the same raw data (kindly made available by the SFT) to examine what they can tell us about translators' earnings and how these earnings are related to various features of translators' profile and activity. In other words, we are aiming less at a descriptive than at an analytical perspective on translators' earnings, which may help to explain how such earnings are determined.

Our approach is in no way intended to be a definitive treatment of the issue, but as a first foray into the economics of translators' incomes, using a well-established tool of education economics and labour economics: earnings equations.[7] To our knowledge, there is very little published information that estimates the impact of several variables on translators' income, which is what we propose to ascertain here.

The SFT survey, like FIT Europe (2010) and CIOL/ITI (2011), is not specifically designed for the type of examination carried out here. The surveys can, however, be used for this purpose, to the extent that the information they contain simultaneously bears upon translators' earnings *and* translators' profile and activity. The statistical relationship between earnings on the one hand, profile and activity on the other, can be investigated, and estimations of this link can plausibly be interpreted in a causal fashion: for example, the coefficient associated with a given feature of a translators' profile (say, level of professional experience) can be seen as the influence of this feature on average and, all other things being equal, on translators' earnings. However, because of the nature of the information collected, the geographical make-up of the sample, and (although this is a lesser concern) the order in which questions appear in the questionnaire, the actual information embodied in the variables may be somewhat unstable, and the range of variables included in the data set only affords a limited range of strategies with which to address this problem. Nevertheless, running ordinary least-square (OLS) regressions with the data set provides some interesting results.

The use of the database for this purpose requires several preliminary steps, of which the main ones are the following:

Computing full-time equivalent income
Nearly all the freelance translators surveyed provided information on their annual income, their number of hours worked per week and the number of weeks' holiday

per year (as per year 2009), even though little of this information appears in the SFT report. For each of them, the corresponding full-time equivalent income (FTEI) is estimated by assuming that a full-time activity consists of 47 working weeks per year and 40 hours' work per week.

Computing hourly rates
We assume that the standard duration of a working day is 8 hours, and 4 hours for half a day. Using this assumption, we estimate, for each respondent, the hourly rate as the average of the self-reported hourly rate, half-day rate divided by 4, and daily rate divided by 8.

Exclusion of extreme values
To avoid bias in the statistical analyses due to extreme values, we removed observations displaying the one per cent highest and the one per cent lowest FTEI from the database. This leaves us with a sample of 875 observations.

It is useful to clarify some of the terms used in the rest of this section.

The term "earnings" is synonymous with "labour income" (as opposed to income from other sources such as property income). In the case of translators, earnings come from freelance work, salaries, or a combination of the two. Freelance work is typically billed in terms of input (by the hour) or in terms of output (by word, line, or page). In what follows, we shall examine the determinants of price charged per word, hourly rate, and full-time equivalent income (FTEI).

Price per word, hourly rate, and FTEI are the dependent variables that we wish to explain. However, in line with usual practice for the estimation of earnings equations, we use the (natural) logarithm of these variables as *dependent* (or "explained") variables in three successive sets of equations, respectively devoted to assessing how these variables are determined.[8]

One implication of this transformation is that the coefficients estimated must also be transformed before they lend themselves to easy interpretation. In practice, if β is the value of the estimated coefficient in an earnings regression where the dependent variable is expressed in log form, this value can be transformed into b, defined as follows:

$$b = e^{\beta} - 1$$

The parameter b can then be interpreted as a percentage: if the independent variable changes by 1 unit, earnings (price per word, hourly rate, or salary) change by b per cent. Suppose for example that our dependent variable is the logarithm of salary income and that in the original equation, the estimated coefficient (β) of variable E (say, the number of years of education) is equal to 0.152. This yields $b = e^{0.152} - 1 = 0.164$. In other words, one extra year of education would be associated, on average and all things being equal, to a 16 per cent increase in the dependent variable.[9] In what follows, all results have been transformed as in the example above, so that estimated coefficients reported here can all be interpreted as percentages.

We have tried out a wide range of independent variables in some 200 equations run with the SFT data set. Not all of them prove equally interesting, and they do not always exert a significant or clear-cut influence on the dependent variables. Our analysis will focus on the role of variables that can be assumed to have *a priori* relevance in the determination of translators' earnings, namely:

- *Language combination*, of which three shall be considered:
    DANGFRA, if a respondent's main language combination is from English to French;
    DFRAANG, if a respondent's main language combination is from French to English;
    DALLFRA, if a respondent's main language combination is from German to French.

These variables are treated as dichotomous variables, informally known as "dummies", which take the value 1 if they apply to a respondent, 0 otherwise; the "default category" is translation in any other language combination.

- *SFT membership*
- *Sex*
- *University education* (in years following a French "baccalaureate" or equivalent)
- *Professional experience* (in years)[10]
- *The square of professional experience* (because including this term allows control of the obsolescence of work-related skills)
- *Other professional activities*, if any, of the translator:
    interpreting
    (language) expertise
    other services
    use of computer-assisted translation (CAT) tools
    seniority (in number of years with the current employer).

We also control, in some equations, for *hierarchy* (but the corresponding dummy variable, "cadre", is a crude one that yields inconclusive results, and caution speaks against trying to interpret its impact), and for *location*, for which a dummy for "Île-de-France" enables us to control for the fact that translators based in or near Paris will typically charge higher rates not because of the nature of the job performed or because of the professional skill they apply to the task, but because the general price level in this region is higher than elsewhere in France. Another dummy, which is set as equal to 1 for respondents based in a country other than France, serves to control for the fact that salaries on average (across occupations and economic sectors) vary across countries – again, independently of the task performed or of how it is performed.

5.2.2. Basic descriptive statistics

As a backdrop to the statistical analysis, it is useful to take a look at some descriptive information in order to become acquainted with the sample. Some of the figures that follow come directly from the SFT report; others have been computed for the purposes of the present report. They all refer to the situation in 2010.

The sample comprises 875 respondents, of whom 681 (78 per cent) are women. The respondents are mainly located in France (77 per cent) and in Île-de-France (24 per cent). The vast majority work as freelancers (91 per cent) and have a university education (94 per cent), but only two thirds of the latter (61 per cent of the sample) have a degree in translation. The average duration of university education is 4.9 years. Respondents also working as interpreters make up 23 per cent of the sample. In 2010, freelance translators charged 14.3 eurocents per word or 44 euros per hour, on average. Their full-time equivalent income averaged 45,221 euros.

One interesting result (not featured in the SFT report) concerns sex-related differences. This figure can be obtained by dividing the (self-reported) number of words translated by the (self-reported) number of hours worked. The resulting ratio is 436 for men and 354 for women. Putting it differently, this suggests that on average, men translators say they translated more than 20 per cent faster than women translators. Of course, this figure needs to be handled with caution, since information about actual translating activity should be viewed in conjunction with the nature of the tasks performed (such as its degree of difficulty of a source text), the frequency of resorting to various types of translation software, and, why not, some indicator of the quality of the output. Nevertheless, this difference is in keeping with a result of the earnings equations presented below: being a woman has a negative (and statistically significant) impact on the earnings of *freelance* translators, but not on the earnings of *salaried* translators. This finding could be explained by different translating speeds between men and women.

5.2.3. Determinants of price per word

The equations in which the logarithm of price per word is treated as the dependent (or "explained") variable are generally less conclusive. This is reflected in a low value of the statistics known as "R^2" and "adjusted R^2", which denote the percentage of total variance in the dependent variable that can be traced back to the variance of the independent variables featured in the equation. For this set of equations, R^2s and adjusted R^2s are always lower than 10 per cent. In the literature across the social sciences, low values in this range are not uncommon; in other words, this result is not shameful, but its import is modest: the data do not go very far towards explaining what determines the price that translators charge per word. Keeping this restriction in mind, we can nevertheless observe the following:

- Professional experience has a consistently positive and statistically significant impact. However, the impact is very small and does not exceed 2 per cent per additional year of experience.
- SFT membership has a positive and statistically significant impact on price charged per word; this "membership premium" is in the region of 7 to 7.5 per cent – lower, as we shall see further on, than in other estimations.

- Translators working from German into French charge significantly more than those who do not work with this combination. Depending on the equation, this price difference ranges from 13 to 17 per cent.
- Likewise, the French-to-English combination generally commands a premium in the 10 per cent range, which holds even when controlling for "region" (including working in Île-de-France, in which foreign residents – as opposed to French nationals with French as an active language – are more likely to reside); since no significant premium applies to the English-to-French combination, the relative scarcity of skills in a language other than the majority language (French) appears to pay off.

Table 6 presents the best performing of the price-per-word equations (in terms of adjusted R^2). Statistically significant coefficients appear in shaded rows.

Table 6. Determinants of the logarithm of price charged per word (N=611, adjusted R^2=0.0943).

VARIABLE	DESCRIPTION OF VARIABLE	ESTIMATED COEFF. IN LOG	STANDARD ERROR	ESTIMATED COEFF. IN %	T-STAT
DANGFRA	translates English to French	0.04260	0.04016	4.4	1.06
DFRAANG	translates French to English	0.09740	0.04719	10.2	2.06
DALLFRA	translates German to French	0.13686	0.05561	14.7	2.46
SEX	= 1 if woman, = 0 if man	−0.04728	0.03824	−4.8	−1.24
EXP	number of years of experience	0.01858	0.00624	1.9	2.98
EXP^2	square of experience	−0.00026	0.00021	−0.0	−1.27
BACPLUS	number of years of study after French or equivalent	0.01266	0.01150	13.5	1.10
IDF	living in the Île-de-France (Paris) region	0.06279	0.03785	6.5	1.66
FOREIGN	living outside of France	0.04069	0.04280	4.2	0.95
MEMBER	SFT membership	0.06966	0.03288	7.2	2.12
INTERPRETER	= 1 if respondent also works as an interpreter, = 0 otherwise	0.01771	0.04004	1.8	0.44
EXPERT	= 1 if respondent also performs other (unspecified) expert work, = 0 otherwise	0.06026	0.04854	6.2	1.24
CONSTANT	constant (= price per word in case of 0 value for all variables)	−2.39173	0.09023	n.a.	−26.51

5.2.4. Determinants of translators' hourly rate

The regression model performs much better for predicting translators' hourly rates, with adjusted R^2s sometimes nearing 20 per cent. This suggests that the variables gathered in the survey are better suited to the study of these variables. The range of variables that have a significant impact on the dependent variable (here, the logarithm of price charged per hour) is also broader. All the technical specifications mentioned in the preceding section apply, and we can move straight to some results.

Sex has a consistently negative impact on the hourly rate. The impact is almost always significant at the 95 per cent level (a conventional criterion of statistical significance) or not much below this threshold, in the 90–95 per cent range). Among the coefficients whose level of statistical significance is 95 per cent or higher, this sex effect ranges from (minus) 7.3 to (minus) 11.8 per cent. Generally, the more variables are included in the equation, the smaller the difference between men and women translators, and the statistical significance of the estimations tends to erode when language combination is taken into account. As noted above, this sex difference may be explained by the fact that the average number of words translated per hour is, in this sample, 20 per cent higher for men than for women. However, this cannot be interpreted as a sign of sex-based differentials in productivity. One would need to control, at least, for the average difficulty of the task and quality of the output, not to mention the frequency with which CAT software is used by men and women translators. Another explanation may be suggested by observing that in these equations, the "experience" term falls just short of conventional criteria of statistical significance (the probability of a non-zero value for the corresponding coefficient generally falls in the 85–95 per cent range). Therefore, the sex-based difference may be linked to the fact that men translators are more likely to devote their time fully to their professional activity, and thus acquire more experience, than women, who are traditionally more likely to interrupt their career or to work part-time for a number of years in order to bear and raise children.[11]

SFT membership has a positive and statistically significant impact. This effect is actually higher for the hourly wage than for the price charged per word, since it ranges from 8.5 to 11.6 per cent. The effect is quite robust and the estimated coefficient is significant in all the equations in which this variable has been included.

The number of years of postgraduate training ("BACPLUS") also has a significant impact on the hourly rate, in all equations but two (but then the probability of a non-zero value is 92 per cent at the lowest). The *average* impact of the additional year of training is extremely stable and ranges from 2.1 to 2.4 per cent. Let us take 2.25 per cent as a mid-point. Considering that university training in translation typically takes from three to five years, let us assume that most of the respondents with university training have had four years of study after a baccalauréat. Hence, we would estimate the labour-market worth of a university degree, for freelance translators, at approximately 9 per cent on average (4 × 2.25), all other things being equal. This value is within the normal range of the rates of return to university education – which, however, varies considerably across disciplines and countries.[12]

Translators who also work as interpreters command a statistically significant premium, ranging from 14.2 to 18.4 per cent. This hefty surcharge is surprising, because one would expect clients to redirect their business towards translators who do *not* also work as interpreters – unless these clients are convinced that translators who are also freelancing as interpreters systematically turn out superior work, by comparison with those who only translate. A more likely interpretation, however, is that we are observing a "halo effect" due to the questionnaire structure. As it happens, the question about translators' earnings turns up immediately after the question about additional professional activities alongside translation (such as interpreting). Although the questionnaire clearly requests respondents to indicate income from translation *only*, it is likely that some respondents have been influenced by the proximity of the question about additional activities, and have therefore indicated an hourly rate referring not just to their work as translators, but also to their (always much more highly paid) work as interpreters. On balance, it seems unlikely that some respondents can impose a surcharge of 15 per cent or more on their translations, just because they also happen to be interpreting at other times.

The effect of language combination, however, is less straightforward than the determination of price per word. This may be connected to the fact that it is probably more difficult for respondents to clearly distinguish hourly rates *by language*, whereas this distinction is immediate for work billed by word translated. The one stable tendency is for the French-to-English combination to command a statistically significant premium, ranging from 13.2 to 15.7 per cent. For the other combinations (English to French and German to French), the coefficients are negative, and generally not statistically significant. Again, the association of hourly rate with a specific language combination is, for the above reasons, probably weak. An explanation may nevertheless be sought in terms of client profile: it may be that in the demand for translations from French to English, traditionally well-paying clients like banks and other financial institutions are more highly represented than in the demand for translation in the omitted categories (say, Italian to French or Spanish to French), which provide the benchmark against which the above effects are estimated.

Finally, the use of CAT software, when significant, is associated with an 8.1 per cent hourly premium. This finding is difficult to interpret. The most straightforward explanation is that CAT use speeds up translation work, allowing for faster delivery of the product and thereby justifying a higher bill. However, many other reasons might be invoked – for example, we may suppose that the nature of relatively well-paying orders is such that it justifies the use of, say, translation memories (e.g. for industrial patents or description of pharmaceutical products).

Table 7 presents the best performing of the hourly rate equations (in terms of adjusted R^2). Statistically significant coefficients appear in shaded rows.

5.2.5. *Determinants of translators' full-time equivalent income (FTEI)*

Other respondents only indicated an aggregate value for their overall yearly earnings. We have therefore pooled this subset of the data with those translators who indicated a price per word or an hourly rate (examined in the preceding sections). In order for the new dependent variable to make sense, it is important to express it in terms of a single unit – such as full-time earnings. It stands to reason that translators working with combinations that are in high demand will, all other things being equal, tend to put in more hours than those who deal with very unusual combinations, and earn more for this reason alone; this point must be controlled for from the outset.

Table 7. Determinants of the logarithm of hourly rate (N=531, adjusted R^2=0.1947).

VARIABLE	DESCRIPTION OF VARIABLE	ESTIMATED COEFF. IN LOG	STANDARD ERROR	ESTIMATED COEFF. IN %	T-STAT
DANGFRA	translates English to French	−0.03978	0.04004	−4.1	−0.99
DFRAANG	translates French to English	0.14598	0.04564	15.7	3.20
DALLFRA	translates German to French	0.22148	0.05097	24.8	0.43
SEX	= 1 if women, = 0 if man	−0.07088	0.03593	−7.3	−1.97
EXP	number of years of experience	0.01067	0.00607	1.1	1.76
EXP^2	square of experience	−0.00003	0.00020	−0.0	−0.16
BACPLUS	number of years of study after French "baccalauréat" or equivalent	0.02322	0.01091	2.3	2.13
IDF	living in the Île-de-France (Paris) region	0.11284	0.03763	11.9	3.00
FOREIGN	living outside of France	0.04340	0.03928	4.4	1.11
MEMBER	SFT membership	0.08614	0.03221	9.0	2.67
INTERPRETER	= 1 if respondent also works as an interpreter, = 0 otherwise	0.13267	0.03877	14.2	3.42
EXPERT	= 1 if respondent also performs other (unspecified) expert work, = 0 otherwise	0.02723	0.04722	2.8	0.58
CAT	use of computer-assisted translation software	0.05794	0.03646	6.0	1.59
CONSTANT	constant (= price per word in case of 0 value for all variables)	3.03608	0.08817	n.a.	38.12

The procedure for computing the FTEI has been described in the 5.2.1 above; other technical aspects are the same as for the preceding sets of results. We end up working, in this section with 640 observations.

With adjusted R^2s ranging from a little under 0.13 to a little over 0.17, the results present a good fit for a transversal dataset, particularly when one takes into account the fact, pointed out above, that the data had not been collected for the purposes of estimating earnings equations. More interestingly, most of the coefficients are statistically significant, suggesting that they are good predictors of a translators' labour income. However, some coefficients are so high that we recommend treating the following results as provisional, pending re-examination with a better, more targeted dataset.

Language combination is always significant. We note that by comparison with the omitted categories (all the other combinations):

— translators working from English to French get a premium ranging from 19.6 to 28.2 per cent, depending on specification;

- for French to English, this premium ranges from 51.9 to 58.1 per cent;
- for German to French, the premium starts at 24.4 per cent and can reach 30.2 per cent.

These results obtain across all the 20 different specifications tested.

Sex always has a negative (and statistically significant) effect; the lowest coefficient stands at 14.7 per cent, while the highest is at 21.7 per cent. Since the results apply to freelance (as opposed to salaried) translators, the sex difference between self-reported translating speeds, discussed earlier, may be part of the explanation (with the reservations already made).

Professional experience is also always significant, with a very stable average contribution of the additional year at just above 6 per cent. Interestingly, this set of results is also the only one in which the square of experience (a term that captures the obsolescence of skills) is always statistically significant (as is normally the case in earnings equations). However, the magnitude of the effect is negligible. One interesting question to examine at closer range is whether this is true independently of participation in retraining or continuing education, or if subgroups of translators divided up according to this criterion present a different value for the EXP^2 coefficient.

Formal education ("BACPLUS") is almost always significant (particularly in more detailed equations featuring a larger number of independent variables), suggesting the relevance of this variable, with an average effect on earnings of the additional year of study ranging from 4.2 to 4.9 per cent, implying a very normal 16 to 20 per cent profitability of university degrees in the translation profession.

SFT membership is mostly significant at the 5 per cent level (or close to it); keeping this conventional criterion, the (positive) contribution of membership to FTEI ranges from 12.1 to 14.4 per cent, that is, higher than in the previous models.

The financial effects of the practice of other activities alongside translation offer a complex pattern: working as an interpreter yields a positive and statistically significant and very substantial premium between 19.6 and 29.1 per cent; however, we can suspect the presence of a halo effect (see discussion above). Where featured, "expert work" has a negative and substantial (minus 24 per cent) impact on earnings, which we find difficult to interpret.[13] The provision of unspecified "other" services has no statistical significance.

Finally, the use of computer-assisted translation software has no significant statistical effect on earnings.

Table 8 presents the best performing of the FTEI equations (in terms of adjusted R^2). Statistically significant coefficients appear in shaded rows.

5.2.6. *Concluding comments*

Several additional tests, not reported above, have been carried out.

First, we have also examined the earnings of salaried translators. However, the subsample is much smaller (N=68) and the robustness of the results is not established

Table 8. Determinants of the logarithm of full-time equivalent income (N=640, adjusted R^2=0.1707).

VARIABLE	DESCRIPTION OF VARIABLE	ESTIMATED COEFF. IN LOG	STANDARD ERROR	ESTIMATED COEFF. IN %	T-STAT
DANGFRA	translates English to French	0.21796	0.06845	24.4	3.18
DFRAANG	translates French to English	0.42009	0.08293	52.2	5.07
DALLFRA	translates German to French	0.24029	0.09029	27.2	2.66
SEX	= 1 if women, = 0 if man	−0.13850	0.06587	−14.9	−2.10
EXP	Number of years of experience	0.05933	0.01099	6.1	5.40
EXP^2	square of experience	−0.00122	0.00036	−0.1	−3.43
BACPLUS	number of years of study after French "baccalauréat" or equivalent	0.04725	0.02044	4.8	2.31
IdF	living in the Île-de-France (Paris) region	0.15081	0.06509	16.3	2.32
FOREIGN	living outside of France	0.17022	0.07195	18.6	2.37
MEMBER	SFT membership	0.09524	0.05648	10.0	1.69
INTERPRETER	= 1 if respondent also works as an interpreter, = 0 otherwise	0.23076	0.06810	26.0	3.39
EXPERT	= 1 if respondent also performs other (unspecified) expert work, = 0 otherwise	−0.21603	0.08370	−24.1	−2.58
CONSTANT	constant (= price per word in case of 0 value for all variables)	9.45963	0.15816	n.a.	59.81

(particularly if one takes into account the fact that the model fit is suspiciously high despite the modest number of observations; few individual variables, however, turn out to be significant). Reassuringly, sex is no longer significant in the determination of income; neither is language combination (both results are expected in the context of salaried employment), but this set of results remains, by and large, insufficiently robust to be reported.

Second, we have attempted further exploratory investigations by carrying out stricter data cleaning. Removing observations displaying, for instance, the 3 per cent (instead of just 1 per cent) highest and lowest FTEI, and/or observations with the 3 per cent highest and lowest prices per word and/or hourly rate, revealed some instability in the levels of significance and signs of the estimations. This affects, in particular, the "education" variable, whose impact on earnings may be significant or not, or even change sign.

Third, we have estimated the same models for SFT members only. The exclusion of non-members affects the results, sometimes substantially, generally blurring the image of the relationship between translators' earnings and the variables that plausibly affect them.

Bearing these reservations in mind, the results obtained generally make sense, suggesting that the variables included in the estimations capture many relevant facets of the determination of translators' income. However, we would like to stress once more that they should be seen as exploratory. It would certainly be worthwhile to carry out a more targeted survey with a tighter grip on the following points:

First, the degree of detail and reliability of the information gathered could be improved to ensure, for example, more consistency within the information (provided by any individual respondent) regarding the rates charged. Many translators bill differently depending on language or client, and answers provided in this respect may not be compatible with information on total annual income (some translators also provide this information). Information on hours worked may also be inadequate; respondents' self-reports may constitute over- or under-estimations, and the data offer few possibilities to track them down and make corrections accordingly.

Second, the survey raises the issue of representativeness. Ideally, one would like to have information on the entire "population" of translators (or not too far from it), but the actual sample necessarily falls short of this ideal. The question, therefore, is whether respondents differ in systematic ways from the population, thereby introducing one bias or another. At any rate, the sample presents a self-selection bias (that is, only those who actually wish to answer have done so), and we may wonder whether translators willing to take part in a survey are similar to "any" translator, or whether some features that contribute to the determination of income are over- or under-represented among them.

Third, in a European Union perspective, a sample covering all the Member States would be particularly relevant.

5.3. Asymmetric Information, Signalling, and Equilibrium on the Market for Translations

The way signalling mechanisms impact the market for translations can be modelled in properly economic terms. Indeed, this modelling is a necessary prerequisite for any serious attempt to state whether individual signals actually have an effect on earnings. For the background development of the economics of language in general, and of translation in particular, see Appendix D. For the equations of the new model developed in this section, see Appendix E.

Consider a market with n translators whose actual level of skills is non-observable. The share or low-skilled translators and high-skilled translators is ω_B and ω_G, where the subscripts B and G stand for "bad" and "good".

Buyers of translation services (TS) do not know the level of skills of translators offering the services required. However, they have an idea of the average quality of the services provided by the market. Quality, denoted by L, ranges from 0 (very poor quality) to 1 (very high quality). Therefore, at market equilibrium, a relationship exists between the average level of quality perceived by buyers, L, the price of services, p, and the strength of demand, z. An increase in the quality perceived by buyers or in the strength of demand leads to an increase in market price applied to a unit of translation services.[14]

This relationship can be represented with an "iso-price" diagram (below), which is read as follows: the translation market will converge towards a certain price level (say, p_0) if demand (z) is strong, but the quality demanded L is low; this is represented by point A in the diagram below. However, even if demand is weak, a translation will command price p_0 if a high level of quality is required, as shown by point B. If, *at that same level of quality*, demand becomes stronger (that is, z increases), the market price for translations will rise, and equilibrium will move from the p_0 to the p_1 iso-price line (where $p_1 > p_0$); this shown by point C:

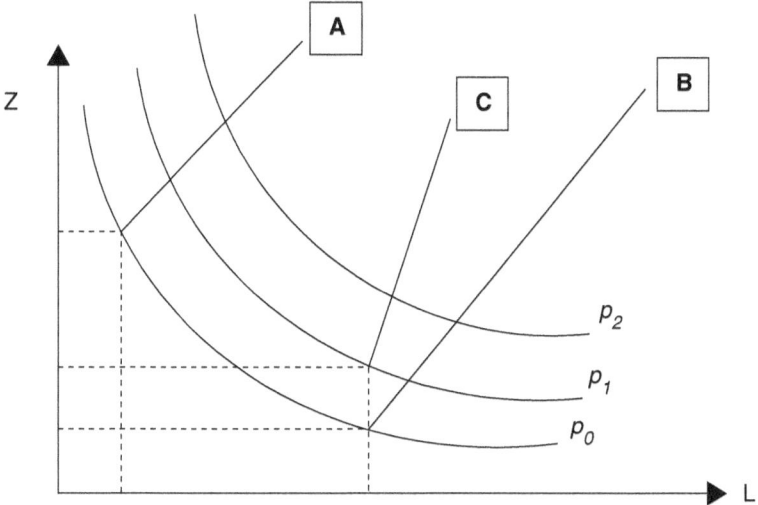

This relationship between demand, quality, and price is central to our analysis of the translation market. In order to explore the implications of this relationship, formal algebraic modelling is useful, but all the corresponding equations have been relegated to Appendix E. For the purposes of this section, an intuitive presentation of the workings of the model will suffice. It is organised in five successive steps:

Step 1. Quality, Price, and Strength of Demand: The quality of a translation is defined as a positive function of the price paid (all other things being equal, a client who wants a better translation will have to pay more), and a negative function of the strength of demand (all other things being equal, strong demand implies that a translator has more clients, will have less time for each, and need not worry too much about finding other clients if one of them is dissatisfied with the performance). Let us nevertheless assume that clients require a minimum quality level (L_{min}) independently of price.

Step 2. Translators' Effort: We have just seen, in step one, that the effort that a translator expends will depend positively on price and negatively on the strength of demand.

This relationship can also be expressed as an equation. However, we can introduce a distinction between "high-skill" (or "good") and "low-skill" (or "bad") translators (the criteria according to which a translator can be assigned to one or the other category remains a separate question). In formal terms, this distinction between the two categories of translators means that even if they all adjust their effort upwards in response to increases in market price, and downwards in response to increases in the strength of demand, the *magnitude* of these adjustments will not be the same in the two groups of translators. It is reasonable to assume, for example, that if price goes up, the increase in quality supplied will be stronger among "good translators" than among "bad translators" (because good translators can aim for high levels of quality, whereas bad translators are limited in that respect). However, just as we have assumed that clients demand a minimum quality level L_{min}, we shall assume that translators will only work if they get a minimum rate (per hour or per word, for example). Because translators are assumed to be aware of their own position (and, possibly, of their reputation on the market), we can suppose that this minimum rate is higher for high-skilled than for low-skilled translators.

Step 3. Connecting Quality to Effort: All other things being equal, more effort means higher quality. But because not all translators are the same, a given level of effort will result in higher quality among "good" than among "bad" translators. The *average* quality found on the translation market will therefore also depend on the statistical distribution of both translator profiles in the profession as a whole.

Step 4. Combining the Formal Relationships: The three preceding steps constitute a system of mutually compatible equations. They can then be combined in order to see, among other things, how the key variable of a market equilibrium model, that is, price, is affected by *all* the other variables in the model considered simultaneously (including, among the latter, the parameters describing actors' behaviour). In our case, this will tell us *how* the market equilibrium price for translations depends on:

- the distribution of translators in "high-skill" and "low-skill" categories;
- the baseline effort transaltors invest in their work, independently of price and strength of demand;
- the effectiveness of translators of both groups at transforming "effort" into "quality";
- the minimum rate respectively demanded by both groups of translators;
- the minimum quality level expected by clients;
- the strength of demand at given time.

Step 5. Using the Model: A model can be used in different ways. The classical, formal way is to running its "comparative statics". This means, in essence, calculating the first-order derivative of the dependent variable (for example, market price) with respect to each of the various independent variables (those listed in step four above), and, given the assumptions made regarding the signs and relative magnitudes of these independent variables, determining the sign (positive or negative) of each of these first-order derivatives. A less formal, but often very convenient way to use a model is to run simulations: fictitious, but plausible and mutually consistent numerical values are assigned to the independent variables, and the value of the dependent variable (in our case, market price) is computed on this basis. Note that this is only possible if Step 4 has been completed, because it is in step four that we generate the equation that defines the dependent variable as a function of the independent variables. The numerical values can be changed at will to simulate the effect of different hypotheses (for example, how does equilibrium price change if demand is weak, strong, or somewhere in between? Or, how does it change depending on whether we assume "good" and "bad" translators to be very, or just a little different from each other in terms of the baseline effort they are prepared to invest in their work *independent* of price and strength of demand?).

In the rest of this section, we have opted for the second, less formal but also more accessible approach. We shall therefore pick a set of numerical values, let them vary, and then assess, on this basis, what this implies for market price and quality provided on the market.

The first thing to check is whether the market naturally converges towards an equilibrium price p, and it helps to represent equilibrium with a diagram, as shown in Figure 10, which is constructed with the following values:

$$\omega_B = \omega_G = 0.5$$

$$\varphi_B = 0.6,\ \varphi_G = 1.0$$

$$b_0 = 0,\ b_1 = 0.03,\ b_2 = -0.003$$

$$g_0 = 0.6,\ g_1 = 0.01,\ g_2 = -0.003$$

$$p_B^{min} = 5,\ p_G^{min} = 10$$

$$a_0 = 0.03,\ a_1 = -0.01$$

$$L_{min} = 0.2$$

$$z = 40$$

Imagine purchasers expect quality to be 0.85. The (green) equilibrium line shows that the equilibrium price will be 42. But at this price, low-skilled translators and high-skilled translators will provide services with an average quality of 0.76. For this quality, in turn, the market will pay a price of 40, and so on.

The dynamics are thus *convergent*: the final equilibrium price will be located at the intersection of the equilibrium line with the average quality line, that is, 38, with an average quality of 0.73. Notice that the equilibrium line and the average-quality line also intersect when price is equal to 12. However, this point represents an unstable equilibrium: any shock that would change the price ever so slightly would push it even further from the equilibrium instead of bringing it back to its initial level.

Figure 10. Converging equilibrium.

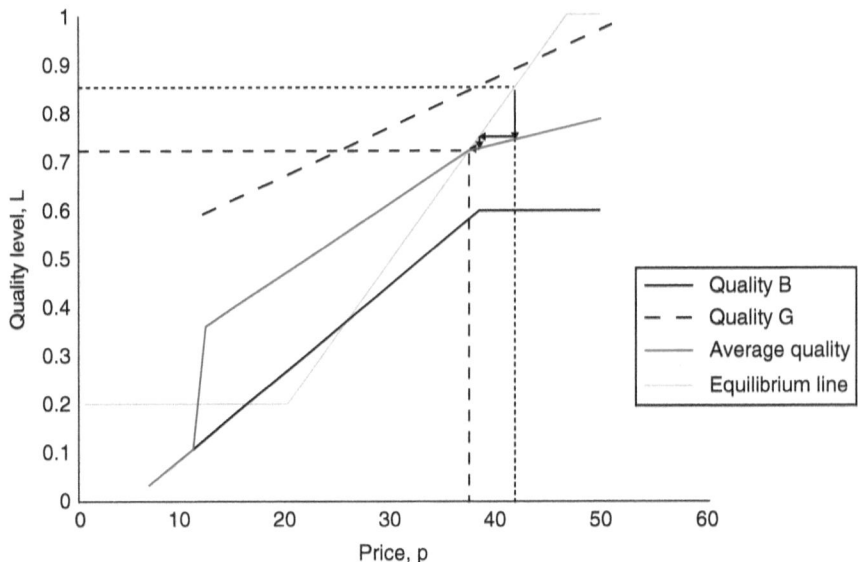

Graphically, these divergent dynamics are due to the fact that, in the vicinity of the (unstable) equilibrium, the slope of the equilibrium line is lower than the slope of the average-quality line.

Figure 10 shows that at the equilibrium price (38), high-skilled translators provide a service with better-than-average quality (0.86 instead of quality level *expected* by purchasers, i.e., 0.73). It also shows that, were the purchasers able to identify the two groups of translators correctly, high-skilled translators would be paid 44 (intersection between the equilibrium line and the quality-G line) instead of 38. In other words, the lack of clear and reliable signals of the quality of the service provided costs high-skilled translators the amount of 6 per unit of service provided.

Interestingly, the model shows that this problem of forgone income does not necessarily disappear following a reinforcement in the demand for translation services. Let us suppose that z increases (remember that parameter z stands for the strength of demand at a given time). In this case, the equilibrium line shifts to the right, since the stronger demand causes prices to rise. But a stronger demand also makes it easier to find clients and thus *might* reduce the overall quality of the service provided. Therefore, the three quality lines shift downwards (or, equivalently on the graph, to the right). Depending on the values of parameters b_2, g_2 and a_1, the equilibrium price can rise, drop, or remain unchanged and so can the foregone income of high-skilled translators.

One of the elements that emerges from the data collected and other findings reported elsewhere in this report is the large number of signals that translators can use to indicate their level of skills, ranging from mere membership of unknown associations to a degree obtained from an "internationally recognised" school of translation and interpreting.[15]

Figure 11. The effect of raising minimum prices.

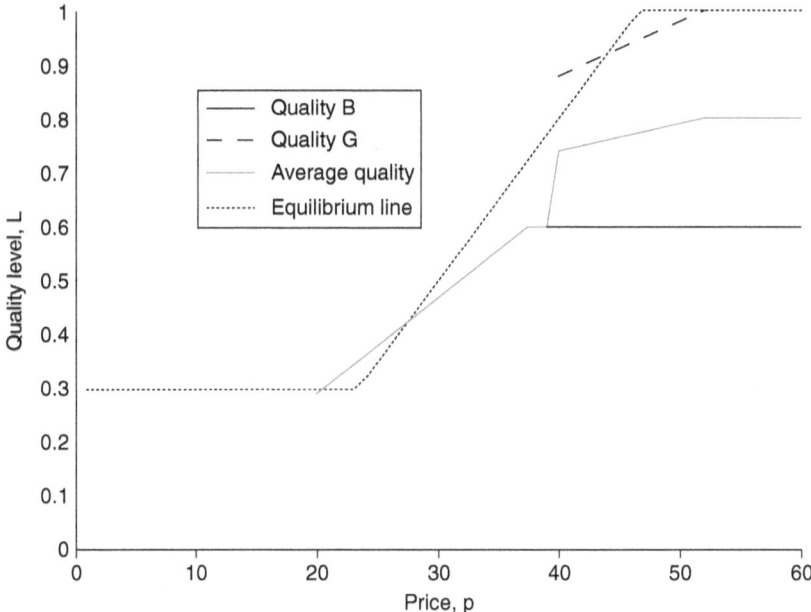

However, two problems arise when acquiring credible signals. First, it can be costly. Secondly, the abundance of diplomas and certificates, the fragmentation of associations and the diversity of national practices create noise, which can eventually reduce the relative value of the signal (obviously without reducing the cost incurred to acquire it).

The acquisition of costly signals requires translators to raise their minimum price. Let us assume an increase in minimum prices to $p_B^{min} = 20$ and $p_G^{min} = 40$ respectively, and the extreme situation where the noise is such that the relative value of signals drops to zero. Taking the same values as for the diagram in Figure 10 (except for minimum prices), we obtain Figure 11.

Figure 11 shows that equilibrium now occurs at a price of 27 and that, at this price, only low-skilled translators stay in the market. The acquisition of signals, instead of raising the value of high-skilled translators, has driven them out of the market. The effect obtained by acquiring the signal is exactly the opposite of what was originally expected, not because the signal is valueless per se, but because the increased abundance of signals is eventually detrimental to the signallers themselves. However extreme this conclusion might sound, it shows that in specific circumstances, despite good skills, despite effort to acquire the right signal, and despite strong demand, high-skilled translators (without an established pool of regular clients) can be underpaid, unemployed, or have to resort to alternative professional activities.

Chapter 6

POLICY OPTIONS FOR ENHANCED SIGNALLING

Here we move from the description of what *is* being done to an outline of what *can* be done, before attempting to formulate what *should* be done.

If there is to be a policy or some kind of public intervention regarding the existing mechanisms for signalling the status of translators, what are the basic options available?

6.1. Free Market or Controlled Entry?

The first fundamental question would seem to be whether this should be an entirely free market, where anyone can translate, or if there should be formal restrictions on who can be allowed to translate in exchange for financial recompense.

Bearing in mind that most people in the world are plurilingual, and since translation is one of the basic things that people do with language (alongside speaking, listening, writing, and reading), there can be little question of restricting the activity of translating. On the contrary, generalised translating should be encouraged, as empowerment in the field of cross-cultural communication. The availability of free online translation memories and machine translation services, together with web-based software for collective volunteer translating ("crowdsourcing"), means that generalised translating can be expected to expand, whether we like it or not. Our question here cannot concern restricting an activity, or controlling who can or cannot be paid for a service. It more exactly concerns the efficiency and effectiveness of the possible mechanisms for signalling status.

As translation generalises, two related problems arise.

The first concerns whether translation can be considered a "regulated profession", such that its signals of status are recognised not only within the home country but also in other EU Member States (in terms of the Professional Qualifications Directive 2005/36/EC).[1] Our general finding must be that most forms of translation do not currently constitute a "regulated profession", and that the provisions of the Directive could at best apply to the field of authorised/sworn translation.[2] This general approach is nevertheless of interest because the focus of attention is first on mobility (cross-border recognition) and only then on specific signalling mechanisms within each country. We consider this to be a valuable approach, and we address the issue below (6.4.2).

The second problem is how to signal *trustworthiness*: as more and more translators become available, and often with very cheap prices, how are purchasers of these services able to judge what they are paying for? In this second area, which does not necessarily concern issues of closed vs. open markets, nor definitions of professions or regulated mobility, there is much to be done.

Indications of inefficient signalling are not hard to find (see a summary in 6.4.1 below). Where they are prevalent, public policy might seek to enhance the mechanisms for signalling trustworthiness.

6.2. One Signal or Many?

Intuitively, it would seem that the strongest signal would come from just one source – a centralised governing body able to test and certify translators in all language combinations and for all segments of the market. In our comparison with IT professionals, however, we found little evidence that a plurality of certifications had a weakening effect on the profession. This merits some reflection.

Classical economists believe that competition is a good thing: the existence of a multiplicity of certifications may have its benefits as well. Competition may prompt the different certification bodies to answer better to market needs. Examples can be drawn from organic food products and testing of English as a foreign language.

For the certification of organically produced foods, it was generally assumed that the government should be the only authority to define what constitutes an organic product. Once the government regulations were in force, the private-sector standards would be redundant and disappear. But the real-world "experiment" has shown that this was not the case: there are some markets where private labelling schemes, representing additional standards, enjoy a very strong position. For example, according to Rundgren (2005), in Sweden almost all organic products sold will carry the private KRAV (Swedish Association for Alternative Cultivation) label. In the United Kingdom and Switzerland, organic food producers seek to obtain both the government seal and the private-sector labels.

Another example can be found in the field of international English testing services. Nowadays, there are two major certification systems for English as a Foreign Language (EFL) students seeking to have their skills evaluated: TOEFL (Test of English as a Foreign Language) and IELTS (International English Language Testing System). TOEFL is administered by Educational Testing (ETS) from the United States and has long been the most popular EFL test taken by students seeking entry to colleges and universities in the US and elsewhere. However, IELTS (currently jointly managed by University of Cambridge ESOL Examinations, the British Council, and IDP Education) entered the market in 2005. As this test assesses both the receptive and productive skills of the English language, it poses a genuine threat to TOEFL. To some extent, this has stimulated the ETS to revamp TOEFL (TOEFL-iBT was introduced in 2005) as the old test used to assess only reading, listening, and grammar but did not test candidates on their writing and speaking abilities. Although the ETS states that more than 24 million students took TOEFL in 2009 alone, 1.4 million candidates took the IELTS test in over 130 countries, and there is some speculation that IELTS may replace TOEFL.

These examples suggest that a degree of competition between certification systems may be beneficial. The examples, however, concern situations where a limited number of strong signalling mechanisms are competing directly, in such a way that all are able to gain some degree of trust. They are a long way from open competition between anyone with a cool website.

A further reason for plurality may be the specificity with which skills can be signalled. In the computer industry, the many certifications available often concern the ability to work with one series of products or another, or to perform specific tasks. In this sense, each certification states what a person can do. In the translation field, one might similarly imagine separate signals for language skills, translation-memory skills, post-editing skills, revision skills, audiovisual skills, legal translation skills, paraprofessional skills, and so on. Of course, those many signalling mechanisms could be built into the one certification system.

A real-world test of plurality in the translation field would be the proliferation of online translator–client portals in recent years (see Appendix C). There can be little doubt that competition between the various signalling mechanisms has maintained considerable variation and innovation in the field. At the same time, this is a service that in theory becomes more valuable as its databases increase, and since the databases increase the more it is used, value and use should constitute a virtuous circle.[3] Thanks to this logic, the field has seen the emergence of just one large dominant player, ProZ. And yet there is a built-in corrective: as the databases of translators on ProZ becomes very large and the prices of translations are thus driven down, the general quality of the translations declines, unhappy clients no longer trust the signal, and the size itself threatens to close down the entire system. This may be why the other portals continue to exist, some in more specialised fields. And it is certainly why ProZ has introduced its own internal certification system. That is, the plurality itself may create the need for some kind of corrective signalling mechanism.

6.3. Signalling as a Commodity or a Service?

A basic philosophical difference concerns the nature of signalling as a commodity. When private companies sell certification, they do so because the certification itself has a market value – people who have it can receive more financial value for their services. This view sits poorly with the traditional role of education systems and government ministries, who see their degrees and authorisations as more of a service provided to society.

The "service" view can be supported by the argument that translation services themselves constitute a (partially) public good, especially in the public sphere. In theory, better information provides non-excludable and non-rival benefits to all members of society. On this view, government should subsidise (in whatever way) the development of the translation profession. One baulks, however, at the idea that this particular kind of service should have *carte blanche* with respect to public funds, and there may be legitimate doubts as to whether all members of society benefit equally from all translation.

The "service" view is also seriously compromised by the changing nature of academic institutions. As education is pushed towards the needs of industry, it itself becomes an industry. In some countries, notably the United Kingdom, programmes are in direct competition with each other and there is a resulting scramble for fee-paying students and any sign of status that can bring fee-paying students.[4] For these institutions, the status they confer on graduates is very much a commodity: high tuition fees are justified in terms of the added income the status will bring to graduates during their professional careers.

In these circumstances, it is difficult to maintain a "service" view across the board. Status signals, especially degrees and professional certifications, should be recognised as having a market value.

In principle, the costs of any efficient signalling system should be borne by the people benefiting from the status signal. In many situations, this will mean the translators themselves should pay for their degrees and certifications.

However, in situations of extreme market disorder where human rights and government interests are directly at stake, the beneficiaries of efficient signalling will not only be the translators. For example, the certification of sworn or authorised translators is in the direct interests of the justice systems and government institutions that generally employ those translators. Further, in the provision of translation services to new immigrant groups and in the interests of border security, a reduction in market disorder first benefits the institutions responsible for supplying those translation services. In these cases, the economics of status as a commodity may indeed justify a service mentality, where it is in the interests of government institutions to fund efficient signalling of translator status because those institutions are themselves the first to benefit (especially when they also legislate the fees paid to translators).

6.4. Modes of Possible Intervention

As we start to outline what could be done, it is good to review the actual policy options available, and some of the established instruments in the European Union context. Here we present some basic options, listed in a rough order of relative difficulty and cost.

6.4.1. Laissez faire

To do nothing is to assume that the current signalling mechanisms are either creating equilibriums or are subject to market forces that will take them in that direction. We have found no consistent evidence of either scenario. On the other hand, we have found signs of market disorder with respect to the following aspects:

- General lack of signalling with regard to translation services in "immigrant" languages;
- Unrestricted web-based marketing of certification as a commodity, with little testing of language skills;

- Very little recognition of the status of sworn or authorised translator in other countries, in a world of increasing professional mobility;
- Lists of authorised translators that far exceed market demands;
- Online lists of professional translators with no checking of qualifications or skills;
- Employers who trust professional experience or their own recruitment tests rather than academic qualifications or professional certification;
- Outsourcing to private companies that have little regard for skills or qualifications (in Spain), or are not trusted by translation professionals (in the United Kingdom);
- Some evidence of declining prices for translations;
- Significant fragmentation of the market in some countries, with a corresponding multiplicity of translator associations.

These features would suggest that the market is not solving all the problems by itself.

6.4.2. A European Professional Card for authorised/sworn translators?

A relatively simply signalling mechanism is a card that identifies that the bearer is a translator. The FIT identity card system has been in place since 2004 and is available to translators, interpreters, and terminologists that belong to FIT member associations.[5] The card costs 25 euros, which in principle is paid by the translator, interpreter, or terminologist.[6] It is not clear whether the card has a market value, but there does appear to be a demand among translators.[7] The card does not address the fact that the member associations have very different membership criteria.

A more substantial signalling mechanism would involve a European Professional Card for Translators.[8] The general idea of professional cards is proposed in the 2011 Green Paper on *Modernising the Professional Qualifications Directive*, which seeks to make the 2005 Professional Qualifications Directive more effective. The basic idea here is that all professionals should have their qualifications recognised in all EU Member States, but that the burden of the recognition process should not fall entirely on the receiving state, as has been the case. Under the proposal, the Member State of departure would first issue a European Professional Card, which would be electronically linked to all the bearer's certifications and academic qualifications. The receiving Member State then only has to check the validity of the card, and they will have access to all the documents concerned. Further, all the authorities involved in this would be members of the Internal Market Information System.

As it stands, the proposal concerns regulated professions: it specifically mentions the professions of doctors, nurses, midwives, pharmacists, architects, and "craft, trade and industry", but not translators. It generally assumes that the profession in question is regulated in both the countries concerned. As such, we can only see this as applying well to authorised/sworn translation, which would appear to constitute a regulated profession in many countries,[9] even though the modes of entry into the profession are quite different (see 2.3 above).

The card proposal also envisages situations where the worker moved from a country where the profession is not regulated to a country where it is. In such cases, specific reference is made to the most problematic feature of status, namely mutual trust:

> To ensure mutual trust, the card would not be issued by any commercial entities. When a profession is not regulated in the Member State of departure it would be up to that Member State to designate a competent public authority to issue the card. (2011: 3)

This placing of trust in public authorities would appear to fall into the "service" mentality outlined above. However, in this case, the Member State of departure can be assumed to have few benefits to gain from issuing the card, so all costs would presumably have to be borne by the main beneficiaries, the authorised/sworn translators.

Several problems might be envisaged with actually having translators accepted in the legal systems of other countries, as has been seen in the case of Peñarroja i Fa's attempts to obtain recognition in France and Switzerland of his Spanish qualifications as a sworn translator (see 2.3.6 above). The recent success of his case in France would nevertheless suggest that at least some of those problems can be overcome.

A more basic problem concerns the very nature of translation. Healthcare workers and architects work with objects that are basically the same in many countries – human bodies, medication, buildings. Language is a secondary consideration, to the extent that "language control can only take place after the end of the recognition procedure and cannot be a reason for refusing recognition of professional qualifications as such" (Green Paper: 14n). Translators, on the other hand, work directly on languages, at least one of which is often not the home language of the place they are working. It is thus harder for authorities and employers to control what they are doing, and all the degree of risk taken when trusting the authority issuing a Professional Card must thus be greater. In some cases, it will be difficult to argue that the languages have always been adequately tested in the Member State of departure. For instance, a sworn translator certified in Spain for work from German into Spanish will have been tested for German as Language B, whereas professional work in Germany will require German as Language A (the translator's strongest language, usually the language one translates into). Further language testing might thus be required.

Many of these issues could be addressed within the framework of a Common Platform.

6.4.3. A Common Platform for authorised/sworn translators?

Article 15 of the Professional Qualifications Directive (2005) aims to facilitate the recognition of professional qualifications on the basis of "Common Platforms". This allows each Member State to regulate access to the profession in its territory, but in principle requires it to recognise the qualifications issued in other Member States.

The nature of these platforms is voluntary, however, which means that "a fully qualified professional who does not satisfy the criteria of the platform would continue to benefit from the rules on recognition" ("Common Platforms": 2),[10] although further requirements may have to be met, such as an aptitude test or an adaptation period.

The establishment of a Common Platform requires an "inventory of national regulations", including the level and type of training and the required experience, the differences between them, and the various compensatory measures that may or may not be required.

With respect to authorised/sworn translation, we would hope to have begun this work in 2.3 above: it is exceedingly difficult to compile and compare the training and experience required of authorised/sworn translators, bearing in mind that this must be done for at least two third of the EU Member States.

Further, if countries compile and maintain public registries of authorised/sworn translators, the risk of fraud and abuse should be minimised.

Quite another question, however, is whether the administrative authorities in the Member States have any real interest in pursuing this. We have found no evidence of a specific shortage of professionals in the field of authorised/sworn translation, and there are several cases where there seems to be a marked over-supply of qualified translators. Further, the specificities of languages and legal systems involve a very local distribution of trust, and resistance can be expected (again, see the issues raised in the Peñarroja cases).

On the other hand, pressure in favour of a Common Platform could probably come from the various professional associations of authorised/sworn interpreters. This need not be because they are actively interested in enhanced mobility. It would more likely be because the Common Platform would retroactively project attention onto the need to improve the signalling mechanisms in many countries, with respect to both training and professional testing, and with particular emphasis on the scandalous situations obtaining in some areas with respect to services in immigrant languages. The active participation of many national associations and training institutions in the European Legal Interpreters and Translators Association (EULITA)[11] would suggest that effective pressure in favour of a Common Platform should come from there.

It is difficult to see a Common Platform evolving for other types of translation, basically because they seem not generally to be covered by the definition of a "regulated profession" as it appears in the Professional Qualifications Directive (2005).[12]

6.4.4. *An apostille for authorised/sworn translations?*

Even when it is difficult to achieve recognition of translators' qualifications, it should not be so difficult to ensure that their translations are recognised as valid. We recall that in Germany, sworn translators registered in one *Land* are not eligible to work as sworn translators in other *Länder*, but their translations are still valid right across Germany.

This could be similar to the Hague apostille by which documents are recognised as being legally valid in the many countries that have signed the convention,[13] and would amount to authorised/sworn translators in many countries sharing a common stamp.

Such a system might be pursued within a Common Platform. The beneficiaries would not only be the authorised/sworn translators, who would have a further signal of status, but also the many authorities who would presumably obtain translations from a wider pool of translators (which can be a real advantage for translations involving smaller languages).

The potential for fraud and abuse should be minimised by open access to the various national registers of authorised/sworn translators. Beyond that, the risks are similar to those of the Hague apostille itself.

6.4.5. Accreditation of certifying bodies

A very different approach to intervention is to recognise that, in practice, signals of status are being emitted by numerous different entities – private companies, associations, academic institutions, courts, and ministries – and that some of those entities do a better job than others. One then sets out to give accreditation to the entities that are doing the best job in certifying translators.

Rather than restrict valid signals to just those sanctioned by public authorities (as is the operative assumption in the Common Platform and Professional Card proposal), the aim here is more modestly to reduce market disorder if and when it is in evidence. In this scenario, a certifying body can be a private company, a government institution, a professional association, or anything in between.

Preference would logically be given to the entities producing the strongest signals, be it on the bases of longevity, size, or accrued authority. The system would thus be inherently conservative, albeit while retaining the advantage that accreditation can be withdrawn from institutions that fail to signal status adequately.

If done outside of intergovernmental institutions, one has the problem of who accredits the accreditor. In the United States, the general answer is to work through an established accreditation agency[14] and to apply the criteria outlined in ISO 17024.[15] In Europe, on the other hand, one instinctively looks to government institutions, and to the prime intergovernmental institution in this case: the European Commission Directorate-General for Translation.

A further initial problem in the translation field would seem to be that few of the generalist certification systems (i.e. those beyond the field of authorised/sworn translation) appear to come close to those ISO 17024: one might list ATA in the United States, the CIOL and ITI in the United Kingdom, the BDÜ in Germany, NAATI in Australia, and the CATTI[16] and NAETI[17] in China.

A real advantage in such a system is that it would implicitly enable mutual recognition of certifications, such that a translator certified by membership of the CIOL, for example, would have that certification automatically recognised by ATA in the United States, NAATI in Australia, and so on.

One could envisage a European Common Platform and/or Professional Card system as being accredited by a wider body, as indeed could a European system for certifying translators beyond the field of authorised/sworn translation.

Translation is a transnational activity by nature, requiring a transnational system of accreditation. And there is no overriding reason why the principle of mobility should stop at the borders of Europe.

6.4.6. Accreditation of training programmes

Yet another approach is to seek to benchmark the academic programmes that train professional translators. This is one of objectives of the European Master's in Translation (EMT), which had 54 training programmes with member or observer status in 2011.[18]

In its current state, the EMT is a label that gives enhanced status to programmes that meet certain formal conditions concerning conditions of access, language levels, range of competences taught, and tracking of graduates. It is not a formal accreditation of these programmes, and its aims do not include the actual testing of graduates through centralised or standard examinations. As far as we can ascertain, its membership criteria do not address the number of contact hours devoted to language-pair-specific tasks within the programmes.[19]

The question is then whether the label should or could feed into a proper accreditation, such that graduates of the member programmes would automatically be certified as professional translators. This seems hard to envisage, given the very loose control over questions of each individual's skills.

The EMT has been associated with TransCert, an initiative to set up a voluntary "European certification system for translators" (EMT Annual Report 2011: 11). The philosophy behind TransCert would nevertheless appear not to involve the accreditation of training programmes as such. Its draft aims are reported as being to:

- Complement existing certifications for companies with certification for individual translators;
- Achieve better comparability of translators' qualifications across Europe;
- Not reinvent the wheel but build on existing systems, e.g. the certification for terminology managers in the framework of ECQA (European Certification & Qualification Association), ATA, OTTIAQ, ISO TC37. (EMT Annual Report 2011: 11)

This sounds closer to the "accreditation of certifying bodies" approach outlined above and would not appear to be headed towards the accreditation of training programmes.[20] Happily, the general proposal for a TransCert consortium comprises a healthy mixture of academy and industry.[21]

6.4.7. Standard European professional examinations

A more radical intervention into the market would be to organise a set of standard European professional examinations, which individual candidates would have to pass in order to receive certification as a professional translator.

Such a move could effectively take its lead from Institute of Linguists Educational Trust (IOLET) Diploma in Translation, the United Kingdom, or the ATA Certification Exams in the United States, the NAATI testing system in Australia, or the recruitment exams used by intergovernmental organisations (Lafeber 2010). The basic model would be that of a professional exam designed for translators with both a degree and experience (but open to those with experience alone) and including a level at which many recent graduates of Master's programmes would generally not pass.

The basic reason for such a professional exam would be that the current academic qualifications are not adequately signalling high professional quality. This is suggested by the very low pass rates at the comparable exams: below 20 per cent for ATA, 27.2 per cent for NAATI in 2009–10, between 41 and 51 per cent for the IOL exams in 2001,[22] and much less for the intergovernmental organisations:

> The formal competitive examinations held by the large IGOs have a reputation for being difficult to pass. For example, of the 38,231 persons who applied to sit the 55 competitive examinations for translators held by the United Nations between 2005 and 2009, 22,938 (60%) were called to the written tests, which are held at designated sites and times around the globe. Only 2,293 candidates (10%) passed the written tests and were called to the interview (the second part of the examination), and of those, only 583 (25%) were placed on the roster – a pass rate of 2.54% for the written and oral examinations combined (DGACM 2011a). Success rates at the European Commission are similarly low: they vary between 1% and 10%, with numbers of applicants for each session ranging from 250 to 1,500 depending on the target language (Wagner et al. 2002: 31–2).
> (Lafeber 2012: 4)

If the examining were left to academic institutions alone, for example by giving a label of this kind to all the member programmes of the EMT, the Directorate-General for Translation might be seen to be endorsing many translators whom it apparently would not employ.

Other arguments in favour of a European standard examination system would be that the Directorate-General for Translation is already engaged in exams, it has at its disposal the world's largest group of professional translators as advisors and graders, it has a direct interest in ensuring the quality of its enlarging catchment of freelance translators, and a stringent system would ensure a resulting market value, such that the costs would willingly be borne by the examination candidates.

That said, a system of this kind would have the drawbacks of the sheer size of the project and its focus on the very top end of the market, which is by no means where all the problems lie. A standard examination system is probably a solution that would work best in combination with other interventions. For example, it should be possible to coordinate procedures with other examining bodies such that there is mutual recognition of the certifications, which would effectively set up a mode of accrediting the certifiers. It might also be possible to have standard exams administered by the member programmes of the EMT, who might even have an interest in seeing how their graduates measure up at the European level. And an examination system could incorporate several different levels, from paraprofessional to advanced, in such a way that the results reflect skills appropriate to the many market segments.

6.4.8. Summary of policy options

The options presented above run from questions of protecting a profession (Professional Card, Common Platform) to the wider question of strengthening signals of status in a situation of market disorder (accreditation of institutions, examinations).

It is not the task of this research to decide among these options. We can, however, attempt an initial SWOT analysis:

Table 9. SWOT analysis of main policy options for action on signalling mechanisms. It is to be noted that the last five of these options can be used in combination.

	Strengths	Weaknesses	Opportunities	Threats
Laissez faire	Zero cost	Uncertainty about market directions; does not address current problems	Market may move to efficient electronic signalling	Market disorder; good translators leave profession
Professional Card/ Common Platform	Low long-term cost (user pays); available information	Limited to authorised/sworn; requires support of many authorities	Will bring attention to the areas of market disorder	Fraud and abuse
Apostille	Low long-term cost (user pays); can be based on the Hague apostille	Limited to authorised/sworn; requires support of many authorities	May support a Professional Card/ Common Platform	Fraud and abuse
Accreditation of bodies	Low long-term cost (user pays); accreditation can be withdrawn; global in scope	High initial cost; requires consensus from many parties	May produce high-strength signalling; may promote wide consensus	May not be sanctioned by an accreditation authority
Accreditation of training	Extends EMT; strengthens value of EMT label	High initial cost; no checking of individuals; no comparison of national training levels	May promote harmonisation of training	Trainers may give easy passes; insufficient testing of language skills
Standard exams	Extends current exams; signals skills of individuals; high degree of control	High initial cost; requires consensus	May lead to harmonisation of all existing certification exams	If narrow in focus, may not address all market segments

Chapter 7

RECOMMENDATIONS

The basic recommendation is that attempts should be made to improve the mechanisms by which the status of translators is signalled, building on the work that has been done by the EMT and Optimale initiatives. This is in view of the many areas in which the current signals of status are not working optimally.

While it is not the task of this study to propose policy, any action in this field should pay some heed to the following criteria and desiderata:

1. *It should address the many paraprofessionals who are translating and interpreting many "immigrant" languages.*
   This implies that a certification system, for example, should have several different levels and types of certification, including a level for segments and languages where little training can be required because the demand far exceeds the supply of trained translators. Translation and interpreting services for the provision of justice in immigrant languages is an area where public policy is scandalously absent in the European Union.[1]
2. *It should involve more than the official languages of the European Union.*
   This concerns not just "immigrant" and "non-territorial" languages, but also the languages of the major trading partners.[2]
3. *In principle, it should be as lean as possible and paid for by the main direct beneficiaries.*
   This implies recognising that status is a commodity, with a market value. Public funds should be invested only to the extent that public administrations are themselves long-term beneficiaries.[3]
4. *It should seek to ensure cross-border recognition of qualifications and certifications.*
   This implies that the signals of status should be strong and as univocal as possible, approaching those of a fully regulated profession. This is most easily done in the general field of authorised/sworn translation and interpreting.[4]
5. *It should be coordinated with certification systems in other countries (particularly the United States, Canada, Australia, and China).*
   Mobility and recognition should be sought not just within Europe, but on the global level as well. Policy should be coordinated with the major associations and companies that are currently reviewing their certification systems.[5]
6. *It should be clear and recognisable for employers.*
   This implies incorporating employer groups into actions concerning qualifications or certifications. If employers cannot see the value of a signal, the signal has little value. In particular, the number of signals should not breed confusion.[6]

7. *It should build on and incorporate the examination and certification systems that currently have a positive market value.*

   This implies working with the existing signalling mechanisms that are efficient and have a market value (the IOL Diploma in the UK, the SFT in France, BDÜ membership in Germany, and the general system of authorised translators in the Scandinavian countries, among others).[7]

8. *In the absence of standard exams and grading mechanisms, it should be wary of granting automatic professional certification on the basis of academic degrees alone.*

   This implies taking heed of the general practice of government employers, private companies, and intergovernmental organisations, all of whom demand experience, post-training professional certification, or an additional exam of some kind.[8]

Appendix A

TRANSLATOR ASSOCIATIONS: YEARS OF FOUNDATION AND NUMBERS OF MEMBERS

The following data have been compiled from the country factsheets, the websites of associations, and information on membership numbers provided by the FIT Treasurer (17/11/2011).

Associations of alumni have been excluded, except in cases where they play an active role on the translation market (as in Greece and Cyprus).

In many cases there are discrepancies in the numbers of members in the associations: the numbers on the associations' website (and even more so on Wikipedia) are often vague and usually higher than the numbers the same associations declare to the FIT (where the more members you have, the higher the fees you pay). Similarly, in cases where a large association has split into two, at least one of the new associations will claim the foundation data of the original association (since longevity is a positive element of status). These are all ways in which associations signal their status.

The data presented here are synthesised in Figure 4 and Table 2 (in 2.4.2 above).

Association	Founded	Members
Austria		
Österreichischer Verband der Gerichtsdolmetscher (ÖVGD)	1920	570
Universitas Austria Interpreters' and Translators' Association (UNIVERSITAS)	1954	440
AIIC-Region Österreich (Austrian chapter of the AIIC)	1966	79
Übersetzergemeinschaft-Interessengemeinschaft von Übersetzern und Übersetzerinnen literarischer und wissenschaftlicher Werke (Austrian Association of Literary and Scientific Translators) (AALST)	1991	246
Österreichischer GebärdensprachdolmetscherInnen Verband (Austrian Sign Language Interpreters Association)	1998	80
Total		1,415
Belgium		
Chambre belge des traducteurs, interprètes et philologues (BKVTF/CBTIP)	1955	380
Bulgaria		
Union of Translators and Interpreters in Bulgaria (BTU)	1974	310

Association	Founded	Members
Association of Interpreters and Translators in Bulgaria (AIT)	1996	49
Total		359
Croatia		
Strukovna udruga stalnih sudskih tumača (Professional Association of Permanent Court Interpreters (SUSST)	–	–
Društvo hrvatskih književnih prevodilaca (Croatian Literary Translators Association) (DHKP)	1953	220
Croatian Association of Scientific and Technical Translators (HDZTP)	1957	247
Udruga prevoditelja za televiziju, kinematografiju i videoprodukciju (Association of Translators for Television, Cinema and Video Production)	1992	49
Društvo sudskih tumača i prevoditelja (Society of Court Interpreters and Translators) (DSTIP)	2007	51
Hrvatska strukovna udruga sudskih tumača (Croatian Association of Professional Court Interpreters) (HSUST)	2007	130
Udruga stalnih sudskih tumača (Association of Permanent Court Interpreters) (USST)	2010	–
Udruga sudskih tumača "TEMPUS" (Tempus Court Interpreters Association) (Tempus)	2010[?]	–
Društvo hrvatskih audiovizualnih prevoditelja (DHAP) (Association of Croatian Audiovisual Translators)	2012	29
Total		726
Cyprus		
Pan Cyprian Union of Graduate Translators and Interpreters (PANUTI)	1999	66
Czech Republic		
Komora soudních tlumočníků České republiky (Chamber of the Court Appointed Interpreters and Translators of the Czech Republic) (KST ČR)	1996	500
Jednota tlumočníků a překladatelů (Union des Interprètes et Traducteurs de la République Tchèque et de la République Slovaque) (JTP)	1990	373
Obec překladatelů (Literary Translators' Guild) (OP)	–	–
Asociace konferenčních tlumočníků (Conference Interpreters' Association) (ASKOT)	–	105
Česká komora tlumočníků znakového jazyka (Sign Language Interpreters' Association) (ČKTZJ)	2000	–
Total		978
Denmark		
Association of Danish Authorised Translators (Translatørforeningen) (TF)	1910	237

Association	Founded	Members
Association for Communication and Language Professionals (Forbundet Kommunikation og Sprog) (KS)	1970	1,000
Danish Authorised Translators and Interpreters (Danske Translatører) (DT)	1990	103
Forum for Billedmedieoversættere (Forum for Screen Translators, within the Danish Journalists Union) (FBO)	1996	100
	Total	1,440
Estonia		
Estonian Association of Interpreters and Translators (ETTL)	1992	215
Estonian Association of Master's in Conference Interpreting and Translation (ETML)	2006	76
	Total	291
Finland		
Suomen kääntäjien ja tulkkien liitto / Finlands översättar- och tolkförbund ry (Finnish Association of Translators and Interpreters) (SKTL)	1955	1,726
Käännösalan asiantuntijat (Translation Industry Professionals) (KAJ)	1979	2,100
Suomen Viittomakielen Tulkit ry (Finnish Association of Sign Language Interpreters) (SVT)	1982	496
	Total	4,322
France		
Société française des traducteurs (SFT)	1947	1,352
Association professionnelle des métiers de la traduction (APROTRAD)	1993	57
Association française des interprètes et traducteurs en langue des signes (AFILS)	1978	100
Association des traducteurs littéraires de France (ATLF)	1973	1,000
Chambre Régionale des Experts-Traducteurs Assermentés d'Alsace (CRETA)	–	106
	Total	2,615
Germany		
Bundesverband der Dolmetscher und Übersetzer (BDÜ)	1955	7,000
Fachverband der Berufsübersetzer und Berufsdolmetscher (ATICOM)	–	180
Verband der Übersetzer und Dolmetscher (VÜD)	1990	150
Assoziierte Dolmetscher und Übersetzer in Norddeutschland (ADÜ Nord)	1997	348
Verband deutschsprachiger Übersetzer literarischer und wissenschaftlicher Werke (VdÜ)	1954	1,200
	Total	8,878

Association	Founded	Members
Greece		
Panhellenic Association of Translators (PAT)	1963	242
Panhellenic Association of Professional Translators Graduates of the Ionian University (PEEMPIP)	2005	140
Hellenic Society of Translators of Literature (EEML)	–	107
Association of Translators-Editors-Proofreaders	2009	240
Society of Greek Playwrights, Musicians and Translators	1894	–
Panhellenic Association of Public Sector Translators & Translators/Interpreters	1985	Inactive
	Total	729
Hungary		
Magyar Fordítók és Tolmácsok Egyesülete (Association of Hungarian Translators and Interpreters) (MFTE)	2009	97
Magyar Műfordítók Egyesülete (Hungarian Association of Literary Translators)	2003	160
	Total	257
Ireland		
Cumann Aistritheoirí agus Teangairí na hÉireann / The Irish Translators' and Interpreters' Association (ITIA)	1986	118
Italy		
Associazione Italiana Traduttori e Interpreti (AITI)	1950	700
Associazioni nazionali interpreti di conferenza professionisti (Assointerpreti)	1974	145
Associazione Nazionale Traduttori ed Interpreti (ANITI)	1956	392
Associazione Nazionale Traduttori Interpreti del Ministero dell'Interno (ANTIMI)	2002	108
Associazione italiana traduttori e interpreti giudiziari (ASSITIG)	2010	18
	Total	1,363
Lithuania		
Lietuvos literatūros vertėjų sąjunga (Lithuanian Association of Literary Translators) (LLVS)	2004	121
Lietuvos vertėjų gildija (Lithuanian Translators' Guild)	–	–
Luxembourg		
Association luxembourgeoise des traducteurs et interprètes (Luxembourg Translators and Interpreters Association) (ALTI)	2011	48
Netherlands		
Nederlands Genootschap van Tolken en Vertalers (Netherlands Society of Interpreters and Translators) (NGTV)	1956	1,625

Association	Founded	Members
SIGV Gerechtstolken en Juridisch Vertalers (Association of SIGV Court Interpreters and Legal Translators) (SIGV)	1988	297
Vereniging Zelfstandige Vertalers (Association of Freelance Professional Translators) (VZV)	1990	63
Vereniging van Schrijvers en Vertalers (Dutch Association of Writers and Translators) (VSenV) (translators section)	1998	355
	Total	2,340
Poland		
Stowarzyszenie Tłumaczy Polskich (Polish Society of Translators) (STP)	1981	579
Polskie Towarzystwo Tłumaczy Przysięgłych i Specjalistycznych (Polish Society of Sworn and Specialised Translators) (TEPIS)	1990	977
Bałtyckie Stowarzyszenie Tłumaczy (Baltic Association of Translators) (BST)	2006	142
Stowarzyszenie Tłumaczy Audiowizualnych (Audiovisual Translators' Association) (STAW)	2007	101
Stowarzyszenie Tłumaczy Polskiego Języka Migowego (Association of Polish Sign Language Interpreters) (STPJM)	2009	40
	Total	1,839
Portugal		
Sindicato Nacional de Atividade Turística, Tradutores e Intérpretes (National Union of Tourist Activity, Translators and Interpreters) (SNAPI)	1936	508
Associação Portuguesa de Intérpretes de Conferência (Portuguese Association of Conference Interpreters) (APIC)	1987	44
Associação Portuguesa de Tradutores (Portuguese Translators Association) (APT)	1988	450
Associação Portuguesa de Tradutores e Intérpretes Jurídicos (Portuguese Association of Legal Translators and Interpreters) (APTIJUR)	2011	–
	Total	1,002
Romania		
Asociaţia Traducătorilor din România (Romanian Translators' Association) (ATR)	2006	112
Uniunea Naţională a Traducătorilor autorizaţi din România (Certified Translators' National Association) (UNTAR)	2008	40
Asociaţia Scriitorilor din Bucureşt (Writers Association of Bucharest)	1972	228
	Total	380
Slovakia		
Slovenská spoločnosť prekladateľov umeleckej literatúry (Slovak Literary Translators´ Society) (SSPUL)	1990	329

Association	Founded	Members
Slovak Association of Translators and Interpreters (SAPT)	2005	82
Slovak Society of Translators of Scientific and Technical Literature (SSPOL)	1990	200
Total		611
Slovenia		
Association of Scientific and Technical Translators of Slovenian (DZTPS)	1960[?]	476
Društvo slovenskih književnih prevajalcev (Association of Literary Translators of Slovenia) (DSKP)	1953	241
Slovenian Association of Conference Interpreters (KTS)	1972	48
Association of Interpreters for the Slovene Sign Language (ZTSZJ)	2004	44
Total		809
Spain		
Asociación Profesional Española de Traductores e Intérpretes (APETI)	1954	–
Asociación de Intérpretes de Conferencia de España	1968	70
Sección Autónoma de Traductores de Libros de la Asociación Colegial de Escritores de España (Acetato)	1983	575
Asociación Profesional de Traductores, Correctores e Intérpretes de Lengua Vasca (EIZIE)	1987	185
Associació de Traductors i Intèrprets Jurats de Catalunya (ATIJC)	1992	166
Asociación Galega de Profesionais da Tradución e da Interpretación (AGPTI)	2001	98
Asociación Aragonesa de Traductores e Intérpretes (ASATI)	2002	50
Asociación española de traductores, correctores e intérpretes (ASETRAD)	2003	601
Red de Traductores e Intérpretes de la Comunidad de Valencia (XARXA)	2003	147
Asociación Profesional de Traductores e Intérpretes Judiciales y Jurados (APTIJ)	2006	81
Associació Professional de Traductors i Intèrprets de Catalunya (APTIC)	2009	598
Asociación de traducción y adaptación audiovisual de España (ATRAE)	2010	50
Total		2,571
Sweden		
Federation of Authorized Translators in Sweden (FAT)	1932	250
Swedish Writers' Union, Translators' Section (SFF)	1954	575
Sveriges Facköversättarförening (SFO)	1990	826
Total		1,651

Association	Founded	Members
United Kingdom		
Chartered Institute of Linguists (CIOL) – Translation Division	1910	2,700
Institute of Translation and Interpreting (ITI)	1986	2,800
Cymdeithas Cyfieithwyr Cymru/Association of Welsh Translators and Interpreters (AWTI)	1976	318
Association of Police and Court Interpreters (APCI)	1974	350
The Translators' Association Society of Authors (TASA)	1958	330
National Union of Professional Interpreters and Translators (NUPIT)	2001	100
Professional Interpreters' Alliance (PIA)	2009	400
Society for Public Service Interpreting (SPSI)	2011	–
Total		6,998
NEIGHBOURING COUNTRIES		
Norway		
Statsautoriserte Translatørers Forening (STF)	1913	205
Norsk Oversetterforening (NO)	1948	308
Norsk Faglitterær Forfatter- og Oversetterforening (NFF)	1978	518
Norwegian Audiovisual Translators Organization (NAVTO)	1997	152
Total		1,183
Switzerland		
Association d'Interprètes et de traducteurs (AIT)	1945	150
Dolmetscher- und Übersetzervereinigung (Interpreters' and Translators' Association) (DÜV)	1951	400
Association suisse des traducteurs, terminologues et interprètes (ASTTI)	1966	209
Association suisse des traducteurs-jurés (ASTJ)	1995	45
Verband der Zürcher Gerichtsdolmetscher und -übersetzer (VZGDÜ)	2003	100
Verband Schweizer Gerichtsdolmetscher und -übersetzer/ Swiss Association of Court Interpreters and Translators (Juslingua)	2007	117
Total		1,021
Turkey		
Translators Association of Turkey (TÜCED)	1992	281
Çeviri Derneği (Association of Translation) (CD)	1999	60
Çevbir: Kitap Çevirmenleri Meslek Birliği (Literary Translators' Society Turkey)	2006	180
Total		521

130 THE STATUS OF THE TRANSLATION PROFESSION

Association	Founded	Members
COMPARISON CASES		
Australia		
Western Australian Institute of Translators and Interpreters (WAITI)	1975	50
Australian Institute of Interpreters and Translators (AUSIT)	1987	586
Australian Sign Language Interpreters' Association (ASLIA)	1991	378
Australian Association for Literary Translation (AALITRA)	2005	68
	Total	1,082
Canada		
Association of Translators and Interpreters of Ontario (ATIO)	1920	1,225
Ordre des traducteurs, terminologues et interprètes agréés du Québec (OTTIAQ)	1940	2,000
Canadian Translators, Terminologists and Interpreters Council (CTTIC)	1970	–
Corporation of Translators, Terminologists and Interpreters of New Brunswick (CTINB)	1970	206
Literary Translators' Association of Canada (ATTTLC)	1975	150
Association of Translators and Interpreters of Alberta (ATIA)	1979	151
Association of Translators and Interpreters of Saskatchewan (ATIS)	1980	65
Society of Translators and Interpreters of British Columbia (STIBC)	1981	452
Association of Translators, Terminologists and Interpreters of Manitoba (ATIM)	1989	50
Association of Translators and Interpreters of Nova Scotia (ATINS)	1990	63
Nunattinni Katujjiqatigiit Tusaajinut: Nunavut Interpreter/Translator Society	1994	76
	Total	4,438
United States		
New Mexico Translators and Interpreters Association (NMTIA)	–	146
American Association of Language Specialists (TAALS)	1957	150
American Translators Association (ATA)	1959	11,000
Delaware Valley Translators Association (DVTA)	1960	72
Northeast Ohio Translators Association (NOTA)	1977	–
American Literary Translators Association (ALTA)	1978	600
National Association of Judiciary Translators and Interpreters (NAJIT)	1978	1,200
Northern California Translators Association (NCTA)	1978	600
Mid-America Chapter of ATA (MICATA)	1979	109
New York Circle of Translators (NYCT)	1979	518
National Capital Area Translators Association (NCATA)	1980	–

Association	Founded	Members
Atlanta Association of Interpreters and Translators (AAIT)	1982	88
El Paso Interpreters and Translators Association (EPITA)	1984	55
Utah Translators and Interpreters Association (UTIA)	1985	42
Northwest Translators and Interpreters Society (NOTIS)	1988	124
Houston Interpreters and Translators Association (HITA)	1993	187
Carolina Association of Translators and Interpreters (CATI)	1993	–
California Healthcare Interpreting Association (CHIA)	1996	–
Austin Area Translators and Interpreters Association (AATIA)	1997	–
National Council on Interpreting in Health Care (NCIHC)	1998	–
Nebraska Association of Translators and Interpreters (NATI)	1999	125
Colorado Association of Professional Interpreters (CAPI)	2001	–
Colorado Association of Professional Interpreters (CAPI)	2001	–
Upper Midwest Translators and Interpreters Association (UMTIA)	2002	153
Michigan Translators/Interpreters Network (MiTiN)	2003	230
Midwest Association of Translators and Interpreters (MATI)	2003	124
New England Translators Association (NETA)	2004	150
Iowa Interpreters and Translators Association (IITA)	2004	66
Tennessee Association of Professional Interpreters and Translators (TAPIT)	2006	112
Nevada Interpreters and Translators Association (NITA)	2008	30
Association of Translators and Interpreters of Florida, Inc. (ATIF)	2009	165
	Total	16,560

Appendix B

WHY THERE ARE ABOUT 333,000 PROFESSIONAL TRANSLATORS AND INTERPRETERS IN THE WORLD

Some of the data collected in the course of this research indicate the need for a reality principle with respect to the rough numbers of professional translators and interpreters that could be working within a given national or regional industry. For example, when the Romanian Ministry of Justice lists 32,856 "certified translators and interpreters", it is difficult to see how so many people could be translating in an economy of that size. Similarly, the 2008–10 statistics for Australia show NAATI certifying 1,856 people a year as translators and interpreters, in a country where the main translator association has only about 500 members. Some kind of measuring stick is needed to tell us when such figures seem incorrect or should be attributed to special factors.

One available instrument is particularly blunt but potentially useful. Parker (2008) estimates the "latent demand" for translation and interpreting services in all the countries (and for 2000 cities!) in the world. This basically means estimating the size of the translation and interpreting industry in "efficient" high-income countries for which data are available, then relating the size of the industry to national income, and finally applying that formula across the globe, as if language services were a function of no more than macroeconomic indicators. Despite those very naïve assumptions, the numbers may act as a *garde-fou* for other cross-country comparisons.

The problem then is that Parker estimates the size of local industries in terms of income; he does not calculate the numbers of translators or interpreters. We have to convert his figures into numbers of people. If we can do that, if we can estimate how many translators and interpreters there are in the world, we can generate an estimate for the *potential* demand for a certain number of them in each country. That potential number of translators and interpreters can then be compared with the actual numbers that we find on the ground.

So how can we find out how many translators there are?

Note that we are looking for the number of *professional* translators. These are taken to be people who declare themselves in an official census or tax declaration as having translation as their main occupation. In this approach, we can offer no more precise definition than that – if we were producing our own data, things would be different.

Unfortunately, many of the official statistics talk about translation and interpreting together, as do most of the previous attempts to answer this question. We are thus obliged to rephrase the question as: How many people declare themselves to have translation or interpreting as their main occupation?

Here are some answers:

- In 1998 Allied Business Intelligence estimated that there were about 140,340 "full-time, salaried translators in the world", plus 253,016 "independent translators" – we cite the numbers from CTISC (2009: 63), which corrected the estimates for Canada. The correction for Canada gives a total of 393,396 translators in the world (not counting interpreters). Of this total, Europe was allocated 40,213 full-timers and 74,650 "independents".
- In 2005 Boucau pointed out that these numbers did not include the technical and administrative staff working in translation companies. He estimated that there were about 250,000 people working in the "global translation industry" (2005: 12), of which about 200,000 were freelancers.
- In 2008 Common Sense Advisory (Beninatto et al. 2008) offered a much higher number, estimating that the number of people in the world who "would call themselves professional translators" was about 700,000.

So there is nothing stable in the previous estimates.

One way to approach this problem is to take countries that give census data for translators and interpreters, and to extrapolate from them on the basis of Parker's estimated shares of the global potential demand for translations. The cases where this is possible are as follows:

- *Australia*: The 2006 census found 1,219 translators and 2,419 interpreters ("main occupation"), giving a total of 3,638 professionals. If Australia had 1.20 per cent of the global potential demand in 2006 (Parker 2008), the number of professional translators and interpreters in the world would be about 303,250.
- *Canada*: The average number of translators, interpreters, and terminologists employed in Canada in 2007–09 was 9,350, with the "total annual needs" for 2010–14 estimated at a further 500 per year. Service Canada (2012) estimates that 95 per cent of the total may be translators (basing their estimate on the membership of the Ordre professionnel des traducteurs et interprètes agréés du Québec). This would give 8,882 translators. Now, if Canada represents 1.92 per cent of the global potential demand for translation services (Parker 2008), then there would be about 444,100 professional translators in the world. In this case, we are not counting interpreters.
- *Germany*: According to the Bundesagentur für Arbeit (Federal Labour Office) in March 2011 there were 6,814 actively employed translators and interpreters registered with the social security system as having fixed employment.[1] Parker (2008) estimates Germany to represent 4.27 per cent of the world total in 2011, which would give a world estimate of 159,578 translators and interpreters with "fixed employment". It is not clear, however, how many freelance translators and interpreters should be added to this number.

- *Norway*: Official numbers from Statistisk Sentralbyrå (Statistics Norway) for the fourth quarter of 2010 give 1,204 "translators, interpreters, etc." (tolker, oversetter mv) (of which 862 are women).[2] Parker (2008) estimates the Norwegian potential market to be 0.40 per cent of the global potential. This would give 301,000 translators/interpreters in the world.
- *Portugal:* The Portuguese Statistics Office states that there were 1,905 companies involved in "translation and interpreting" activities in 2009. The figures for 2007 show 4,471 companies involved in "secretarial, translating and mailing activities", of which 91.7 per cent (4101) were one-person companies. If we assume that the same proportion applies to the 2009 figure, this gives 1,746 self-employed translators and interpreters. In the remaining 159 companies, we might allow for 1.58 in-house translators and revisers per company,[3] which gives an additional 235 translators and interpreters. So we estimate that there are 1,981 professional translators and interpreters in Portugal.[4] If the Portuguese potential market is 0.35 per cent of the global total, there are 566,000 professional translators and interpreters in the world.
- *United States* (cf. Wooton 2009): In 2006 the United States Bureau of Labor Statistics counted 41,000 employed translators and interpreters. In 2005, the US Census counted 30,000 "non-employers" in the translation industry.[5] If the number of non-employers roughly indicates the number of freelancers, there would have been about 71,000 professional translators and interpreters in the US in those years.[6] If the US accounted for 22.13 per cent of the global potential demand at that time (Parker 2008), there would be about 322,727 translators and interpreters in the world.

   However, in 2012 the United States Department of Labor estimated that "interpreters and translators held about 58,400 jobs in 2010".[7] Of these, about 23 per cent were self-employed. The baseline figure of 58,400 for the US would give about 264,000 translators and interpreters in the world.

A problem in all these estimates is that many translators also work as interpreters, so we are not really sure how many people are being counted twice. Strangely, the one case where we can separate out the interpreters (Canada) gives a relatively high estimate for the world. We can thus only talk about "translators and interpreters" here, without accounting for overlaps.

Summing the above calculations (and using the higher estimate for the United States),[8] we have a total of 86,705 translators and interpreters in 26 per cent of the potential global market. That gives 333,480 professional translators and interpreters in the world.

For the purposes of the estimates here, and for the sake of a memorable number, we will round this down to 333,000 translators and interpreters in the world, awaiting better data.

This method gives an unfair weight to the largest economy in our sample, that of the United States, especially since there is reason to believe that the relative demand for translators is higher in smaller countries (see Table 3 in 2.4.3). The resulting number is nevertheless within the general range of the estimates based on individual countries.

ProZ, an online site for contracting translators, claimed in 2011 that it listed "over 300,000 professional translators and translation companies".[9] One doubts, however, that the translators listed there all have translation as their main activity (basic listing is free, and membership costs just US$129 a year).

The important point is that our figure for the world is much lower than the 700,000 estimated by Common Sense Advisory (Beninatto et al. 2008).

Appendix C

ONLINE TRANSLATOR–CLIENT CONTACT SERVICES: NEW MODES OF SIGNALLING STATUS

The focus of this study is mainly on the more traditional signalling systems, the ones attached in some way to political states. It would be naïve, however, to overlook the reasons why new systems are developing, notably through Internet technologies.

Informants in various countries, especially in central Europe, report that translators are receiving information and networking less through national associations and more through online sites. Some sites, like LinkedIn and Facebook, provide social networking. Other sites, however, provide an additional range of services for translators and basically function as marketplaces where clients can find translators. Here we review the way status is constructed in the main sites, presented in order of claimed number of translators.

ProZ

Founded in New York in 1999, ProZ.com claims to have "over 300,000 professional translators and translation companies" in 2011.[10] Anyone can sign up for free, but full membership costs US$129 a year. Since the huge number of "translators" listed (i.e. everyone who has signed up for free) would seem to exceed market demands, there must be doubts that all the translators have the same professional status. ProZ has been particularly innovative in the development of signalling devices, which come with their own names-for-things. Members ask questions about translation problems, and when a member answers a question satisfactorily, they gain kudos (or KudoZ) points; the number of points accumulated thus signals relative expertise. Members may also gain "BrowniZ" points for good community services such as translating part of the ProZ site, introducing new members, or organising discussions (powwows).

In 2011, the points hierarchies are being complemented by a system of "ProZ certification".[11] You can become a certified ProZ translator by passing an exam (assessed by "peers") assessing your translation ability, proving "business reliability", and showing "good citizenship" (basically by not abusing the ProZ rules). Translation ability is defined in terms of Quality Standard EN15038 (intended for translation service providers) and unnamed "industry credentials" are accepted. Significantly, no mention is made of academic qualifications (which are only one option in EN15038), and the available academic models of translation competence or expertise are avoided. It is envisaged that ProZ certification should be retained by members taking courses of some kind ("ongoing professional development") but this had not been finalised in 2011.

TranslatorsCafé

TranslatorsCafé was launched in 2002 and claims to have 143,717 registered users in 2011. Anyone can register for free, but "Master Membership" costs US$135 or 95 euros a year (for which you get priority listing). It has a "TCTerms stars" system similar to ProZ's kudos system. It has a "Hall of Fame and Shame" indicating the highs and lows of status, although those lists are available to paying members only. A study on the use of TranslatorsCafé (McDonough 2007: 805) showed that "fewer than a quarter of the members" actually visited the site in a 30-day period and only 7 per cent of registered members "had ever posted a question in the discussion forum". That is, the use of social networking has distinct levels of involvement, with a hard core of frequent users and a vast majority of passive followers. One would imagine that the heaviest users are those with the highest internal status, although McDonough gives no information on this.

Trally

Trally claims to have 110,000 registered freelance translators and agencies.[12] Anyone can join for free, but "Level 3" membership for freelance translators is 114 euros a year. It offers no discussion groups or other networking activities. Instead, it carries online articles on translation and links to academic books on translation.

Aquarius

Aquarius was founded in 1995 and claims to have 47,818 translators registered in 2011.[13] It targets the market for localisation as well as translation. Anyone can join for free, but "business class" membership costs 100 euros a year. This includes membership of the TAUS Data Association (TDA), which "hosts translation memories and glossaries in all languages structured by industry domains and company indexes".[14] So, in theory, members are able to share databases.

GoTranslators

GoTranslators is registered in Belgium. Anyone can sign on for free for one month, but the annual "GoMembership" fees are 60 euros, 30 euros, or free, depending on the economic status of your country.[15] Its website is available in 30 languages and claims that the organisation "helps UNICEF".

Table 10. Main online translator networking sites.

	Founded	Registered translators	Fees (euros)	Networking
ProZ	1999	330,000	94	Yes
TranslatorsCafe	2002	143,717	95	Yes
Trally	–	110,000	114	No
Aquarius	1995	47,818	100	Some
GoTranslators	–	–	60	No

The main features of these services are summarised in Table 10, to which we add the following notes:

- None of these sites uses educational qualifications as signals of status; they borrow authority exclusively from industry associations and standards.
- They all advertise huge numbers of "registered translators" who have signed on for free, thus creating a kind of zero-degree status (many people say they are translators but may have no training or qualification as such).
- They all offer paying membership for a smaller (undisclosed) number of privileged translators, thus creating an initial "one-up" level of status.
- Some then create further hierarchies of translator status among the paying members.
- Some offset the commercial nature of their service by referring to "good causes", which may evoke a kind of moral status: ProZ says it links its database with Translators without Borders; Aquarius links to a database-sharing project; GoTranslators "helps UNICEF" and does not charge fees in poorer countries.

These sites were once regarded as little more than sweatshops producing cheap-and-nasty translations, and they are still often accused of using globalisation to drive down the going rates for translations. Nevertheless, they have generally been innovative in finding ways to signal the relative status of translators and in providing a range of social, educational, and technical services of real interest to translators. In many respects they are doing what many national translator associations would probably like to be doing, albeit in bed with the one service that the traditional associations have generally stayed clear of:[16] they are putting clients and translators in direct contact with each other.

Appendix D

TYPES AND USE OF ECONOMIC PERSPECTIVES ON TRANSLATION

Translation has received very little attention in economics. Existing contributions can first be arranged in two main categories as follows:

DESCRIPTIONS, backed up by more or less extensive quantitative data, of translation as an economic sector; the quantitative information, which is usually arranged by target language or by country, variously contains estimates of:

– the number of persons involved in the profession;
– the annual turnover of more or less narrowly defined translation services;
– the volume of output (words, pages, etc.).

Such descriptions are usually not produced by (academic) economists and are generally due to professional associations.

ANALYTICAL WORK providing theory-based explanations of some aspect or other of translation perceived as a "product" in the economic sense of the term. This work is more likely to be due to academic economists, although some contributions have come from scholars in sociology or in the language disciplines, who have adopted an economic perspective in their research on translation.

The expression "analytical work" should also be understood in a broad sense, encompassing both strictly theoretical work (usually in the form of algebraic modelling, with a focus on investigating the nature of the relationships between variables) and empirical work, in which statistical data are used to test the propositions generated by theoretical models.

This analytical work is what is chiefly of interest to us here, because we are turning to economics in order to find (or, if necessary, develop) an analytical framework that can help organise factual observations.

The analytical work can be further broken down in two main categories:

– First, some contributions aim at explaining the volume of translation produced, whether in total or for some specific combinations, whether for translation "in general" or for some types of translation (such as literary translation). In these contributions, the focus is on demand, and supply is simply assumed to follow. Putting it differently, most of the attention is devoted to explaining the amount of translation taking place as a result of a process, which is not, as such, investigated

economically; this amounts to assuming that the translation production process is an essentially technical one that does not raise particular economic questions.
- Second, some categories focus instead on the production process, emphasising the idea that translation may not be such a straightforward process and does, rather, present features that not only deserve attention but can be relevantly investigated through the prism of economic analysis.

It is this latter line of thought that will interest us here, and to which the economic analysis that is part of this work will be devoted. It is through an analysis of translation as a production process that we expect an economic analysis to:

- generate a plausible explanation of some features that characterise the work of translators and, by implication, some aspects of their status;
- provide an explanatory framework that help make sense of observations and information regarding the activity of translators.

Economics and Language

Economic perspectives on language can be split in two groups. A very small branch of the speciality studies language (in the singular). One of the earliest papers in the area ("Economics of language" by Jacob Marschak, 1965) belongs to this family, as does a recent book ("Economics and language" by Ariel Rubinstein, 2000). This line of work investigates language (either as tool for communication, or in terms of its structure) as the result of a complex process that is, in turn, driven by forces that may be deemed "economic". This, however, constitutes a decidedly minority branch of language economics. In the main, language economics addresses questions that have to do with the respective position of *languages* (in the plural) with respect to one another.

Early work in language economics was spurred on by socioeconomic problems in the outside world: in the 1960s, economists were invited to study socioeconomic inequality between Anglophones and Francophones in Québec in order to assess if this inequality was really correlated with language. The answer: yes, it was – Francophones did earn less than Anglophones, even if they had equivalent education, comparable professional experience, and were working in the same economic sectors; this disadvantage could be observed even for Francophones with a good command of English (see work by Vaillancourt 1996; Vaillancourt, Lemay and Vaillancourt 2007). Thus, economists could establish that there was *language-based* discrimination. This type of findings provided some of the backing for language legislation that aimed at redressing the balance, with the result (attributable at least in part to the language legislation) that some 30 years later, these earnings differentials had vanished.

Likewise, it was not just academic interest, but also political concern over continuing earnings differentials between some groups of immigrants in the US (particularly Hispanics/Latinos) and the mainstream "white" population that gave rise to a large body of econometric research in the US (for a review, see Bloom and Grenier 1996; Grin 2003a), mostly in the 1970s and 1980s (after which US economists seem to have largely lost interest, with the exception of labour economists like Barry Chiswick). While most of this econometric work used US data, it has spawned similar studies in Germany, Israel, and Australia (see Chiswick and Miller 2007 for an extensive review).

In such work, therefore, the emphasis was very much on economic issues, with "language" (usually in the form of a somewhat crude estimate of language *skills*) little more than a variable that wasn't considered intrinsically interesting, but that was taken into account simply because it could explain (*better* than *other* variables could) what happened to economic variables like earnings.

In parallel to empirical econometric (or statistical) work, other economists were developing theoretical models to propose explanations of earnings differentials. Identifying their causes, thanks to modelling, could help targeting policies that could eliminate language-based inequality (see for example work by Migué 1970, Raynauld and Marion 1972, or Lang 1986).

This tradition is still going strong, with a steady production flow of estimations of language-based earnings differentials.

The traditional way of looking at such differentials still dominates: they serve to track down inequality, and perhaps injustice. However, another way of looking at them has emerged since then: language-based earnings differentials may be linked to foreign language skills: instead of investigating whether immigrants tend to earn less because they have inadequate skills in the dominant language, the same techniques can be used to assess whether some people earn more because they have learned foreign languages. Putting it differently, earnings differentials can also be a labour market reward for a sensible investment. At this time, returns to second language skills are regularly estimated for Québec, sometimes Canada as a whole; and there exist one-off studies, with more or less extensive samples, for a small number of countries, including Switzerland, Luxembourg, Ukraine, and Israel.

The reason why research on the value of second or foreign language skills remains relatively rare is simply that it requires data which few countries collect (let alone collect *on a regular basis*, and with *adequate degree of detail*); and even fewer countries are in a position to compare the returns to skills in *different* foreign languages (e.g. as in Switzerland, to compare the value of "English" and "[other] national languages"; Grin 1999).

Already in the 1980s, however, a few papers in language economics had appeared which, in a sense, turned the specialty on its head.

Work by Hocevar (1975, 1983) and by Carr (1985), for example, proposed to use economic analysis *not* in order to understand economic phenomena like "wage inequality", but in order to understand language-related processes like language decline and language spread. In a sense, these economists were returning to some of the early inspirations in language economics – not just the Jacob Marschak paper of 1965, but much earlier forerunners, including no less an author than Adam Smith himself, who's considered one of the founding fathers of the discipline of economics, and who had ventured some hypotheses about the connections between the development of language and the development of trade, back in the 1740s (taken up again and published in *Considerations Concerning the First Formation of Language*, published in 1761).

This opened up a whole new range of issues. From the 1990s onwards, new studies started to appear, with language playing a much more central analytical role than in earlier work. Either language was *the* dependent (or "explained" variable), for example in theoretical models of minority language dynamics (e.g. Grin 1992 on language use by bilinguals, whose linguistic behaviour at time t affects the vitality of a language at time $t+1$), or of the choice of official languages as an economic decision (Pool 1991).

Even in studies (quite popular around the turn of the 1990s; see e.g. Ó Cinnéide and Keane 1988) of the role of language in local economic development, where the dependent variable ("development") is an economic one, the true focus of the investigation was on language and the ways in which language (whether language skills, language use, language attitudes, all possibly mediated through large-scale social, political, and economic processes) would affect society at large.

The past decade has witnessed an increasing focus, in language economics, and on language policy issues. As part of this process, economists have had to confront their findings with the vision of scholars from other disciplines – most centrally, sociolinguists, of course, but also language education specialists, as well as political theorists working on language rights and principles of justice. True, not everybody does, and some papers in language economics, though published in the most prestigious economic journals, remain very crude in sociolinguistic terms (e.g. Lazear 1999), but as can be seen in recent work, increasing effort is expended in order to accommodate linguistic realities in economic analyses. Examples include Ginsburgh and Weber (2011), who recognise the multidimensionality of the reasons a society might have for preserving diversity; or Grin, Sfreddo, and Vaillancourt (2010), where the fundamental models of mainstream economics like the theory of production are being re-visited and "augmented" through the explicit inclusion of linguistic variables (e.g. language skills of suppliers, language profile of clients, language use among workers, etc.); understanding the role of language in core economic processes opens new avenues for language policy. Language planning bodies can then learn to harness market forces for the purposes of language policy, instead of (as often seems to be the case) waging an exhausting battle *against* such forces.

Finally, one might add that this also holds for recent, still marginal developments, in which language economics connects (pretty much for the first time – the movement is only at its beginnings) with the questions of theorists of management and communication (e.g. "does the way in which linguistic diversity in working teams affect productivity, creativity or innovation?"): here again, knowledge of the processes at hand could deliver powerful levers in the hands of language planning bodies.

Economics of Translation

Against this backdrop, it is surprising that so little work has been done on translation. The main orientations of this line of work have been sketched out above;

Chan (2008, 11–18) provides an overview of contributions by scholars in translation studies in which economic aspects have been brought into the analysis, and proposes explanations for the relative lack of interest affecting translation.

To our knowledge, only a small number of economic models actually focus on translation. In what follows, we shall briefly account for three such models in addition to those reviewed in Chan (2008), namely:

- the demand for translation (Hjorth-Andersen 2001);
- the links between language dynamics and translation flows (Mélitz 2007);
- the determination of the magnitude of translation flows in different language combinations (Ginsburgh and Weber 2010).

Let us briefly examine them in turn.

Hjorth-Andersen (2001) is concerned with intercultural contact and the transmission of, or between, cultures. Considering that goods are more mobile than people, that people's foreign language skills are usually limited, and that books are primary carriers of culture, much of the burden of ensuring inter-cultural contact befalls translation. Hjorth-Andersen's model focuses on the flow of translations emanating from a linguistic/cultural sphere. It starts out by estimating the number T_i of (new) titles published in country i in a given year (which implies the assumption of a one-to-one correspondence between "country" and "language", a problem later dealt with by adjusting the figures in order to focus on actual languages). A certain percentage of these publications will be translated into other languages (but the percentage is likely to be a negative function of the total "production" of books in language i); and translations from other languages make up a certain share of the total offer of publications in any given year. The model is then used to estimate these shares for Denmark, Germany, and the United States, in total and by source language. One intriguing result of the model, supported by the data, is that larger language areas produce relatively less titles, but that relatively more translation will take place from these larger language areas (for example, the relatively large English-speaking sphere will produce fewer titles relative to absolute GDP than much smaller Denmark does, but Danish publishers will tend to translate and publish proportionally more works coming from that sphere than from smaller language spheres). The two tendencies appear to compensate each other, with the result that "translated works from a country will basically be roughly in proportion to its GNP [gross national product]" (Hjorth-Andersen, 2001: 214; recall that GNP and GDP both proxy the size of an economy).

Owing to its very compact expository style, the paper's line of argument is not always fully transparent. In any event, the thrust of the paper is quite removed from the concerns of the present study; it does not bear upon the conditions under which the service itself is produced; at best, it may allow the interpretation that translators will get more work from publishers if their L2, L3, etc. – or their "language A", "language B", etc., that is, the languages *from* which they translate are associated with language spheres with a high absolute GDP.

Turning now to the second model, Jacques Mélitz's (2007) paper on the impact of English dominance on literature and welfare emphasises the role of translation not only as a means to convey information from one language to another, but also as the vehicle of a "commodity" (literature) which is valuable in its own right because it generates welfare (or, in standard economic parlance, "utility"). Literature, however, must not be seen as an undifferentiated whole, but as a set of linguistically differentiated inputs, whose variety itself is conducive to welfare. Therefore, it is not indifferent in what language literature is produced. The data used by Mélitz to test his model suggest a significant over-representation of English as a source language, leading Mélitz to express concern about the over-representation of English as a literary language and the concomitant risk to the genuine accumulation of capital in the form of literature.

Another economic perspective on translation can be found in Ginsburgh, Weber, and Wyers (2007), who take issue with Mélitz's approach (which had already been put forward in earlier working papers before its formal publication in the prestigious *Journal of Economic Behavior and Organization*), particularly with his interpretation of his results as proof that English is over-represented in translation flows. We shall devote a little more space to the Ginsburgh, Weber, and Wyers (GWW) model than to the preceding two, because it features a wider range of variables referring to actors' behaviour. Their demonstration goes as follows.

Consider a world where citizens speak languages that belong to a set $S = \{1, 2, 3..., k, ... s\}$. Each citizen is assumed to speak *one* of these languages. Each language J is characterised by a certain population P_j (in other words, P_j represents the population with J as an L1), an average level of literacy in the population (called L_j), and an average disposable income W_j. J-speakers have access to works published in language J, but also to translations of works published in other languages (1, 2, ..., j–1, j+1, ..., s). Let us by convention denote variables referring to the source language with subscript i, and variables referring to the target language with subscript j.

For any language J, there exists a "typical" or archetypal reader A_j, who belongs to population group P_j (indicating the size of the group) and devotes R_j of his time to the reading of translated works. The number of translations from language I to language J that A_j reads is denoted by t_{ij}. GWW then assume that the amount of time R_j that A_j spends reading translations will (positively) depend on L_j and W_j. They further assume that reading works in translation requires a specific effort – in particular, openness and adaptation to the source language's cultural references – and that this effort is positively correlated with intercultural "distance" between I and J, which will be noted D_{ij}.

In general, the time required for reading a book translated from I to J is given by $r(1+D_{ij})$. This generates a *time constraint* on reading time that can be written as:

$$R_j = r(1+D_{1j})t_{1j} + ... + r(1+D_{ij})t_{ij} + ... + r(1+D_{sj})t_{sj}$$

Reading positively affects welfare (or "utility"); however, GWW introduce the assumption that reading translations from an important source language has a stronger effect on welfare than reading translations from a "small" source language. The utility function is given by:

$$U(t_{1j},...,t_{ij},...t_{sj}) = t_{1j}^{\gamma_1} \times ... \times t_{ij}^{\gamma_i} \times ... \times t_{sj}^{\gamma_s} \text{ where } 0 < \gamma_i < 1, \forall i \in S.^{17}$$

This utility function is what actors are assumed to maximise, under a set of constraints (including technical relationships) provided by preceding definitions and equations. In practice, maximizing U under the various constraints generates a system of equation, the solutions of which include *optimal values* for t_{ij}, that is, the number of translated titles that the *average* reader A_j will read, for each source language. This solution reads:

$$t_{ij}^* = \frac{R_j}{r(1+D_{ij})} \frac{\gamma_i}{\sum_{k \neq j}^{s} \gamma_k} \equiv \frac{R_j}{r(1+D_{ij})} \Gamma_i$$

Beyond the complexity of the algebraic expression, the model generates several straightforward propositions, starting with the prediction that the demand for translations from I to J depends:

- positively on J speakers' average income
- positively on the demolinguistic size of the I-speaking population
- negatively on linguistic/cultural distance between I and J

The above expression simply provides a stylised specification of these relationships.

In addition, the model suggests that if the J-speaking population is very homogeneous, everyone will tend to read the same works, with the implication that the number of works actually translated will tend towards t_{ij}^*; if, however, the population is very heterogeneous, with every one making sharply personal reading choices, the number of titles translated will go up, and could theoretically reach $P_j \times t_{ij}^*$.

Thus, in order to predict the magnitude of translation flows, and more specifically the number of works translated, what matters is not so much the size of the target-language population as its degree of internal heterogeneity, noted H_j (and which is, of course, positively correlated to P_j); it follows that the total number of works translated will be given by:

$$t_{ij} = H_j t_{ij}^*$$

This makes it possible to reason not with *individual*, but with *aggregated* demand functions applying to any {i, j} language combination:

$$t_{ij} = \frac{R_j(L_j, W_j)}{r(1+D_{ij})} \Gamma_i$$

where Γ sums up, in a condensed way, a more complex term featuring the parameters intervening in the various definitions and equations presented earlier. The model predicts that total demand for translation will depend:

- positively on P_j, that is, the population having J as a mother tongue (because P_j positively affects H_j);
- positively on P_i, that is, the population having I as a mother tongue (because P_i positively affects γ_{ij});
- negatively on D_{ij}, the inter-linguistic / inter-cultural distance between I and J;
- positively on L_j, the average literacy level of the J-speaking population;
- positively on W_j, the average income of the J-speaking population.

These results can be tested using multivariate analysis, in order to assess if the coefficients associated with each of the explanatory variables just listed have the expected sign (plus or minus) and are statistically significant. The estimation results are presented in Table 11, and they confirm the assumptions made. They are expressed in terms of "elasticities", that is, the sensitivity of a variable with respect to changes in another.

Let us take a couple of examples:

- If the Norwegian population increases by 2 per cent, the number of translations from Norwegian into other languages varies by 1.40 × 2 per cent, that is, by 2.80 per cent (both for literary and other types of translation);
- If the target language population varies by 3 per cent, literary translations into this language will vary by 0.52 × 3 per cent, that is, by 1.56 per cent; however, "other" types of translation (e.g. technical, legal, etc.) will increase by 1.08 × 3 per cent, that is, by 3.24 per cent.

Table 11. Estimated elasticities of variables (all the reported coefficients are significant at the 1 per cent level).

Types of translation	Literary	Other
Constant	3.17	−1.74
Source language population: 19 languages, including:	NOR: 1.40; DSK: 1.38; SVE: 1.29; FRÇ: 1.09; ENG: 0.99; DEU: 0.84; SUO: 0.79; ITA: 0.78	NOR: 1.40; DSK: 1.38; SVE: 1.29; FRÇ: 1.09; ENG: 0.99; DEU: 0.84; SUO: 0.79; ITA: 0.78
Target language population	0.43	0.63
Interlinguistic distance	−1.05	−1.31
Literacy score of target language population	3.93	0.88
Per capita income of target population	0.52	1.08
N	471	471
R^2	0.774	0.739

As regards the impact of linguistic distance, this point is taken up again below. These results lead the authors to the conclusion that, contrary to Mélitz's claims, English is not over-represented in translation flows, once population figures are duly taken into account; it might even be under-represented, considering that an increase in the population of English-speaking countries of, say, x per cent, results in an increase of translations from English of *less* than x per cent (although this under-representation would be very slight, given the 0.99 value of the elasticity, that is, barely below 1).

This result, however, is open to debate for two reasons.

First, it incorporates a definition (and an interpretation) of linguistic distance that is questionable in two different ways. The interlinguistic distance variable is based on the Dyen index, which records some 200 basic terms in 95 languages and checks if they are related (as "water" in English and "Wasser" in German are, while "water" and "acqua" in Italian are not, even though their meaning is essentially the same). The problem lies with the choice of words in the list, which prioritise terms from kinship and everyday life, as opposed to abstract concepts. This results in biases, yielding among others the odd prediction that French is closer to the German than to English. Inappropriate characterisation of distance may cause an over- or an underestimation of its effect on translations, and, by implication, lead to errors in the estimation of the coefficient of other variables in the model. As regards the interpretation of interlinguistic distance (even if it has been measured correctly), it is debatable if the admittedly major distance between Swedish and Finnish really implies that Swedish readers would have to make significantly higher adaptation efforts to read a Finnish novel (in Swedish translation) than to read (also in Swedish translation) an Italian novel (because Italian, like Swedish, also is an Indo-European language) or even a German novel (which is not just part of the Indo-European language family, but also part, as Swedish of its Germanic branch).

Another problem with the model is that it ignores a major fact, namely, that non-native speakers of English often write in English (for non-literary production). One may of course dispute the syntactic and stylistic quality of their writing, but the fact remains that these texts are drafted in English, not in their respective native language. Thus, the dominance of English that Mélitz is concerned with may very well exist without being reflected in figures regarding translation flows.

Finally, one remark may be made about this third model that also applies to the preceding two. As suggested above, the approaches just reviewed mainly concern the demand side in translation. They focus on determining and interpreting the magnitude of translation flows. To a large extent, one might say that they assume translation away, in the sense that they apparently view it as a purely technical process that will simply follow demand, whatever it might be. Relatively little attention has been devoted to the *production function* characterising translation, or to those aspects of interplay between supply and demand that take place before, or *upstream* from the determination of an "equilibrium" quantity of translation. It is precisely these aspects that deserve closer attention as part of an economic perspective on translator status.

Pym (2004) and Chan (2008), however, have already suggested that the processes at hand deserve more attention, owing to some specificities of the production process of translation. Pym (2004) stresses the translation costs that attach to localisation, an activity that rests, among others, on translation skills. Transaction costs are likely to be positively correlated with the extent of diversity that an organisation needs to handle. Controlling such transaction costs requires paying closer scrutiny of the translation production process and of the decisions that surround it, including in particular the *quality* aimed at in translation.

Quality emerges as a key variable in an economic perspective on translation, because contrary to the assumption made in most economic analyses of market exchange, it is very difficult for the client (whom we may also refer to as the "principal") to be sure about the quality provided by the translator acting as his supplier (whom we may also call the "agent", acting, as it were, on behalf of the principal). There is an asymmetry between the two with respect to the information they have about the quality of the good.

This issue has been explored by Chan (2008), who proposes to examine translation in the perspective of information economics. This field of specialisation in economics was opened by a celebrated paper by Akerlof (1970), whose basic argument runs as follows: in a market where some suppliers offer quality goods while others don't, and where consumers cannot (or not fully) separate the grain from the chaff, buyers will only be ready to pay a low price for the goods on offer. The low price reflects the risk of acquiring a low-quality good (and if the good is of decent quality, the buyer will have made a bargain). However, sellers of genuinely good products will (rationally) turn down offers at an excessively low price and eventually exit the market. Only "bad" goods will remain on the market, and the market price, while appropriate for the low-quality segment of the market, will be less than adequate for the high-quality segment of supply. While asymmetric information characterises second-hand goods (like the cars referred to in Akerlof's original paper), it can be said to apply to a host of other goods and services, from medical acts to translation; the mechanism whereby "bad" goods drive out the "good" ones from the market is known as adverse selection.

A standard solution to this problem is signalling (Spence 1974): "good" sellers may issue a signal credibly establishing the quality of their products, thus distancing or even shutting themselves off from the "bad" sellers. This creates the conditions for the market to stabilise at a "fairer" price. Unfortunately, this merely shifts the problem, since signals are easy to fake, and the buyer is then saddled with the problem of distinguishing between "good" and "bad" signals. Buyers can then engage in "screening" procedures (Arrow 1973; Stiglitz 1975), resorting to other characteristics of the seller as indicators of the likely quality of the good or service offered; only sellers presenting the requisite traits will be hired, or retained as trustworthy suppliers of the good or service concerned.

Even effective screening, however, may not constitute a sufficient guarantee, since another problem may turn up in the form of moral hazard. This is linked not to the intrinsically poor quality of a good or service, but on the unobservable, or "un-monitorable" character of the effort that even a perfectly competent provider may put into discharging his duties.

Summing up, it is very difficult for a market like translation to completely eschew the difficulties associated with asymmetric information. While signalling remains necessary and is an important feature of the market for translation services, the profusion of signalling devices (certification, specialised programmes, membership in professional organisations, client references, etc.) may create as much noise as *bona fide* information.

Appendix E
EQUILIBRIUM ON THE TRANSLATION MARKET

Here we give the formulas underlying the analysis of asymmetric signalling in section 5.3 of the report.

At equilibrium, the relationship between p, z, and L (assumed to be linear for simplicity), can be represented as follows:[18]

$$L = a_0 \cdot p + a_1 \cdot z, \quad \text{with } a_0 > 0,\ a_1 < 0. \tag{1}$$

We also assume a minimum quality level required by purchasers (L_{min}), independently of price.

To provide a service, *individual* translators expend an effort which depends positively on the price received and negatively on the strength of demand. This reflects the fact that, for a given price, the incentive to do a "good job" depends on the risk of losing (or not finding) a client; this risk decreases when demand is strong.[19] (This is reminscent of the concept of "efficient wages".)

The effort expended by low-skill translators, e_B, is given by:

$$e_B = b_0 + b_1 \cdot p + b_2 \cdot z, \quad \text{with } b_0 < 0,\ b_1 > 0,\ b_2 < 0 \tag{2}$$

Similary, the effort exerted by high-skill translators, e_G, is given by:

$$e_G = g_0 + g_1 \cdot p + g_2 \cdot z, \quad \text{with } g_0 < 0,\ g_1 > 0,\ g_2 < 0 \tag{3}$$

We assume that translators operate only if price is above a minimum level (which differs between the two groups) and that the maximum level of effort is 1. Minimum prices for low-skilled translators and high-skilled translators will be noted p_B^{min} and p_G^{min}, respectively.

The quality of the services provided (L_B, L_G) depends on the level of skills and on the effort expended. This can be expressed as follows:

$$L_B = \varphi_B \cdot e_B \text{ and } L_G = \varphi_G \cdot e_G, \quad \text{with } \varphi_G = 1,\ 0 < \varphi_G < 1. \tag{4}$$

The average quality provided by the market is therefore:

$$L = \omega_B \cdot L_B + \omega_G \cdot L_G \tag{5}$$

Combining (4) with (2) and (3), expression (5) can be rewritten as:

$$L = \omega_B \cdot \varphi_B \cdot (b_0 + b_1 \cdot p + b_2 \cdot z) + \omega_G \cdot \varphi_G \cdot (g_0 + g_1 \cdot p + g_2 \cdot z) \qquad (6)$$

Equilibrium requires that (1) hold. The system describing the market is therefore made up of equations (1) and (6), which gives:

$$a_0 \cdot p + a_1 \cdot z = \omega_B \cdot \varphi_B \cdot (b_0 + b_1 \cdot p + b_2 \cdot z) + \omega_G \cdot \varphi_G \cdot (g_0 + g_1 \cdot p + g_2 \cdot z) \qquad (7)$$

Solving for p yields the market equilibrium price:

$$p = \frac{\omega_B \varphi_B b_0 + \omega_G \varphi_G g_0 + (\omega_B \varphi_B b_2 + \omega_G \varphi_G g_2 - a_1)z}{a_0 - \omega_B \varphi_B b_1 - \omega_G \varphi_G g_1}$$

This solution is valid away from maximum and minimum equilibrium quality and if both types of translators do not operate at strictly maximum or minimum quality levels.

NOTES

1. Methodological Issues

1 http://translationinstitute.org. Accessed November 2011.
2 http://translationcertification.org. Accessed November 2011.
3 http://www.becomeatranslator.com. Accessed November 2011.
4 http://www.aipti.org. Accessed November 2011.
5 Note that this view of status differs from approaches that identify a group of well-qualified professional translators, then set out to measure their relative salaries, education, visibility, and power (as in Dam and Zethsen 2008, 2009a, 2009b, 2011, 2012). In keeping with the more uncertain world where apparent status can be bought from a website, here we ask how translators are identified as such, and how some are signalled as being more trustworthy than others.
6 http://www.linguaeshop.com/. Accessed 14 June 2013.
7 Katan (2009: 128–9) reports that class 74.85 of the "General Industrial Classification of Economic Activities within the European Communities" (2008) was for "Secretarial and translation activities", where "translation and interpretation" appeared alongside typing, transcribing, proofreading, and photocopying.
8 http://circa.europa.eu/irc/dsis/nacecpacon/info/data/en/. Accessed November 2011.
9 Note that in conceptualising "status" in this way, we have little need to offer a restrictive definition of "profession", beyond its general understanding as regularly remunerated activity (making "voluntary" the opposite of "professional"). The various signals of status themselves indicate what a "profession" is held to be in a given place and at a given moment – our task is merely to describe those signals. For example, when we attempt to say how many professional translators and interpreters there are in the world (Appendix B), the actual definitions of "professional" are those used 1 by the statistical services of the United States, Australia, Canada, Germany, Norway, and Portugal, whose numbers we draw on. Put more simply, "profession" is the thing we set out to discover, not the thing we assume.
10 Information supplied by Andrew Evans, FIT Treasurer, 17/11/2011.
11 http://www.aipti.org/eng/speaks-out/art3-aati-expels-members-for-founding-iapti.html. The international association replies that one of the main differences between the two associations is that "many colleagues from a variety of different countries do not possess translating or interpreting diplomas. But these are professionals who should indeed be included in any association that wishes to genuinely reflect the broader professional community and to work to correct a number of irregularities that exist today in Italy, the United Kingdom, the United States, Argentina, Brazil, India and so many other countries around the world. AATI, on the other hand, with very few exceptions, does not admit translators and interpreters who do not hold a degree."
12 See http://isg.urv.es/publicity/isg/projects/2011_DGT/reports.html. Accessed November 2011.
13 See http://isg.urv.es/publicity/isg/projects/2011_DGT/factsheets.html.
14 Translation and Interpreting Summit Advisory Council: http://www.tisac.org. Accessed April 2012.

2. Results

1 http://en.enace.eu/d-74.3.html. Accessed November 2011.
2 As mentioned previously, Katan (2009: 128–9) reports that class 74.85 of the NACE (2008) was for "Secretarial and translation activities", where "translation and interpretation" appeared alongside typing, transcribing, proofreading, and photocopying. This should explain why there are reports of the categories changing, for example in Poland.
3 http://www.ilo.org/public/english/bureau/stat/isco/isco88/index.htm. Accessed November 2011.
4 *Libro Blanco de la traducción y la interpretación institucional* (2011: 81): http://ec.europa.eu/spain/pdf/libro_blanco_traduccion_es.pdf. Accessed November 2011.
5 Information from Sunniva Whittaker, 7/10/2011.
6 Information from Janet Fraser, 21/10/2011.
7 Information from Sunniva Whittaker, 7/10/2011.These terms are in addition to the title "Statsautoriseert translator", which is protected and can only be used by authorised translators.
8 Information from Fernando Ferreira-Alves, 15/11/2011. The main complication in Portugal is that the register is actually of translation companies, most of which only have one employee.
9 http://www.literar.at/pages/uu/sf_s1100.aspx. Accessed November 2011.
10 Jurgita Mikutyte, 5/10/2011.
11 Danuta Kierzkowska, 17/10/2011.
12 Nike K. Pokorn, 8/10/2011.
13 The restrictions of the licence can be circumvented in the following ways: 1) translators who received an unrestricted licence prior to 2007 can continue to use it; 2) licences are granted to translators who have stayed for 10 years in the country where the official language is the one they wish to translate from; 3) companies employ secretaries to translate for them (so no invoice is necessary); 4) an unregulated work agreement (*dohoda o vykonaní práce*) can be issued for temporary work as a translator, for example by students. (Djovčoš 13/02/2012). The restricted title might thus result in an increase in translations done by secretaries and students.
14 OTTIAQ (Ordre des traducteurs, terminologues et interprètes agréés du Québec) (2009) *Demande de modification de statut et de réserve d'actes professionnels présentée le 5 mars 2009 à l'Office des professions du Québec*, http://www.ottiaq.org/extranet/pdf/memoire_opq.pdf, accessed November 2011.
15 http://ec.europa.eu/translatores/documents/factsheet_recruitment_en.pdf. Accessed November 2011.
16 This might appear to contradict the DGT's promotion of a European Master's in Translation (EMT). However, the EMT could also be seen as an attempt to standardise translator training to the point where the Master's in Translation can be a prerequisite for employment.
17 International Annual Meeting on Language Arrangements, Documentation and Publications.
18 http://www.iamladp.org/PDFs/2009_docs/R8_WG_on_Training2009Report.pdf, p. 79.
19 Translators recruited at the United Nations need "a first-level degree from university or institution of equivalent status, where, normally, the language of instruction is the translator's main language". http://www.unlanguage.org/Careers/Translators/Qualification/default.aspx.
20 Anne Lafeber, United Nations Office at Geneva, personal communication, 6/11/11.
21 This question was not asked in our initial questionnaire but has been addressed in follow-up interviews and email exchanges.
22 http://ec.europa.eu/spain/pdf/libro_blanco_traduccion_es.pdf. Accessed November 2011.
23 Our thanks to Kyriaki Kourouni for this information. It seems that the 2008 "Kassimis law" allows that graduates with a first university degree in other disciplines may be candidates for the position of sworn translator in Greece. We are told that the law has yet to be applied.
24 According to Jørgen Christian Wind Nielsen (09/03/12), the trade-off was "a necessary prerequisite to reach a compromise, the countries with 'strong' academic traditions on the one

hand arguing for academic qualifications as a criteria, other countries with no such tradition arguing for practical experience."
25 Directive 2010/64/EU of the European Parliament and of the Council of 20 October 2010 on the right to interpretation and translation in criminal proceedings. (Online: http://eur-lex.europa.eu/LexUriServ/LexUriServ.do?uri=OJ:L:2010:280:0001:0007:EN:PDF.) The directive states that interpreting and/or translation services should be provided free of charge to suspected or accused persons. It does not specify into what languages those services should be provided (i.e. there is no reference to an L1 or mother tongue). The criterion is merely that the suspected or accused person be able "fully to exercise their right of defence and safeguarding the fairness of the proceedings" (17).
26 http://www.eulita.eu/. Accessed April 2012.
27 In Italy, "the translator goes to the court house with the original and the translation, and the court clerk makes you sign a declaration where you swear to have translated 'faithfully', and then puts a stamp on every page" (Chiara Salce, 5/10/2011).
28 The entry in EUATC 2009 states: "Members of the ATC [Association of Translation Companies] and the Institute of Translating and Interpreting are recognised by the Home Office, other government bodies and the courts. This means that members have a stamp with a unique number which we can use to stamp the translations. This is accepted as evidence of an official translation. (But there is no checking process on the suitability of that particular member to carry out a legal translation.)". The respondents to our own survey did not mention this recognition.
29 http://www.appliedlanguage.com. Accessed November 2011.
30 Our thanks to Christine Schmit (12/02/2012) for the exact information, as follows: "The current criteria for becoming a sworn translator are: a) a degree in translation/interpreting (this needs to be at least a 4-year degree, a 3-year BA in translation is not considered sufficient), b) a degree in languages plus 5 years of professional experience as translator/interpreter or language teacher, c) people who hold a degree in another field (law, business, etc.) are only accepted exceptionally, if they can demonstrate several years of experience in translation, as a sworn translator in another country, etc." Cf. Kanelliadou 2011.
31 In Spain, article 441 of the Ley de Enjuiciamiento Criminal (1882/2004) states: "El intérprete [including translators] será elegido entre los que tengan títulos de tales, si los hubiere en el pueblo. En su defecto, será nombrado un maestro del correspondiente idioma, y si tampoco lo hubiere, cualquier persona que lo sepa." That is, for criminal proceedings, first you look for a translator with a degree (the nature of the required degree remains vague); if none is found, you look for a teacher of the foreign language; and if no teacher is found, you settle for anyone who "knows the language". http://noticias.juridicas.com/base_datos/Penal/lecr.l2t5.html#a441. Accessed November 2011.
32 "Graduates of university departments for translator and interpreter training must furnish proof of two years of professional work, all other applicants proof of five years of professional work during the years immediately preceding registration." Austrian Association of Certified Court Interpreters, http://www.gerichtsdolmetscher.at. Accessed November 2011.
33 Our thanks to Łucja Biel of the University of Gdansk, 10/02/2012.
34 http://www.peempip.gr/index.php/en. Accessed November 2011.
35 Our thanks to Dee Shields of Danske Translatører, 23/11/11.
36 "For Romania, there is clearly a discrepancy between the protection markers as noted by Hertog, which are indeed present, and the underlying application criteria." (Anca Greere, private communication, 16/05/12).
37 http://www.gerichtsdolmetscherverzeichnis.de/suche.jsp. Accessed April 2012.
38 Eva Gorgolová, 28/05/2012.
39 The potential numbers here are calculated on the basis of Parker (2008) estimates of the total demand for translation services, as explained in Appendix B. With respect to the percentages,

note that 100 per cent would indicate that the real supply of sworn T/Is corresponded exactly to the potential demand for professionals in all fields.
40 For the information in this paragraph, our thanks to Łucja Biel of the University of Gdansk, 10/02/2012.
41 According to Iliescu Gheorghiu of the Universitat d'Alacant (19/05/12), the Spanish authorities do not always accept sworn translations done by translators authorised in Romania. This may be because the translators first have to be included in the list of sworn translators issued by the Spanish Ministry of Foreign Affairs.
42 If a sworn translator moves from one *Land* to another, they may apply for new accreditation. That said, the basic admission criteria are the same, requiring a state exam or a degree in translation.
43 According to information from the Romanian Ministry of Justice, the translators authorised by them must be citizens of "an EU Member State, a member of the European Economic Area, or Switzerland" (trans. Catalina Iliescu Gheorghiu 19/05/12). This may allow for a limited reciprocity with Spain, since the Romanian ministry issues the authorisation on the basis of educational qualifications. Non-Romanian candidates nevertheless have their knowledge of Romanian certified in Romania. See 3.2.5.
44 http://eur-lex.europa.eu/LexUriServ/LexUriServ.do?uri=OJ:C:2011:139:0005:01:EN:HTML. Accessed November 2011.
45 Only six translators were listed at the time of writing: http://www.bulgarianembassy-london.org. Accessed November 2011.
46 http://www.proz.com/forum/translators_associations/38224-certified_sworn_translators_around_the_world.html. Accessed November 2011.
47 This conclusion may not be universal: in Uruguay and Argentina, academic degrees qualify "public translators" (*traductores públicos*), who can then work as sworn translators.
48 This would appear to be the logic behind the 2011 change in the Polish system, where a university qualification in translation is no longer required as a prerequisite.
49 http://translatorforeningen.dk/om-translatoerforeningen/. Accessed April 2012. Note that the two main institutions that train translators in Denmark are traditionally known as business schools (the Aarhus school has since been incorporated into Aarhus University). There are two associations for authorised translators in Denmark: Translatørforeningen (http://translatorforeningen.dk/) and Danske Translatører (http://www.dtfb.dk/, accessed November 2011). Both associations require that one be an "authorised translator" to become a member.
50 http://www.dtfb.dk/?mode=c_page&pageID=1574&parent_page_ID=0. Accessed April 2012.
51 http://www.iol.org.uk/qualifications/exams_diptrans.asp. Accessed November 2011.
52 http://www.atanet.org/membership/. Accessed November 2011.
53 This concerns only the field covered in this survey. The giant of the worldwide field may be the Translators Association of China, which claims some 30,000 members. The Canadian Conseil des traducteurs, terminologues et interprètes du Canada had 2831 members in 2011 (FIT source).
54 http://dvud.de/. "Wir… das sind 8 Übersetzer und ein Anwalt und noch ein paar mehr Menschen, die endlich etwas bewegen wollen" (We… that is eight translators and a lawyer and a few others who just want to get something moving"). Accessed November 2011.
55 http://uepo.de/2011/11/12/dvud-neuer-verband-fur-ubersetzer-und-dolmetscher-gegrundet/. Accessed November 2011.
56 See Appendix A for the membership numbers of each association. The larger FIT numbers are approximate, since FIT data are only designed to calculate the fees each association pays to the FIT. In cases where the number of members is not available, the association has been counted in the number of associations but not in the total membership.
57 US figures include regional chapters and affiliates of the ATA, listed as separate associations.
58 http://www.cttic.org. Accessed November 2011.

59 Conselho Nacional de Tradução (CNT): http://associacao-portuguesa-de-tradutores.blogspot.com/2011/02/nova-seccao.html. Accessed November 2011.
60 A further development is the Translation and Interpreting Summit Advisory Council (TISAC) (http://www.tisac.org/), which is mainly North American. The TISAC, however, was set up to advise, not to represent the interests of translators.
61 Note that this means that our working definition of "professional translator and interpreter" is in effect a composite of the definitions used in official statistics in Australia, Canada, Germany, Norway, Portugal, and the United States, which provide the components for our estimate of 333,000 professional translators and interpreters in the world (see Appendix B).
62 Applying this logic, the more worrying data are from the smaller countries where the memberships do *not* exceed the prediction: Cyprus (where there is no training programme), Malta (where we have found no association), and Latvia (where attempts are being made to set up an association).
63 CIOL/ITI (2011: 5) reports that 22 per cent of the respondents to its major survey were members of both the CIOL and the ITI.
64 http://www.iti.org.uk/indexMainG.html. Accessed November 2011.
65 http://www.iol.org.uk/membership. Accessed November 2011.
66 http://www.proz.com/forum/translators_associations/29683-which_is_better_iti_or_iol.html. Accessed November 2011.

3. Case Studies

1 Our thanks to Dr Radegundis Stolze for her review of this section and invaluable suggestions.
2 See http://www.aticom.de/a-abschluesse.pdf. (updated March 2009).
3 The Germersheim institute alone has about 2,000 students. We thank Professor Michael Schreiber, director of the Germersheim institute, for this information and for his help with our consciously rough estimate of the total number of students in Germany. Note that a survey conducted in 1994 (Caminade and Pym 1995) suggested there were some 11,850 students enrolled in translator-training institutes in Germany, so the current estimate may be conservative.
4 http://www.literaturuebersetzer.de/pages/uebersetzer/wirsindwer.htm: "Im Juli 2011 zählen wir über 1200 Mitglieder". Accessed November 2011.
5 The BDÜ is a member of various German institutions engaged in pertinent fields of activity: the Bundesverband mittelständische Wirtschaft – BVMW e.V. (Federal Association of Small and Medium-Sized Enterprises), the Institut für Sachverständigenwesen (IfS) (Institute for Expert Affairs), the Zentrale zur Bekämpfung unlauteren Wettbewerbs e.V. (WBZ) (Centre for Combating Unfair Competition), the European Legal Interpreters and Translators Association (EULITA), and the Conférence internationale permanente d'Instituts universitaires de Traducteurs et Interprètes (CIUTI).
6 http://www.adue-nord.de/. Accessed November 2011.
7 http://www.aticom.de/. Accessed April 2012.
8 http://www.vued.de/. Accessed November 2011.
9 The member companies offer "graduates of the various universities and training institutes for translators and interpreters with the relevant language combinations a practical training placement, lasting between two and six months. The practical training placements initially involve an introduction to the company organisation, the company philosophy and the quality management system, which operates in accordance with the current standards, and extends to all aspects of translation work in a translation company." http://www.qsd.de/eng/ausbildung/index.html. Accessed November 2011.
10 Note that the VdÜ is omitted from accounts such as Stejskal (2003) and was not mentioned by our own informants.

11 http://dvud.de/. Accessed November 2011.
12 http://www.bdue.de/index.php?page=020000&id=552. The data also indicate that some 70 per cent of the translators and interpreters are women, and 42 per cent have a university-level degree. This does not appear to be a majority, despite what is said in the BDÜ report: "Die Mehrheit der angestellten Dolmetscher und Übersetzer hat einen Fach- oder Hochschulabschluss. Dies war auch schon im Jahr 2005 der Fall, doch ist die Zahl der angestellten Sprachexperten mit einem Studium noch einmal um 5,2 Prozent gestiegen und liegt 2011 bei 2.890 Personen."
13 A succinct description of this field is given by Stejskal (2003a), whom we merely update here.
14 A complete comparison of the terms and systems used in each *Land* is available at the EULITA website: http://www.eulita.eu/sites/default/files/Loi%20de%20la%20ville%20libre%20et%20hanseatique%20de%20Hambourg%20relative%20aux%20interpretes%20et%20traducteurs_landervergleich.pdf. Accessed November 2011.
15 As proposed by Natascha Dalügge-Momme, "Loi de la ville libre et hanséatique de Hambourg relative aux interprètes et traducteurs – un modèle pour l'Europe?", http://www.eulita.eu/loi-de-la-ville-libre-et-hanseatique-de-hambourg-relative-aux-interpretes-et-traducteurs-un-modele. Accessed November 2011.
16 http://www.gerichtsdolmetscherverzeichnis.de. The list is actually maintained by the Hesse Ministry for Justice, Integration and Europe.
17 The position of the BDÜ is expressed in an open letter to the Federal Minister for Justice: http://vbdu.de/Download/BDU-StellungnahmeJVEG.pdf. The position of the Bavarian Association for Sworn Translators and Interpreters (VbDÜ) is similar: http://vbdu.de/Download/VbDU-StellungnahmeJVEG.pdf. Accessed November 2011.
18 For example, the Gesetz über die öffentliche Bestellung und allgemeine Vereidigung von Dolmetscherinnen und Übersetzerinnen sowie Dolmetschern und Übersetzern (2006) in Hamburg (http://www.eulita.eu/sites/default/files/Loi%20de%20la%20ville%20libre%20et%20hanseatique%20de%20Hambourg%20relative%20aux%20interpretes%20et%20traducteurs2.pdf), or the Gesetz über die öffentliche Bestellung und allgemeine Beeidigung von Dolmetschern und Übersetzern (2009) in Bavaria: http://vbdu.de/Download/Bayr-Dolmetschergesetz.pdf. Accessed November 2011.
19 Our thanks to Dr Radegundis Stolze for this information. The survey is only available on the BDÜ intranet.
20 http://www.bdue.de/index.php?page=020000&id=552. Accessed November 2011.
21 http://www.gerichtsdolmetscherverzeichnis.de/suche.jsp. Accessed November 2011.
22 Our thanks to Anca Greere of Babeş-Bolyai University of Cluj-Napoca, Cristiana Cobliş of the Romanian Translators Association, and Catalina Iliescu Gheorghiu of the Universitat d'Alacant for providing a wealth of information and for checking this section.
23 Constantin 2004: http://www6.gencat.net/llengcat/noves/hm04tardor/docs/constantin.pdf. Accessed November 2011.
24 Anca Greere, 15/05/12.
25 Catalina Iliescu Gheorghiu, 20/05/12, 21/05/12.
26 www.atr.org.ro. Accessed April 2012.
27 http://www.untar.ro, especially http://www.untar.ro/brosura_UNTAR.pdf. Accessed November 2011.
28 Stefan Macovei, personal communication, 05/05/2012.
29 Romanian Ministry of Justice. Our thanks to Catalina Iliescu Gheorghiu (19/05/12) for the translation of this document.
30 Information from Delia Radu, 27/10/2011. The number of certifications should be greater than the number of certified translators who are alive and professionally active. Greere and Tătaru state that the number of authorised translators in Romania is "over 15,000" (2008: 103).
31 Romanian Ministry of Justice. Our thanks to Catalina Iliescu Gheorghiu (19/05/12) for the translation of this document.

32 http://legestart.ro/Monitorul-Oficial-208-din-01.04.2009-(M.-Of.-208-2009-14032).htm. Accessed November 2011.
33 Anca Greere, personal communication, 16/05/12.
34 Our thanks to Nike Pokorn of the University of Ljubljana for providing much useful information and for checking this section.
35 http://www.prevajalstvo.net/. Accessed November 2011.
36 http://www.ff.uni-mb.si/oddelki/prevodoslovje/studijski-programi.dot. Accessed November 2011.
37 http://www.slovenskavojska.si/en/structure/genneral-staff-commands-and-units/doctrine-development-educational-and-training-command/school-of-foreign-languages/. Accessed November 2011.
38 http://www.dskp-drustvo.si/. The number is given as 210 in Fock et al. 2008.
39 http://www.dztps.si/. Accessed November 2011.
40 http://www.zkts.si/news.php. Accessed November 2011.
41 http://www.tolmaci.si/?id=3&c=21. Accessed November 2011.
42 http://zpp.gzs.si/slo/. Accessed November 2011.
43 Nike K. Pokorn, 8/10/2011.
44 "Court interpreters and sworn translators of legal language" http://www.eulita.eu/sites/default/files/Court%20interpreters%20and%20sworn%20translators%20of%20legal%20language_0.pdf. Accessed November 2011.
45 http://www.direct.gov.uk/en/Governmentcitizensandrights/LivingintheUK/DG_10012519. Accessed November 2011.
46 http://theinterpreterdiaries.com/2011/05/18/the-university-of-westminster-closes-its-training-program/. Accessed November 2011.
47 http://www.iol.org.uk/. Accessed November 2011.
48 http://www.iol.org.uk/membership/CriteriaforMembershipOct08.pdf. Accessed April 2012.
49 See, for example: http://www.city.ac.uk/courses/cpd/institute-of-linguists-educational-trust-iolet-diploma-in-translation-module-1, and http://2009.westminster.ac.uk/schools/humanities/professional-courses/diploma-in-translation. Accessed November 2011.
50 http://www.iol.org.uk/membership/CL%20Rules/CLRules11.pdf. Accessed November 2011.
51 According to Alan Peacock, joint acting CEO and director of membership of the CIOL (personal communication 26/04/12): "When we were drawing up the criteria for the CL scheme, it was felt that the content of some Master's degrees in Translation might require exploration, to ensure that the modules taken were sufficiently robust in terms of professional practice: for example, a degree with heavy emphasis on technology or theory might not be considered sufficient to fulfil the practice element expected of a Chartered Linguist. There is no list of degrees which are not accepted; it was a case of keeping our options open to seek information about the contents of qualifications with which we are not familiar."
52 http://www.iti.org.uk/. Accessed November 2011.
53 http://en.wikipedia.org/wiki/Institute_of_Translation_%26_Interpreting. Accessed November 2011.
54 http://www.unitetheunion.org/nupit. Accessed November 2011.
55 http://en.wikipedia.org/wiki/List_of_UK_interpreting_and_translation_associations. Accessed November 2011.
56 http://www.atc.org.uk/. Accessed November 2011.
57 http://www.profintal.org.uk/. Accessed November 2011.
58 http://nopeanuts.wordpress.com/resistance/uk-interpreters-boycott/police-rip-up-contract/. Accessed November 2011.
59 http://www.spsi.org.uk/. Accessed November 2011.
60 http://www.nomisweb.co.uk/articles/ref/abi/ETApr03Jones.pdf. Accessed November 2011.

61 http://www.ons.gov.uk/ons/guide-method/classifications/current-standard-classifications/standard-industrial-classification/index.html. Accessed November 2011.
62 http://www.ons.gov.uk/ons/rel/ppi2/services-producer-price-indices/quarter-2-2011/tsd-services-producer-price-index---quarter-2-2011.html. Accessed November 2011.
63 http://www.nrpsi.co.uk/. Accessed February 2012.
64 http://www.appliedlanguage.com/. Accessed November 2011.
65 http://www.iol.org.uk/nrpsi/NRPSIRepWeb0511.pdf. Accessed November 2011.
66 http://epetitions.direct.gov.uk/petitions/8290. Accessed November 2011.
67 http://www.iol.org.uk/news/news_article.asp?r=PB63KS11093. Accessed February 2012. This statement gives links to parliamentary debate and question on the issue, including that the reasons for the outsourcing were to improve the quality of the previous system and to save money: "the expected saving would be about £18 million on an annual budget of £60 million".
68 Letter from the Chairman of the NRPSI to the Minister of Justice: http://www.nrpsi.co.uk/pdf/NRPSI%20%20letter%20to%20MoJ%2019.12.2011.pdf.
69 See e.g. http://www.solicitorsfirm.com/90-of-interpreters-boycott-applied-language-solutions.
70 http://www.linguistlounge.com. Accessed November 2011.
71 CIOL/ITI (2011: 5) reports that 22 per cent of the respondents were members of both the CIOL and the ITI.
72 This could become an important consideration for the European Master's in Translation, if and when degrees issued by members of the EMT network are not recognised as professionally valid within the domestic market.
73 http://www.act.es/empresas.htm. Accessed November 2011.
74 Real Decreto 2002/2009: http://www.boe.es/boe/dias/2009/12/24/pdfs/BOE-A-2009-20767.pdf.
75 http://www.maec.es/es/menuppal/ministerio/tablondeanuncios/interpretesjurados/Paginas/Intrpretes%20Jurados.aspx. Accessed November 2011.
76 "…resulta muy descorazonador constatar que en todo lo relacionado con nuestra profesión, somos el único país de Europa que tiene una norma que permite el reconocimiento de nuestros colegas europeos, sin que ninguno de esos países exista reciprocidad" (2012). For some four years Peñarroja i Fa used himself as a "guinea pig", requesting European recognition of his Spanish qualifications. His 2012 *Butlletí* incudes refusals from France and Geneva.
77 "En las actuaciones orales se podrá habilitar como intérprete a cualquier persona conocedora de la lengua empleada, previo juramento o promesa de aquélla." Text as in Ley Orgánica 1/2009, modifying the Ley Orgánica of 1985: http://noticias.juridicas.com/base_datos/Admin/lo1-2009.html. Cf. article 441 of the Ley de Enjuiciamiento Criminal (1882/2004): "El intérprete [including translators] será elegido entre los que tengan títulos de tales, si los hubiere en el pueblo. En su defecto, será nombrado un maestro del correspondiente idioma, y si tampoco lo hubiere, cualquier persona que lo sepa." http://noticias.juridicas.com/base_datos/Penal/lecr.l2t5.html#a441. Accessed February 2012.
78 http://www.seprotec.com.
79 "Ministry of the Interior Privatizes the Translation Services of the Police and the Civil Guard" http://www.elmundo.es/elmundo/2008/05/31/espana/1212207586.html; An interpreter is sent to the Barajas airport to work for the police and is arrested by the police because he is in their list of wanted persons: http://ccoomir.blogspot.com/2010/02/seprotec.html; "Ministry of the Interior uses Translators without Guarantees of their Qualifications": http://www.publico.es/espana/122671/interior-emplea-traductores-sin-garantias-en-sus-investigaciones; "Paying 10 euros an hour, it is difficult to ensure the desirable professionalism [among interpreters working for the police]": http://www.magdabandera.com/archives/000771.html; "Police are sent interpreters with criminal records": http://www.20minutos.es/noticia/384035/antecedentes/

traductores/policia/; "Police interpreters arrested": http://www.interviu.es/reportajes/articulos/varios-traductores-policiales-han-sido-detenidos.
80 http://www.elgasconjurado.com/2010/02/15/informe-de-la-magistrada-pilar-de-luna-jimenez-de-parga/.
81 http://www.abc.es/20120113/madrid/abcp-juzgados-retiran-traductores-lenguas-20120113.html.
82 http://www.fit-europe.org/vault/FIT_Europe_Rates_report_fr.pdf. Accessed November 2011.
83 http://www.us-english.org/view/9. Accessed November 2011.
84 http://www.census.gov/hhes/socdemo/language/data/acs/ACS-12.pdf. Accessed November 2011.
85 http://www.tisac.org/programs/. Accessed November 2011.
86 http://www.atanet.org/aboutus/history.php. Accessed November 2011.
87 http://www.taals.net/apply.php. Accessed November 2011.
88 http://www.aboutus.org/Najit.org. Accessed November 2011.
89 http://www.najit.org/index.php. Accessed November 2011.
90 http://www.ncihc.org/. Accessed November 2011.
91 http://www.netaweb.org/. Accessed November 2011.
92 http://www.aciaonline.org/. Accessed November 2011.
93 http://www.coloradointerpreters.org/. Accessed November 2011.
94 http://www.iitanet.org/. Accessed November 2011.
95 http://www.natihq.org/. Accessed November 2011.
96 https://www.tapit.org/. Accessed November 2011.
97 http://www.aatia.org/. Accessed November 2011.
98 http://www.hitagroup.org/user/find. Accessed November 2011.
99 http://alcus.org/. Accessed November 2011.
100 http://www.tisac.org/. Accessed November 2011.
101 http://www.bls.gov/ooh/Media-and-Communication/Interpreters-and-translators.htm#tab-5. Accessed May 2012.
102 Federal Trade Commission Decision and Consent Order, issued 31 August 1994. http://www.federalregister.gov/articles/1994/09/23/94-23579/the-american-association-of-language-specialists-prohibited-trade-practices-and-affirmative. The Order allows the association to express opinions: "nothing contained in Paragraph IV of this Order shall prohibit respondent [TAALS] from providing information or its non-binding and non-coercive views concerning interpretation equipment, the hours of work or preparation, or the number of language specialists used for types of jobs." The prohibition was restated in 1996, against the AIIC, the United States chapter of the AIIC, and TAALS. See: http://www.ftc.gov/os/1996/07/9270_id.pdf. Accessed November 2011.
103 15 November 2011. Holly Mikkelson is Adjunct Professor at the Monterey Institute for International Studies.
104 Factsheet survey data, 15 November 2011.
105 http://www.atanet.org/certification/eligibility_faqs.php. Accessed November 2011.
106 Ibid.: "You do technically qualify, but the examination is designed for someone with a significant amount of experience working as a professional translator. It will be very difficult to pass the examination without that experience. If you do not have that experience, it would be a very good idea to attempt a practice test first to get an indication of how you might perform on the examination."
107 http://www.atanet.org/certification/aboutcert_overview.php. Accessed November 2011.
108 http://www.atanet.org/certification/aboutcert_overview.php. Accessed November 2011.
109 http://info.cetra.com/blog/bid/47367/Translation-Interpreting-Summit-Advisory-Council-2011-Meeting. Accessed November 2011.

110 Principal Foreign Language and Area Advisor, Office of the Under Secretary of Defense for Intelligence.
111 http://www.bls.gov/oco/ocos175.htm. Accessed November 2011.
112 We might have some reason to doubt the figure. The same report states that "interpreters and translators held about 50,900 jobs in 2008" (http://www.bls.gov/oco/ocos175.htm), whereas the 2005 US Census counted 30,000 "non-employers" in the translation industry (http://www.bls.gov/oco/ocos175.htm).
113 http://www.bls.gov/ooh/Media-and-Communication/Interpreters-and-translators.htm#tab-6. Updated 26 April, 2012.
114 http://www.bdue.de/index.php?page=020000&id=552. The data also indicate that some 70 per cent of the translators and interpreters are women, and 42 per cent have a university-level degree. This does not appear to be a majority, despite what is said in the BDÜ report: "Die Mehrheit der angestellten Dolmetscher und Übersetzer hat einen Fach- oder Hochschulabschluss. Dies war auch schon im Jahr 2005 der Fall, doch ist die Zahl der angestellten Sprachexperten mit einem Studium noch einmal um 5,2 Prozent gestiegen und liegt 2011 bei 2.890 Personen."
115 http://www.servicecanada.gc.ca/eng/qc/job_futures/statistics/5125.shtml
116 *Official Language Policies of the Canadian Provinces. Costs and Benefits in 2006.* http://www.fraserinstitute.org/uploadedFiles/fraser-ca/Content/research-news/research/publications/official-language-policies-of-canadian-provinces.pdf. Accessed April 2012.
117 http://en.wikipedia.org/wiki/Official_Languages_Act_%28Canada%29.
118 http://www.btb.gc.ca/btb.php?lang=eng&cont=282.
119 http://www.thecanadianencyclopedia.com/articles/language-policy. Accessed March 2012.
120 http://www.uottawa.ca/associations/csict/represum.pdf, p. 45. Accessed March 2012.
121 http://www.uottawa.ca/associations/csict/represum.pdf. Accessed March 2012.
122 http://www.cttic.org/mission.asp. Accessed April 2012.
123 http://www.cttic.org/president.asp. Accessed April 2012.
124 http://www.languagemarketplace.ca/ATIO%20Bill%20Pr36%20English.PDF. Accessed April 2012.
125 http://www.cttic.org/. Accessed 25/07/12. At the time of writing, we are not aware of the reasons for the withdrawal.
126 http://www.servicecanada.gc.ca/eng/qc/job_futures/statistics/5125.shtml. Accessed April 2012.
127 http://www.cttic.org/certification.asp. Accessed April 2012.
128 http://www.cttic.org/certification.asp. Accessed April 2012.
129 http://www.ottiaq.org/extranet/pdf/memoire_opq.pdf. Accessed April 2012.
130 "Unfortunately our petition did not get a very positive response. The following paragraph is taken from the letter we received from the Office des professions, in July 2010: 'L'Office ne peut donner suite à votre demande dans la mesure où nous n'avons pas évalué toutes les implications qu'engendreraient une telle mesure du fait notamment des nombreux textes législatifs qui seraient touchés…'"
131 http://www5.hrsdc.gc.ca/NOC/English/NOC/2011/QuickSearch.aspx?val65=5125. Accessed April 2012.
132 http://www.servicecanada.gc.ca/eng/qc/job_futures/statistics/5125.shtml Accessed March 2012.
133 Our thanks to Barbara McGilvray 11/02/2012; also see the list of NAATI approved courses reproduced at http://isg.urv.es/tti/tti.htm.
134 http://www.aiti.edu.au/english/. Accessed November 2011.
135 http://www.siit.nsw.edu.au/. Accessed November 2011.
136 www.ausit.org. Accessed November 2011.
137 http://home.vicnet.net.au/~aalitra/. Our thanks to Professor Brian Nelson for this information.

138 www.waiti.org.au. Accessed November 2011.
139 http://aslia.com.au. Accessed November 2011.
140 As many as 27 per cent may be accredited as both translators and interpreters (McGilvray 11/02/2012), although this does not mean they actually work as both.
141 "In reality this is restricted to AITC for Advanced Translator and Adv. Tr. (Senior), and for the professional level the CIOL (Member or Fellow)" (McGilvray 10/02/2012).
142 See Accreditation by Overseas Qualification: http://www.naati.com.au/accreditation.html, updated December 2010.
143 http://www.naati.com.au/PDF/Misc/Improvements%20to%20NAATI%20Testing%20flyer.pdf. Accessed May 2012.

4. Sociological Modelling

1 The importance of certification had been mentioned in a previous analysis of community interpreting by Roberts (1994): "The respect of other professionals for community interpreters will certainly increase if the latter's competency is guaranteed by a rigorous accreditation system. Indeed, it is not enough to evaluate a potential interpreter's abilities at the end of training; what is also required is national recognition of their interpreting skills by means of an accreditation procedure established by a professional body" (Roberts 1994: 136).
2 While the role of the "Professional Association" seems fairly clear in Ju's revision of Tseng's model, we note that it is not without political ramifications. According to a report dated April 2012, the Translators Association of China (TAC) is now offering its certification programme in Taiwan: http://w3.cpbae.nccu.edu.tw/news/?nid=1130&utm_source=feedburner&utm_medium=twitter&utm_campaign=Feed%3A+cpbaenews+%28%E6%94%BF%E5%A4%A7%E5%85%AC%E4%BC%81%E4%B8%AD%E5%BF%83%E6%9C%80%E6%96%B0%E6%B6%88%E6%81%AF%29.
3 Fraser and Gold (2001: 685) report the ITI membership to be 61 per cent women.
4 http://www.bdue.de/index.php?page=020000&id=552. Accessed April 2012.
5 http://www.servicecanada.gc.ca/eng/qc/job_futures/statistics/5125.shtml. Accessed April 2012.
6 http://statbank.ssb.no/statistikkbanken/Default_FR.asp?PXSid=0&nvl=true&PLanguage=0&tilside=selectvarval/define.asp&Tabellid=04858.
7 http://aiic.net/ViewPage.cfm/page2195.htm. Accessed April 2012.
8 http://www.sft.fr/clients/sft/telechargements/file_front/4c45ab788dee5.pdf. Accessed April 2012.
9 "… as many as 91 percent are done by women, only 3 percent by men, and the rest by mixed teams" (Wolf 2007: 136).
10 Liu's online survey of 193 Chinese translators in the greater China region (2011: 108) found that 56.5 per cent were women. This was relatively young sample, including many translators in public-relations companies.
11 Pym (2009) suggests that Wolf's view of translation as a non-field might apply better to larger cultures than to smaller ones. In a language like Czech, for example, where translations might constitute over 80 per cent of published fiction (CEATL 2008: 10), literary translators are indeed well-known and are in direct competition with each other, admittedly as experts in literature as well as in their capacity as translators. We know that translation plays a greater cultural role in smaller cultures than in larger ones (Pym 2004: 42).
12 Brown's 2001 survey of 374 AIIC interpreters found that 68 per cent of them also do written translations.
13 European Commission, *Translating for a Multilingual Community* (2009: 5).
14 http://www.mendeley.com/c/4276785753/p/8195983/lagoudaki-2006-translation-memories-survey-2006-users-perceptions-around-tm-use/. Accessed May 2012.

15 Liu (2011: 59) finds younger translators in the greater China region working with job titles such as "Account Executive", "Communication Consultant", "Corporate Communications Specialist", "Marketing Communications Executive" and "Public Affairs Specialists", which would indicate an increasing disposition to mix translation with other professional activities in an entrepreneurial vein.
16 http://www.lawgazette.co.uk/news/row-erupts-over-police-interpreters. Accessed April 2012.
17 www.translator-training.eu (for the project).
18 Now available at http://www.translator-training.eu/optimale/attachments/article/36/PPT_WP5_survey%20results.pdf. Accessed April 2012.
19 Our thanks to Daniel Toudic for supplying the PowerPoint of the preliminary report and a draft of the final report. Some of the numbers remain difficult to interpret. For example, Figure 8 shows that "professional ethics and standards" are actually more important to employers than is a university degree, even though it is presumably difficult for an employer to assess ethics at the moment of recruitment (if not from a certification or degree of some kind), so the two are hardly comparable (for that matter, few employers would admit to accepting anything unethical). Similarly, the Optimale survey found that what employers most value is "100% accuracy", but it is hard to imagine a translation company willing to admit that it would accept reduced accuracy in favour of high speed or a cheap price. One might compare this with Renato Beninatto's claim that, for most companies, what matters is indeed speed and price, not quality: http://www.l10n411.com/2007/11/quality-still-doesnt-matter-ata-san.html (accessed April 2012). Business is one thing; public surveys are another.
20 This version of the table has been copied from the draft final report "The OPTIMALE employer survey and consultation" (Toudic 2012: 6).
21 http://en.wikipedia.org/wiki/ISO/IEC_17024. Accessed November 2011.
22 This took the form of the seminar "A global certification system for translators?" at ELIA's networking days in Madrid, 3–4 May 2012. The seminar included representatives of some 24 language-service providers and was followed up by numerous informal discussions.
23 A good example of discussion and cooperation with industry was the seminar on the "translator profile" held in Brussels on 29 September 2011, with the corresponding report.
24 According to the US National Research Council (2001: 4), IT workers are "engaged primarily in the conception, design, development, adaptation, implementation, deployment, training, support, documentation, and management of IT systems, components or applications."
25 Department for Professional Employees AFT/CIO. "The Professional Computer Workforce" http://dpeaflcio.org/professionals/professionals-in-the-workplace/the-professional-computer-work-force/. Updated August 2011.
26 In Katan's survey of over 1000 translators and translation professionals, predominantly in Italy, some 73 per cent of respondents reported having university training in "'languages', 'translation' or 'interpreting'" (2009: 120), and yet only a handful said that translation was a profession "because it requires specific training/special education" (2009: 124). This would suggest that, for these respondents, university training is present but is not seen as signalling sufficient market status.
27 http://www.servicecanada.gc.ca/eng/qc/job_futures/statistics/5125.shtml. Accessed April 2012.
28 http://www.bdue.de/index.php?page=020000&id=552. Accessed April 2012.
29 http://www.sdl.com/en/language-technology/training-and-certification/. Accessed April 2012.
30 http://www.tilponline.net/. Accessed April 2012.
31 http://www.pmi.org/. Accessed April 2012.
32 Department for Professional Employees AFT/CIO. "The Professional Computer Workforce" http://dpeaflcio.org/professionals/professionals-in-the-workplace/the-professional-computer-work-force/. Updated August 2011.

5. Economic Modelling

1 http://www.fit-europe.org/vault/FIT_Europe_Rates_report_fr.pdf. Accessed April 2012.
2 In the report, "'professional literary translator' applies to all literary translators who work full time on literary translation and who earn their living mainly from literary translation and occasionally from translation-related literary activities (lectures and talks, readings, book publishing, literary criticism, etc.)" (2008: 6).
3 Germany is excluded from the comparison because fewer than 100 respondents from Germany answered this question. This may be because translations in Germany are usually paid by the page, not the word, and since the words are long, the conversion is not easy.
4 The CIOL/ITI report had 26.4 per cent of its respondents located outside of the United Kingdom, while 36 per cent of the earnings of the respondents were coming from outside the United Kingdom (2011: 8).
5 http://www.servicecanada.gc.ca/eng/qc/job_futures/statistics/5125.shtml. See also, for example: http://kv-emptypages.blogspot.com.es/2010/04/falling-translation-prices-and.html; http://www.wintranslation.com/articles/decliningrates/. Accessed April 2012.
6 http://www.sft.fr/clients/sft/telechargements/file_front/4c45ab788dee5.pdf. Accessed April 2012.
7 See Mincer (1974) for the methodological presentation of the approach, and Grin (1999) for an application to foreign language skills by type and level.
8 The fundamental reason for using a log scale is that the variance of untransformed earnings data typically increases with the level of earnings, whereas one condition that must be met for the statistical analysis to perform well is precisely that the variance of the dependent variable is constant. Converting earnings into the log of earnings homogenises the variance of the dependent variable, and therefore increases the appropriateness of the statistical method used – in this case, ordinary least squares (OLS). Another advantage of using a log scale is that it magnifies the distance between two points at lower values of the variable relative to a similar distance between two points at higher values; the influence on the dependent variable of a change in an independent variable may be indiscernible if the former is expressed in "raw" terms; a change in an independent variable will have a much greater impact on the *logarithm* of the dependent variable.
9 Note that if β is small, say, less than 0.1, the difference between b and β is minor, and the transformation could, for all practical purposes, be omitted.
10 This variable proceeds from a questionnaire item that refers to professional experience in translation. It differs from common definitions of "experience" in earnings equations, where it is routinely computed (lacking more specific information) as "current age minus number of years of schooling minus average age of entry into the education system".
11 Note that a survey of 1,140 interpreters in North America (Kelly et al. 2010: 41) finds that men interpreters earn 6 per cent more than women interpreters. This might similarly be explained in terms of different years of experience. The American sample, however, is heavily weighted in favour of healthcare interpreters (only 9.1 per cent are members of the AIIC), and it would seem useful to know what percentage of the men work as conference interpreters (who tend to earn much more than healthcare interpreters, to the extent that the survey is mixing two quite different economic milieux).
12 The actual benefit of a university education for translators, however, is probably higher. As shown in the following section, the average contribution of the additional year of university study is in the 6 to 10 per cent range for salaried translators; other tests (see section 5.3.5) run on an estimate of full-time equivalent income among freelance translators indicate a very stable and usually significant premium of a little over 4 per cent, implying a return on university education between 16 and 20 per cent.
13 One possible explanation is that some of the expertise provided by translators may be of the near pro-bono type (for example, offering translation services to human rights NGOs).

Another is that expert work, even if commanding a decent lump-sum honorarium, ends up taking much more time than planned, an effect that will come through strongly if incomes are converted to full-time equivalent.
14 Whether the unit is expressed in amount charged per (source or target language) word, line, or page is not important here, as long as one unit is chosen.
15 Game theorists would identify *the acquisition of a signal* as a dominant strategy: when translators compete with each other, each of them is better off acquiring the signal, whichever strategy is chosen by their competitors, that is, whether their competitors choose to acquire the signal or not.

6. Policy Options for Enhanced Signalling

1 http://eur-lex.europa.eu/LexUriServ/LexUriServ.do?uri=OJ:L:2005:255:0022:0142:en:PDF. Accessed April 2012.
2 This issue seems to be at stake in debates that involve an "all or nothing" approach to signals of professional status. According to one report, which we find difficult to interpret, "in relation to the implementation process of the EU service directive in 2008, Danish authorities tried to do away with the system of authorisation of translators. Their line of arguments was that it constituted a barrier to free competition and the free right to exercise a profession" (Jørgen Christian Wind Nielsen, 09/03/12). Dam and Zethsen (2010: 201) cite a respondent talking about "the recent [failed] attempt by authorities to abolish the authorisation system for translators".
3 One might compare this with the early use of mobile telephony, which started as an expensive service for professionals, then increased with value as more people used it, thus entering a logic that required lower prices for the service. A similar comparison can be made with free online statistically driven translation memory and machine translation services, which improve performance the more they are used. But if they are used indiscriminately (which is what happened with Google Translate), the databases get dirty and the performance declines. This led Google to make its Application Programme Interface app a pay-service in December 2011.
4 This is where a status signal like the European Master's in Translation itself becomes a commodity, which could be sold to academic institutions for an annual fee adequate to cover actual control over the quality of translation graduates.
5 http://www.jtpunion.org/spip/IMG/pdf/IDcard_new_procedure_EN.pdf. Accessed April 2012.
6 "During the 2005 FIT World Congress in Tampere, delegates from a number of associations indicated their interest in sponsoring members of other associations who are not able to obtain the FIT ID Card on their own due to economic circumstances." http://www.cttic.org/InfoLangIndustry/FIT/FIT_ID_Card_Memo_EN.pdf. Accessed April 2012.
7 Some 550 cards had been sold by 2008: http://www.fit-europe.org/vault/minutes/FITEC-26-27jan08-en.pdf. Accessed April 2012.
8 See Green Paper 367 "Modernising the Professional Qualifications Directive", http://eur-lex.europa.eu/LexUriServ/LexUriServ.do?uri=COM:2011:0367:FIN:en:PDF. Accessed April 2012.
9 This could be a moot point. One recalls the difficulties faced by Peñarroja i Fa (see 2.3.6 above) in attempting to gain cross-country recognition of his qualification as a sworn translator in Spain. The preliminary ruling by the European Court (17 March 2011) maintained that qualifications from another EU member state must be recognised, and that this generally had more weight than the right of each court to compile its own list of translators and to require a certain number of years' experience of the judicial system in question. However, the ruling held that "court expert translators" are not covered by the definition of "regulated profession", and that would seem to be the main issue at stake here. The definition in question is as follows: "regulated profession: a professional activity or group of professional activities, access to which, the pursuit of which, or one of the modes of pursuit of which is subject, directly or indirectly, by virtue of legislative, regulatory or administrative provisions to the possession of specific

professional qualifications; in particular, the use of a professional title limited by legislative, regulatory or administrative provisions to holders of a given professional qualification shall constitute a mode of pursuit" (Article 3(1)(a), Directive 2005/36/EC). Without going into legal complexities, it seems to us that authorised/sworn translation is (or could become) a regulated profession in many countries, and that the issue at stake in the above ruling is the status of "expert", not that of "translator": a judge at the Cour de cassation can indeed call any person at all as an expert, with or without qualifications as a translator.

10 See http://ec.europa.eu/internal_market/qualifications/docs/future/platforms_en.pdf. Accessed April 2012.
11 http://www.eulita.eu/members-admitted-executive-committee-eulita. Accessed April 2012.
12 This is with the exception of Slovakia – and one exception is not enough for mobility.
13 The Hague apostille does not normally legalise translations as such: it is attached to the original document, which is then translated with the apostille as part of the document.
14 This option has been proposed by Professor Alan K. Melby with respect to the TISAC discussions of certification (see 3.6.6 above), under the working name of "TransCertGlobal" (personal communications November 2011, March 2012). Possible agencies include the International Accreditation Service (http://www.iasonline.org) and the International Accreditation Forum (http://www.iaf.nu). Accessed April 2012.
15 http://en.wikipedia.org/wiki/ISO/IEC_17024. Accessed November 2011.
16 The CATTI (China Aptitude Test for Translators and Interpreters) dates from 2003: http://www.tac-online.org.cn/en/tran/2009-10/09/content_3174954.htm. Accessed November 2011.
17 The NAETI (National Accreditation Examinations for Translators and Interpreters) date from 2001. http://www.albaglobal.com/article-print-1403.html. Accessed November 2011.
18 EMT Annual Report 2011: http://ec.europa.eu/dgs/translation/programmes/emt/key_documents/emt_annual_report2011_en.pdf. Accessed April 2012.
19 This could be of some concern in the context of the CIOL's doubts about the capacity of some theory-based one-year Master's courses to qualify professional translators (see 3.4.3 above).
20 It is intriguing to read that "as an indirect and long term goal, a successful project would also have the potential to secure the EMT's financial sustainability as an independent association" (EMT Annual Report 2011: 10). One would have thought that the member academic institutions, as the main beneficiaries, would themselves be paying for the EMT label, and it is difficult to imagine that a group of training institutions could work through a certification scheme to effectively turn themselves into the instance able to accredit all other certification systems.
21 "The University of Vienna (EMT member) would be the leader of the project and lead the consortium of European stakeholders, which include: BDÜ, GALA, FIT Europe, EULITA, EUATC, Intertext, BQTA and ESIT, ISIT, Aarhus among the EMT member programmes" (EMT Annual Report 2011: 11).
22 Our thanks to Rannheid Sharma, 13/06/12. The High Entry Languages Unit pass rate was 41 per cent; the Small Entry Languages Unit pass rate 51 per cent; there was nevertheless significant variation for specific languages.

7. Recommendations

1 See 2.3.7; 3.1.6; 3.4.5; 3.5.6; 3.8.1; 3.8.2.
2 The languages can be grouped as follows: 1) official languages of the EU; 2) CRSSLs (constitutional, regional, and small state languages, including Basque, Faroese, Frisian, etc.; 3) "immigrant" languages; 4) non-European languages of wider communication (Chinese, Arabic, Japanese); 5) languages of countries whose economies are closely integrated with the EU (Norwegian, Romansch, Icelandic).
3 See 1.1; 5.3; 6.3; 6.4.5 above, and Appendix D.
4 See 2.3.6; 3.1.6; 6.1; 6.3.3 above.

5   See 2.4.2; 3.8.6; 6.4.4.
6   See 3.1.3; 3.8.6; 4.4; 6.4.5.
7   See 2.4.2; 3.1.6; 3.4.3; 3.6.3; 3.8.6.
8   See 2.2.2; 2.2.3; 2.2.4; 3.4.3; 6.4.5.

Appendices

1 http://www.bdue.de/index.php?page=020000&id=552. The data also indicate that some 70 per cent of the translators and interpreters are women, and 42 per cent have a university-level degree. This does not appear to be a majority, despite what is said in the BDÜ report: "Die Mehrheit der angestellten Dolmetscher und Übersetzer hat einen Fach- oder Hochschulabschluss. Dies war auch schon im Jahr 2005 der Fall, doch ist die Zahl der angestellten Sprachexperten mit einem Studium noch einmal um 5,2 Prozent gestiegen und liegt 2011 bei 2.890 Personen."
2 http://statbank.ssb.no/statistikkbanken/Default_FR.asp?PXSid=0&nvl=true&PLanguage=0&tilside=selectvarval/define.asp&Tabellid=04858. Accessed November 2011.
3 Figure based on a study of 12 translation companies in northern Portugal (Ferreira-Alves 2012).
4 Ferreira-Alves (2011: 268) states there were 2,865 "people associated with translation companies" in Portugal in 2007, and 2,153 in 2008. This would include owners, project managers, secretaries, and technicians. The huge difference in the numbers does not inspire confidence in this particular part of the Portuguese statistics.
5 http://www.bls.gov/oco/ocos175.htm. Accessed November 2011.
6 http://www.census.gov/epcd/nonemployer/2005/us/US000_54.htm. Accessed November 2011.
7 http://www.bls.gov/ooh/Media-and-Communication/Interpreters-and-translators.htm#tab-3. Accessed May 2012.
8 We use the higher estimate in order to partially counterbalance the apparent tendency, in the above numbers, for smaller countries to have higher percentages of translators and interpreters (see also see Table 3 in 2.4.3).
9 http://www.proz.com/. Accessed November 2011.
10 http://www.proz.com/. Accessed November 2011.
11 http://www.proz.com/pro-tag/info/about/freelancers. Accessed November 2011.
12 http://www.trally.com. Accessed November 2011.
13 http://www.aquarius.net. Accessed November 2011.
14 http://www.translationautomation.com/best-practices/solid-foundation-for-taus-data-association.html. Accessed November 2011.
15 http://www.gotranslators.com. Accessed November 2011.
16 This is with the exception of the ATA, which has had online directories of "Translation and Interpreting Services" and "Language Services Companies" (http://www.atanet.org/onlinedirectories/) for more than 15 years. (Alan K. Melby 12/05/12).
17 This function is a very standard one in microeconomics and is known as a "Cobb-Douglas" function, named after the economist Paul Douglas and the mathematician Richard Cobb who introduced it in 1928.
18 To be fully consistent with the rest of the model, this relation should be adjusted in such a way as to be consistent with the additional assumption that one group of translators leaves the market as soon as the price drops below a certain level. However, omitting this adjustment does not affect the general results of the model.
19 Buy assuming frictions of this kind, we depart from the standard assumption of free entry and exit of perfect-competition models.

REFERENCES

Adelman, Clifford. 2000. *A Parallel Postsecondary Universe: The Certification System in Information Technology*. Washington, DC: US Department of Education.
Akerlof, George. 1970. "The Market for Lemons: Quality Uncertainty and the Market Mechanism". *Quarterly Journal of Economics* 84 (3): 488–500.
Allied Business Intelligence. 1998. *Language Translation: World Market Overview, Current Developments and Competitive Assessment*. Oyster Bay, NY: ABI.
Arora, Ashish and Alfonso Gambardella. 2004. "The Globalization of the Software Industry: Perspectives and Opportunities for Developed and Developing Countries". National Bureau of Economic Research Working Paper Series, Number 10538. Stanford, CA: National Bureau of Economic Research. http://www.nber.org/papers/w10538. Accessed April 2012.
Arrow, Kenneth. 1973. "Higher Education as a Filter". *Journal of Public Economics* 2: 193–216.
Bartlett, Donald L. and James B. Steele. 2011. "Offshoring Stole Many U.S. Programming Jobs." *Philly Online*. 1 May.
Beninatto, Renato S. and Donald A. DePalma. 2008. "The Top 25 Translation Companies and Some Really Big Revenue Numbers". http://www.globalwatchtower.com/2008/06/20/top-25-revenue-08. Accessed April 2012.
Birchler, Urs and Monika Bütler. 2007. *Information Economics*. London: Routledge.
Bloom, David and Gilles Grenier. 1996. "Language, Employment and Earnings in the United States: Spanish-English Differentials from 1970 to 1990". *International Journal of the Sociology of Language* 121: 45–68.
Boucau, Fernand. 2005. *The European Translation Industry – Facing the Future*. Brussels: EUATC. www.guilde.net/fr/news/euatc.pps. Accessed April 2012.
Bourdieu, Pierre. 1997. "The Forms of Capital". In A. Halsey, H. Lauder, P. Brown and A. Stuart Wells (eds), *Education: Culture, Economy and Society*, 46–58. Oxford: Oxford University Press.
Bowker, Lynne. 2005. "Professional Recognition in the Canadian Translation Industry: How Is It Perceived by Translators and Employers?" *Translation Watch Quarterly* 1: 19–116. http://www.translocutions.com/tsi/twq/tranlsation_watch_quarterly_December2005_issue1_sample.pdf. Accessed April 2012.
Brookshire, Robert G. 2000. "Information Technology Certification: Is This Your Mission?". *Information Technology, Learning and Performance Journal* 18 (2): 1–2.
Brown, Sara A. 2001. "Do Interpreters Translate? Results of an E-mail Survey of AIIC Members to Determine if Interpreters Also Work as Translators". Consortium for Training Translation Teachers. http://isg.urv.es/cttt/cttt/research/browncorrected.pdf. Accessed July 2011.
Canadian Translation Industry Sectoral Committee. 1999. *Survey of the Canadian Translation Industry. Sectoral Reports*. http://www.uottawa.ca/associations/csict/represum.pdf. Accessed October 2011.
Carmel, Erran and Paul Tjia. 2005. *Offshoring Information Technology: Sourcing and Outsourcing to a Global Workforce*. Cambridge: Cambridge University Press.
Carr, Jack. 1985. "Le bilinguisme au Canada: l'usage consacre-t-il l'anglais monopole naturel?" In F. Vaillancourt (ed.), *Économie et langue*, 27–37. Québec: Conseil de la langue française.
Carr-Saunders, Alexander Morris. 1928. *Professions: Their Organization and Place in Society*. Oxford: Clarendon Press.

Chan, Andy Lung Jan. 2008. "Information Economics, the Translation Profession and Translator Certification". PhD thesis, Universitat Rovira i Virgili. Tarragona: Intercultural Studies Group. http://tdx.cat/handle/10803/8772. Accessed April 2012.

———. 2009. "Effectiveness of Translator Certification as a Signaling Device: Views from the Translator Recruiters". *Translation and Interpreting Studies* 4 (2): 155–71.

———. 2012. "Signal Jamming in the Translation Market and the Complementary Roles of Certification and Diploma in Developing Multilateral Signaling Mechanisms". *Translation and Interpreting*.

Childs, Karl. 2002. "Conquering the IT Job Market – Find the Right Job for You!" *Certification Magazine* 4 (2).

Chiswick, Barry R. and Paul W Miller. 2007. *The Economics of Language. International Analyses*. London and New York: Routledge.

CIOL/ITI. 2011. *2011 Rates and Salaries Survey for Translators and Interpreters*. Chartered Institute of Linguistics and Institute of Translation and Interpreting.

Dale, Madeleine L. 1999. "Alphabet Soup: Licensing, Certification, and Credentialing". http://www.naswnyc.org/l15.html. Accessed April 2012.

Dam, Helle V. and Karen Korning Zethsen. 2008. "Translator Status – a Study of Danish Company Translators". *Translator* 14 (1): 71–96.

———. 2009a. "Who Said Low Status? A Study on Factors Affecting the Perception of Translator Status". *Journal of Specialised Translation* 12: 2–36. http://www.jostrans.org/issue12/art_dam_zethsen.pdf

———. 2009b. "Translators and (Lack of) Power: A Study of Danish Company Translators' Occupational Status". In *Language at Work – Bridging Theory and Practice* 6. http://www.languageatwork.eu/readarticle.php?article_id=27.

———. 2010. "Translator Status. Helpers and Opponents in the Ongoing Battle of an Emerging Profession". *Target* 22 (2): 194–210.

———. 2011. "The Status of Professional Business Translators on the Danish Market: A Comparative Study of Company, Agency and Freelance Translators". *Meta*.

———. 2012. "Translators in International Organizations: A Special Breed of High-Status Professionals? Danish EU Translators as a Case in Point". *Translation and Interpreting Studies*.

District Court of Western Australia. 2011. *Language Services Guidelines*. Circular to Practitioners GEN 2011-12. 27 September.

Djovčoš, Martin. 2011. "Prekladateľ v kontexte doby: sociologické aspekty prekladu a prekladania". [The Translator in the Context of their Time: Sociological Aspects of Translation and Translating]. PhD thesis, Comenius University in Bratislava. Bratislava: FF CU.

Educational Testing Service. 2010. "Record Number of 2009 TOEFL Test Takers in China". http://www.ets.org/newsroom/news_releases/record_number_2009_toefl_test_takers_china. Accessed April 2012.

EduChoices.org. 2009. "IT Professional: Education and Job Training Requirements for Becoming an IT Professional". http://educhoices.org/articles/IT_Professional_Education_and_Job_Training_Requirements_for_Becoming_an_IT_Professional.html. Accessed April 2012.

EUATC. 2009. "Practice in Parts of Europe on Sworn Translations, Notarisation and Apostille". European Union of Associations of Translation Companies. http://ec.europa.eu/translation/LID/index.cfm?fuseaction=main.PublicationDetail&PBL_ID=363. Accessed November 2011.

European Commission. 2011. "Green Paper: Modernising the Professional Qualifications Directive". COM(2011) 367 final. http://eur-lex.europa.eu/LexUriServ/LexUriServ.do?uri=COM:2011:0367:FIN:en:PDF. Accessed December 2011.

Ferreira-Alves, Fernando Gonçalves. 2011. "As faces de Jano: Contributos para uma cartografia identitária e socioprofissional dos tradutores da região norte de Portugal". PhD thesis, Braga: Universidade do Minho.

Ferreira-Alves, Fernando Gonçalves. 2012. "Translation Companies in Portugal". *Anglo-saxónica*. Special issue on translation studies.

FIT Europe (Fédération Internationales des Traducteurs). 2010. *Enquête européenne sur les conditions d'exercice des traducteurs*. http://www.fit-europe.org/vault/FIT_Europe_Rates_report_fr.pdf. Accessed November 2011.

Fock, Holger, Martin de Haan and Alena Lhotová. 2008. *Comparative Income of Literary Translators in Europe*. Brussels: Conseil Européen des Associations de Traducteurs Littéraires. http://www.ceatl.eu/docs/surveyuk.pdf. Accessed April 2012.

Fraser, Janet and Michael Gold. 2001. "'Portfolio Workers': Autonomy and Control amongst Freelance Translators". *Work, Employment and Society* 15: 679–97.

———. 2011. "Weathering the Storm". *ITI Bulletin*. September–October: 18–21.

Freidson, Eliot. 1986. *Professional Powers: A Study of the Institutionalization of Formal Knowledge*. Chicago, IL: University of Chicago Press.

Fulford, Heather and Joaquín Granell-Zafra. 2005. "Translation and Technology: A Study of UK Freelance Translators". *Journal of Specialised Translation* 4: 2–17. http://www.jostrans.org/issue04/art_fulford_zafra.pdf. Accessed April 2012.

Ginsburgh, Victor and Shlomo Weber. 2011. *How Many Languages Do We Need?* Princeton, NJ: Princeton University Press.

Ginsburgh, Victor, Shlomo Weber and Sheila Wyers. 2007. "Economics of Literary Translation: A Simple Theory and Evidence". *CORE Discussion Paper* 2007: 62.

Greenwald, Bruce and Joseph E. Stiglitz. 1986. "Externalities in Economies with Imperfect Information and Incomplete Markets". *Quarterly Journal of Economics* 101 (2): 229–64.

Greere, Anca. 2008. "Quality Issues in Romanian Translator and Interpreter Training: Investigating the Validity of the Standards Proposed by the Romanian Agency for Quality Assurance in Higher Education [ARACIS]". *Studia Universitatis Babes-Bolyai Philologia* 8 (3): 81–94.

———. 2010. "Translation in Romania: Steps towards Recognition and Professionalization". *Meta* 55/4: 789–816. http://www.erudit.org/revue/meta/2010/v55/n4/index.html. Accessed April 2012.

Greere, Anca and Cristina Tătaru. 2008. "Training for the translation professions: What do Romanian University Programmes Have to Offer?" *Studia Universitatis Babes-Bolyai Philologia* 8 (3): 95–122.

Grin, François. 1992. "Towards a threshold theory of minority language survival", *Kyklos* 45, 69–97.

———. 1999. *Compétences et récompenses. La valeur des langues en Suisse*. Fribourg: Editions Universitaires de Fribourg.

———. 2003. "Economics and language planning", *Current Issues in Language Planning* 4, 1–66.

———. 2005. "Grundzüge der volkswirtschaftlichen Bildungsökonomie". In V. Bank (ed.), *Vom Wert der Bildung*, 61–148. Bern, Stuttgart and Wien: Haupt.

———. 2010. "Economics". In J. Fishman and O. García (eds), *Handbook of Language and Ethnic Identity. Disciplinary and Regional Perspectives*, vol. 1, 70–88. Oxford: Oxford University Press.

Grin, François, Claudio Sfreddo and François Vaillancourt. 2010. *The Economics of the Multilingual Workplace*. New York and London: Routledge.

Hale, Sandra. 2011. *Interpreter Policies, Practices and Protocols in Australian Courts and Tribunals. A National Survey*. Melbourne: The Australasian Institute of Judicial Administration Inc.

Haralambos, Michael and Martin Holborn. 2008. *Sociology: Themes and Perspectives*. London: Harper Collins.

Hertog, Erik, ed. 2001. *Aequitas: Access to Justice across Language and Culture in the EU*. Antwerp: Lessius Hogeschool.

———, ed. 2003. *Aequalitas: Equal Access to Justice across Language and Culture in the EU*. Antwerp: Lessius Hogeschool.

Hertog, Erik and Jan van Gucht, eds. 2008. *Status Quaestionis. Questionnaire on the Provision of Legal Interpreting and Translation in the EU*. Antwerp, Oxford and Portland, OR: Intersentia.

Hjorth-Andersen, Christian. 2001. "A Model of Translations". *Journal of Cultural Economics* 25: 203–17.

Hočevar, Toussaint. 1975. "Equilibria on Linguistic Minority Markets". *Kyklos* 28: 337–57.

———. 1983. "Les aspects économiques de la dynamique fonctionnelle des langues". *Language Problems and Language Planning* 7: 135–47.

Hodson, Randy and Teresa A. Sullivan. 2001. "Professions and Professionals". In R. Hodson and T. A. Sullivan (eds), *The Social Organization of Work*, 287–314. Belmont, CA: Thomson Higher Education.

Houle, Cyril O. 1980. *Continuing Learning in the Professions*. San Francisco: Jossey-Bass Publishers. http://www.ceatl.eu/docs/surveyuk.pdf. Accessed November 2011.

IAMLADP. 2009. "Results of Survey on Recruitment and Testing of Translators and Interpreters". Annex V of *Report to IAMLADP Working Group on* Training, 79–94. http://www.iamladp.org/PDFs/2009_docs/R8_WG_on_Training2009Report.pdf. Accessed July 2011.

Information Technology Association of America. 2003. *Workforce Survey*. Arlington, VA: Information Technology Association of America.

Ju, Elma Mingli. 2009. "The Professionalization of Interpreting in Taiwan: A Critical Review of Tseng's Model". *Compilation and Translation Review* 2 (2): 105–25. http://ej.nict.gov.tw/CTR/v02.2/ctr020215.pdf. Accessed April 2012.

Kanelliadou, Polyxeni. 2011. "La procédure de certification des traducteurs et interprètes assermentés au Grand-duché de Luxembourg: situation actuelle et perspectives". Paper presented to the Dixième forum international sur la déontologie et les bonnes pratiques. Paris, 19–21 May.

Katan, David. 2009. "Translation Theory and Professional Practice: A Global Survey of the Great Divide". *Hermes* 42: 111–54. http://download2.hermes.asb.dk/archive/download/Hermes-42-7-katan_net.pdf. Accessed April 2012.

Keijzer-Lambooy, Heleen and Willem Jan Gasille, eds. 2005. *Aequilibrium: Instruments for Lifting Language Barriers in Intercultural Legal Proceedings*. Utrecht: ITV Hogeschool voor Tolken en Vertalen.

Kelly, Nataly, Robert G. Stewart and Vijayalaxmi Hegde. 2010. *The Interpreting Marketplace. A Study of Interpreting in North America*. Common Sense Advisory/InterpretAmerica. http://www.interpretamerica.net/publications. Accessed May 2012.

Knapp, Lenora G. and Joan E. Knapp. 2002. *The Business of Certification: A Comprehensive Guide to Developing a Successful Program*. Washington, DC: ASAE.

Lafeber, Anne. 2010. *Results of the Survey on the Testing of Translators at International Organizations*. IAMLADP: http://www.iamladp.org/PDFs/2010_docs/Testing%20Survey_Report_for_IAMLADP-Anne_Lafeber.pdf.

———. 2012. "Translation at Inter-governmental Organizations: The Set of Skills and Knowledge Required and the Implications for Recruitment Testing". PhD thesis, Universitat Rovira i Virgili. Tarragona: Intercultural Studies Group.

Lagoudaki, Elina. 2006. *Translation Memories Survey 2006: Users' perceptions around TM use*. Imperial College London. http://www.mendeley.com/c/4276785753/p/8195983/lagoudaki-2006-translation-memories-survey-2006-users-perceptions-around-tm-use/. Accessed May 2012.

Lang, Kevin. 1986: "A Language Theory of Discrimination". *Quarterly Journal of Economics* 101: 363–82.

Larson, Magali Sarfatti. 1977. *The Rise of Professionalism: A Sociological Analysis*. Berkeley: University of California Press.

Lazear, Edward. 1999: "Language and Culture". *Journal of Political Economy* 107: 95–126.

Libro Blanco de la traducción y la interpretación institucional. 2011. Ministerio De Asuntos Exteriores y de Cooperación; Comisión Europea Dirección General de Traducción y Representación de la Comisión Europea en España; Comisión Europea Dirección General de Traducci. http://ec.europa.eu/spain/pdf/libro_blanco_traduccion_es.pdf. Accessed November 2011.

Liu, Fung Ming Christy. 2011. "A Quantitative and Qualitative Inquiry into Translators' Visibility and Job-Related Happiness: The Case of Greater China". PhD thesis. Tarragona:

Intercultural Studies Group. http://tdx.cat/bitstream/handle/10803/37347/LIU_thesis_very%20definitive_TOSEND.pdf?sequence=1. Accessed April 2012.

Lo Bianco, Joseph. 1987. *National Policy on Languages*. Canberra: Australian Government Publishing Service.

———. 1990. "Making Language Policy: Australia's Experience". In Richard B. Baldauf Jr. and Allan Luke (eds), *Language Planning and Education in Australasia and the South Pacific*, 47–79. Clevedon and Philadelphia: Multilingual Matters. http://www.multiculturalaustralia.edu.au/doc/lobianco_1.pdf. Accessed October 2011.

Lönnroth, Karl-Johan. 2005. "How to Ensure Total Quality in a Changing Translation Market: A European Approach". In Leena Salmi and Kaisa Koskinen (eds), *Proceedings of the XVII World Congress*, 30–34. Tampere, Finland.

———. 2009. "Translation and Quality Control. How to Get the Message Across". Paper presented at Öppenhet och klarspråk i EU. Stockholm, 8 September. http://ec.europa.eu/dgs/translation/publications/presentations/speeches/20090908_translation_quality_control_en.pdf.

LTC (Language Technology Centre). 2009. *Study on the Size of the Language Industry in the EU*. DGT-ML-Studies 08. Brussels: European Commission, Directorate-General for Translation.

Marschak, Jacob. 1965. "Economics of Language". *Behavioral Science* 10: 135–40.

Mayoral, Roberto. 2003. *Translating Official Documents*. Manchester: St Jerome.

McDonough, Julie. 2007. "How Do Language Professionals Organize Themselves? An Overview of Translation Networks". *Meta* 52 (4): 793–815.

Mélitz, Jacques. 2007. "The Impact of English Dominance on Literature and Welfare". *Journal of Economic Behavior and Organization* 64: 193–215.

Migué, Jean-Luc. 1970. "Le nationalisme, l'unité nationale et la théorie économique de l'information". *Revue canadienne d'économique* 3: 183–98.

Mikkelson, Holly. 1996. "The Professionalization of Community Interpreting". In Muriel Jérôme-O'Keeffe (ed.), *Global Vision: Proceedings of the 37th Annual Conference of the American Translators Association*, 77–89. Alexandria, VA: American Translators Association.

Mincer, Jacob. 1974. *Schooling, Experience and Earnings*. New York: National Bureau of Economic Research.

National Research Council, United States. 2001. *Building a Workforce for the Information Economy*. Washington, DC: National Academy Press.

Ó Cinnéide, Mícheál and Michael Keane. 1988. *Local Socio-economic Impacts Associated with the Galway Gaeltacht*. Gaillimh/Galway, Eïre/Irland: Coláiste na hOIllscoile Gaillimhe.

Office of Multicultural Interests. 2008. *The Western Australian Language Services Policy 2008*. Perth: Office of Multicultural Interests. http://www.omi.wa.gov.au/omi_language.cfm. Accessed October 2011.

Ozolins, Uldis. 1993. *The Politics of Language in Australia*. Cambridge and New York: Cambridge University Press.

———. 2007. "The Interpreter's 'Third Client'". In Cecilia Wadensjö, Birgitta Englund Dimitrova and Anna-Lena Nilsson (eds), *The Critical Link 4: Professionalisation of Interpreting in the Community*, 121–31. Amsterdam: John Benjamins.

Parker, Philip M. 2008. *The 2009–2014 World Outlook for Translation and Interpretation Services*. San Diego, CA: ICON Group International.

Peñarroja i Fa, Josep. 2012. Presentation and editing of *Iurata Fides. Butlletí de l'Associació de Traductors i Intèrprets jurats de Catalunya*. 1 trimestre 2012.

Phelan, Mary. 2001. *The Interpreter's Resource*. Clevedon: Multilingual Matters.

Podkalicka, Aneta Monika. 2007. "Lost in Translation? Language Policy, Media and Community in the EU and Australia: Some Lessons from the SBS". PhD thesis, Queensland University of Technology. http://eprints.qut.edu.au/16696/. Accessed October 2011.

Pool, Jonathan. 1991. "The Official Language Problem". *American Political Science Review* 85: 495–514.

Pym, Anthony. 2000. *Negotiating the Frontier. Translators and Intercultures in Hispanic History*. Manchester: St Jerome.

———. 2004. *The Moving Text: Localization, Translation, and Distribution*. Amsterdam and Philadelphia: John Benjamins.

Pym, Anthony, Miriam Shlesinger and Zuzana Jettmarová, eds. 2006. *Sociocultural Aspects of Translating and Interpreting*. Amsterdam and Philadelphia: John Benjamins.

Randall, M. and C. Zirkle. 2005. "Information Technology Student-Based Certification in Formal Education Settings: Who Benefits and What is Needed". *Journal of Information Technology Education* (4): 287–306. http://jite.org/documents/Vol4/v4p287-306Randall78.pdf. Accessed April 2012.

Raynauld, André and Pierre Marion. 1972. "Une analyse économique de la disparité interethnique des revenus". *Revue économique* 23: 1–19.

Roberts, Roda. 1994. "Community Interpreting Today and Tomorrow". In Peter Krawutschke (ed.), *Proceedings of the 35th Annual Conference of the American Translators Association*, 127–38. Medford, NJ: Learned Information.

Romaine, Matthew and Jennifer Richardson. 2009. *State of the Translation Industry: Smarter, More Casual*. Tokyo: myGenko.

Rowe, Julie. 2003. "IT Certifications: Lessons from Other Industries". *Certification Magazine* April. http://www.certmag.com/read.php?in=171. Accessed July 2012.

Rubinstein, Ariel. 2000. *Economics and Language*. Cambridge: Cambridge University Press.

Rundgren, Gunnar. 2005. "Break-out Group: The Role of Certification Services in Organic Produce Market". Paper delivered to the Conference on Standards and Conformity Assessment: Minimising Barriers and Maximising Benefits. Berlin, 21–22 November. http://www.grolink.se/Resources/studies/513_Trade_in_Organic_certification_OECD_paper.pdf. Accessed April 2012.

Sela-Sheffy, Rakefet and Miriam Shlesinger, eds. 2011. *Identity and Status in the Translational Professions*. Amsterdam and Philadelphia: John Benjamins.

Service Canada. 2012. *Translators, Terminologists and Interpreters. Analytical text*. http://www.servicecanada.gc.ca/eng/qc/job_futures/statistics/5125.shtml. Accessed 13 February 2012.

Setton, Robin and Alice Guo Liangliang. 2011. "Attitudes to Role, Status and Professional Identity in Interpreters and Translators with Chinese in Shanghai and Taipei". In Rakefet Sela-Sheffy and Miriam Shlesinger (eds), *Identity and Status in the Translational* Professions, 89–118. Amsterdam and Philadelphia: John Benjamins.

Société Française des Traducteurs (SFT). 2010. *Enquête tarifs traducteurs 2009*. http://www.sft.fr/clients/sft/telechargements/file_front/4c45ab788dee5.pdf. Accessed November 2011.

Spence, A. Michael. 1973. "Job Market Signalling". *Quarterly Journal of Economics* 87: 355–74.

Stejskal, Jiri. 2001a. "International Certification Study: Accreditation Program in Brazil". *ATA Chronicle* (July). http://www.cetra.com/uploads/Files/2001-07.pdf. Accessed August 2013.

———. 2001b. "International Certification Study: Accreditation by the South African Translators' Institute". *ATA Chronicle* (August). http://www.cetra.com/uploads/Files/2001-08.pdf. Accessed August 2013.

———. 2001c. "International Certification Study: Non-Degree Professional Certificates for Arabic". *ATA Chronicle* (September). http://www.cetra.com/uploads/Files/2001-09.pdf. Accessed August 2013.

———. 2001d. "International Certification Study: Accreditation in Australia". *ATA Chronicle* (October). http://www.cetra.com/uploads/Files/2001-10.pdf. Accessed August 2013.

———. 2001e. "International Certification Study: Czech Republic". *ATA Chronicle* (November/December). http://www.cetra.com/uploads/Files/2001-11&12.pdf. Accessed August 2013.

———. 2002a. "International Certification Study: OTTIAQ". *ATA Chronicle*. January. http://www.cetra.com/uploads/Files/2002-01.pdf. Accessed August 2013.

———. 2002b. "International Certification Study: Finland and Sweden". *ATA Chronicle* (February). http://www.cetra.com/uploads/Files/2002-02.pdf. Accessed August 2013.

_____. 2002c. "International Certification Study: Canada Revisited". *ATA Chronicle* (March). http://www.cetra.com/uploads/Files/2002-03.pdf. Accessed August 2013.

_____. 2002d. "International Certification Study: Austria". *ATA Chronicle* (April). http://www.cetra.com/uploads/Files/2002-04.pdf. Accessed August 2013.

_____. 2002e. "International Certification Study: U.K. and Ireland". *ATA Chronicle* (May). http://www.cetra.com/uploads/Files/2002-05.pdf. Accessed August 2013.

_____. 2002f. "International Certification Study: Argentina". *ATA Chronicle* (June). http://www.cetra.com/uploads/Files/2002-06.pdf. Accessed August 2013.

_____. 2002g. "International Certification Study: Norway". *ATA Chronicle* (July). http://www.cetra.com/uploads/Files/2002-07.pdf. Accessed August 2013.

_____. 2002h. "International Certification Study: Denmark". *ATA Chronicle* (August). http://www.cetra.com/uploads/Files/2002-08.pdf. Accessed August 2013.

_____. 2002i. "International Certification Study: Japan". *ATA Chronicle* (September). http://www.cetra.com/uploads/Files/2002-09.pdf. Accessed August 2013.

_____. 2002j. "International Certification Study: Spain and Portugal". *ATA Chronicle* (October). http://www.cetra.com/uploads/Files/2002-10.pdf. Accessed August 2013.

_____. 2002k. "International Certification Study: Ukraine". *ATA Chronicle* (November/December). http://www.cetra.com/uploads/Files/2002-11&12.pdf. Accessed August 2013.

_____. 2003a. "International Certification Study: Germany" *ATA Chronicle* (January). http://www.cetra.com/uploads/Files/2003-01.pdf. Accessed August 2013.

_____. 2003b. "International Certification Study: ATA's Credential". *ATA Chronicle* 22 (7): 13–16. http://www.atanet.org/certification/article_stejskal.php. Accessed July 2011.

_____. 2003c. "International Certification Study: South America Revisited" *ATA Chronicle* (March). http://www.cetra.com/uploads/Files/2003-03.pdf. Accessed August 2013.

_____. 2003d. "International Certification Study: Belgium and the Netherlands" *ATA Chronicle* (April). http://www.cetra.com/uploads/Files/2003-04.pdf. Accessed August 2013.

_____. 2003e. "International Certification Study: The Arab Countries" *ATA Chronicle* (May). http://www.cetra.com/uploads/Files/2003-05.pdf. Accessed August 2013.

_____. 2003f. "International Certification Study: The United States" *ATA Chronicle* (June). http://www.cetra.com/uploads/Files/2003-06.pdf. Accessed August 2013.

_____. 2003g. "International Certification Study: ATA's Credential". *ATA Chronicle* 22(7): 13–16. http://www.atanet.org/certification/article_stejskal.php. Accessed July 2011.

_____. 2003h. "Lessons Learned" *ATA Chronicle* (August) http://www.cetra.com/uploads/Files/2003-08.pdf. Accessed August 2013.

_____. 2003i. *International Certification Study*. Alexandria, VA: American Translators Association.

_____. 2004. "Certification of Translators and Interpreters: Seminars on Standards and Certifications in the T&I Industry". http://www.jtpunion.org/historie/certif.ppt. Accessed July 2011.

_____. 2005. *Survey of the FIT Committee for Information on the Status of the Translation & Interpretation Profession*. Fédération Internationale des Traducteurs. http://www.cetra.com/uploads/Files/FIT_Report.pdf. Accessed August 2013.

Stiglitz, Joseph. 1975. "The Theory of 'Screening', Education, and the Distribution of Income". *American Economic Review* 65: 283–300.

Toudic, Daniel. 2012. "Employer Consultation Synthesis Report". OPTIMALE Academic Network Project on Translator Education and Training, Université Rennes 2, Rennes. http://www.translator-training.eu.

Tseng, Joseph. 1992. *Interpreting as an Emerging Profession in Taiwan – A Sociological Model*. MA thesis, Fu Jen Catholic University. Taipei, Taiwan. http://isg.urv.es/publicity/isg/projects/2011_DGT/references/1992_Tseng.pdf. Accessed April 2012.

United States Department of Labor. 2010. *Occupational Outlook Handbook, 2010–11 Edition. Interpreters and Translators*. http://www.bls.gov/oco/ocos175.htm. Last modified 21 July 2010.

United States National Center for Education. 1997. *Teacher Professionalization and Teacher Commitment: A Multi-Level Analysis*. Washington, DC: US Department of Education.

Vaillancourt, François. 1996. "Language and Socioeconomic Status in Quebec: Measurement, Findings, Determinants, and Policy Costs". *International Journal of the Sociology of Language* 121: 69–92.

Vaillancourt, François and Olivier Coche. 2009. *Official Language Policies at the Federal Level in Canada: Costs and Benefits in 2006*. Fraser Institute. http://www.fraserinstitute.org/researchandpublications/publications/6667.aspx. Accessed April 2012.

Vaillancourt, François, Dominique Lemay and Luc Vaillancourt. 2007. "Laggards No More: The Changed Socioeconomic Status of Francophones in Quebec". *C.D. Howe Institute Backgrounder* 103.

Vaillancourt, François, Olivier Coche, Marc Antoine Cadieux and Jamie Lee Ronson. 2012. *Official Language Policies of the Canadian Provinces. Costs and Benefits in 2006*. Fraser Institute. http://www.fraserinstitute.org/uploadedFiles/fraser-ca/Content/research-news/research/publications/official-language-policies-of-canadian-provinces.pdf. Accessed April 2012.

Valverde, Estela. 1990. *Language for Export. A Study of the Use of Language and Language Related Skills in Australian Export Companies*. Canberra: Office of Multicultural Affairs, Department of the Prime Minister and Cabinet.

Venuti, Lawrence. 1995. *The Translator's Invisibility. A History of Translation*. London and New York: Routledge.

Vigier Moreno, Francisco Javier. 2010. "El nombramiento de Traductores-Intérpretes Jurados de inglés mediante acreditación académica". PhD thesis, Universidad de Gradada, Departamento de Traducción e Interpretación.

Vorstermans, Louis. 2010. "Green Paper on Elementary Strategic Issues for AUSIT". 28 July. http://www.ausit.org/page/essays_and_articles.html.

Wilensky, Harold L. 1964. "The Professionalization of Everyone?" *American Journal of Sociology* 70 (2): 137–58.

Wilss, Wolfram. 1999. *Translation and Interpreting in the 20th Century: Focus on German*. Amsterdam and New York: John Benjamins.

Witter-Merithew, Anna and Leilani Johnson. 2004. "Market Disorder within the Field of Sign Language Interpreting: Professionalization Implications". *Journal of Interpretation* 19–55.

Wolf, Michaela and Alexandra Fukari, eds. 2007. *Constructing a Sociology of Translation*. Amsterdam and Philadelphia: Benjamins.

Wooten, Adam. 2009. "What is the Total Number of Translators and Interpreters in the World?" http://tandibusiness.blogspot.com/2008/02/what-is-total-number-of-translators-and.html. Accessed October 2011.

Yılmaz Gümüş, Volga. 2012. "Translator Training and the Translation Market. A Survey of Academics and Professionals in Turkey". Draft PhD project. Tarragona: Intercultural Studies Group, Universitat Rovira i Virgili.

ACKNOWLEDGEMENTS

We are extremely grateful to Harro Glastra of the Directorate-General for Translation for his guidance and patience throughout this research.

We are especially thankful to those who have given permission to draw on and reproduce results of previous studies: Jiri Stejskal, now with the FIT, for his vast pioneering study of the field; Andrew Evans, FIT treasurer, for data on memberships of associations (Appendix A); Erik Hertog, of EULITA, for information on the regulation of legal translators (Figure 2); Elma Mingli Ju for her extension of Tseng's model (Figure 7); Daniel Toudic, of the Optimale project, for data on employers of translators (Figure 8); and Anne-Marie Robert, vice president of the Société Française des Traducteurs, for the raw data from their 2009 survey (analysed in Tables 6, 7, and 8).

We would like to extend our very sincere thanks to all the following translators, academics, and administrators who have assisted us with our survey:

Alvstad, Cecilia, PhD, University of Oslo
Amalaine Diabova, chair, JTP
Arnall, Annamaria, acting president, AUSIT
Aulenback, Joyce, administrative assistant, ATIA
Aymerich, Neus, ATRAE
Bacak, Walter, CAE, executive director, American Translators Association
Balci, Alev, Dokuz Eylül University, Turkey
Baloti, Kirstine, Dansk Journalistforbund
Bargan, Oana, certified translator, Romania
Bertholet, Catherine, executive director, Association of Translators and Interpreters of Ontario
Biel, Łucja, University of Gdansk
Boucher, Johanne, directrice générale/executive director, Ordre des traducteurs, terminologies et interprètes agréés du Québec
Brunke, Anne, Associação Portuguesa de Tradutores e Intérpretes Jurídicos
Caciagli, Flavia, ASSITIG, Italy
Caldera, Simona, board member, Assointerpreti, Italy
Chesterman, Andrew, professor, University of Helsinki
Cobliş, Cristiana, president, Romanian Translators' Association
Cormier, Faith J., certified translator, NB Translation
Cruz, Dora Saenger da, Cruz Communications GmbH, University of Vienna

Dam, Helle V., professor, Aarhus University, Denmark
Dejica, Daniel, PhD, Politehnica University of Timisoara, Romania
Diabova, Amalaine, president, JTP, Czech Republic
Dion, Yves, coordinator, Literary Translators' Association of Canada
Djovčoš, Martin, PhD, Matej Bel University, Banská Bystrica, Slovakia
Durban, Chris, director of translation company, Paris
Dyson, Stephen, professional translator, Lisbon
Esselink, Bert, Lionbridge, Amsterdam
Evans, Andrew, treasurer, FIT
Fernández Costales, Alberto, Universidad de Oviedo
Ferreira-Alves, Fernando, PhD, Universidade do Minho, vice president, Conselho Nacional de Tradução
Foote, Robert, manager of accreditation, NAATI
Fortin, Joe, Dutch Association of Writers and Translators
Fraser, Janet, University of Westminster, Chartered Institute of Linguists, Institute of Translation and Interpreting (Admissions Committee, Fellowship Committee)
García, Ignacio, PhD, University of Western Sydney
Geus, Marcus de, VZV Netherlands
Ghivirigă, Teodora, Al. I. Cuza University of Iasi
Gorgolová, Eva, chair, Chamber of the Court Appointed Interpreters and Translators of the Czech Republic
Greere, Anca, PhD, Babeş-Bolyai University of Cluj Napoca, Romania
Griessner, Florika, Karl-Franzens-Universität Graz, Universitas member
Hernández, Nuria, APTIJ Secretariat
Hertog, Erik, Lessius Hogeschool, Antwerp
Hinchliffe, Inga-Beth, SFÖ, Swedish Authors' Union, Institute of Translation and Interpreting
Horváth, Péter Iván, Hungary
Iliescu Gheorghiu, Catalina, PhD, Universitat d'Alacant, Spain
Jettmarová, Zuzana, PhD, Charles University, Prague
Johnsen, Åse, University of Bergen
Katschinka, Liese, President EULITA
Kierzkowska, Danuta, President, TEPIS
Kolb, Waltraud, University of Vienna
Kourouni, Kyriaki, Aristotle University
Leal, Alice, PhD, University of Vienna
Liu, Fung-ming Christy, Hong Kong
Lundbo, Thomas, vice chair, Norwegian Association of Literary Translators
MacArthur, Ian, treasurer FAT, Sweden
Macovei, Stefan, vice president, UNTAR, Romania
Mallia, Janet, translator, Malta
Maskaliuniene, Nijole, head of the Department of Translation and Interpretation Studies, Vilnius University
Massey, Gary, Zurich University of Applied Sciences

McGilvray, Barbara, NAATI Professional Reference Group, AUSIT National Council, Australia
McMahon, Melissa, NAATI-accredited translator, AUSIT member
Melby, Alan K., PhD, professor of linguistics, Brigham Young University; board of directors, ATA; chair, TISAC
Metsis, Toomas, ETTL, Estonia
Metzger, Michael, American Translators Association
Mikkelson, Holly M., Monterey Institute of International Studies
Mikutyte, Jurgita, president, Lithuanian Association of Literary Translators
Mullamaa, Kristina, PhD, University of Tartu
Nelson, Brian, PhD, professor of French Studies, Monash University, Melbourne; president, Australian Association for Literary Translation
Nielsen, Jørgen Christian Wind, Forbundet Kommunikation og Sprog
Nikolic, Kristijian, Association of Croatian Audiovisual Translators
Nunn, Angela, registration manager, National Registers of Communication Professionals working with Deaf and Deafblind People
Ozkaya Saltoglu, Esra, İstanbul University
Paloposki, Outi, professor, Department of English (Translation and Interpreting), University of Turku
Pappel, Triin, Estonian Association of Master's in Conference Interpreting and Translation
Pavlovic, Natasa, PhD, University of Zagreb, Croatia
Phelan, Mary, ITIA, Ireland
Pilottou, Anastasia, PanUTI
Pöchhacker, Franz, PhD, University of Vienna
Pokorn, Nike K., PhD, University of Ljublana
Polanskis, Sergejs, Latvia
Robert, Anne-Marie, vice president, SFT
Roggen, Rita, for Agnès Feltkamp, president of the Belgian Chamber of Translators and Interpreters
Rognlien, Jon, Norwegian translator, journalist and literary critic
Sakellis, Sophia, director, Delphi Translations, Australia; NAATI-accredited professional translator, member of AUSIT
Salce, Chiara, MIIS
Salmi, Leena, Lecturer, University of Turku, Finland
Santamaría, Arturo Peral, Secretaría de ACE TRADUCTORES
Schreiber, Michael, professor, University of Mainz at Germersheim
Schwartz, Ros, Translators' Association of the Society of Authors, chair of English PEN's Writers in Translation Programme
Sengo, Susana Valdez, Universidade Nova de Lisboa
Sharma, Rannheid, Chartered Institute of Linguists (trustee, Educational Trust)
Shields, Dee, executive committee member, Danske Translatører
Somló, Ágnes, Pázmány Péter Catholic University
Springer, Christine, president, ÖVGD

Stejskal, Jiri, PhD, FIT, director of translation company
Stolze, Radegundis, PhD, Diplom-Übersetzerin, BDÜ, Germany
Teresa Intrieri, SFT, expert près la Cour d'Appel de Nîmes
Tokić, Marijan, HDZTP, Croatia
Vecchione, Flavia, ANTIMI, Italy
Verberk, Susanne, translator, director of Nevero audiovisual translation company, Brussels
Way, Catherine, PhD, Universidad de Granada
Whittaker, Sunniva, NHH-Norwegian School of Economics

NOTES ON THE RESEARCH TEAM

Anthony Pym
Professor of Translation and Intercultural Studies and coordinator of the Intercultural Studies Group at the Rovira i Virgili University in Tarragona, Spain. He runs a doctoral programme in Translation and Intercultural Studies. He is also president and fellow of the Catalan Institution for Research and Advanced Studies, and visiting researcher at the Monterey Institute of International Studies. He is a Harvard alumnus.

François Grin
Professor of Economics at the Faculty of Translation and Interpreting of the University of Geneva. François Grin received a PhD in Economics from the University of Geneva and worked at the University of Montreal and the University of Washington. From 1998 to 2001, he was the deputy director of the European Centre for Minority Issues (ECMI) in Flensburg, Germany. He heads the "Observatoire Économie-Langues-Formation" at the University of Geneva.

Claudio Sfreddo
PhD in Political Economy and a diploma in Economics and Finance from the University of Geneva, as well as a Bachelor's in Business Management from the University of Lausanne. After a year as visiting researcher at Simon Fraser University in Vancouver, Canada, Dr Sfreddo worked for several years as an adjunct faculty member at the University of Geneva while continuing his research activities. He also undertook a consulting mission in Tadjikistan for the World Bank. He has been a faculty member at EHL in Lausanne since 2003.

Andy Lung Jan Chan
PhD in Translation and Intercultural Studies from the Rovira i Virgili University in Tarragona, Spain as well as a Master's in Economics from the University of Virginia, USA. His doctoral dissertation looks into how the theoretical framework of information economics can be used to analyse the translation profession. He currently teaches translation theory and practice at the City University of Hong Kong.

Carlos Teixeira
Carlos da Silva Cardoso Teixeira has BAs in Electrical Engineering (1996) and Linguistics (1998) from the University of Campinas (Unicamp), SP, Brazil, and a Master's in Translation and Intercultural Studies (2011) from the Universitat Rovira i Virgili (URV). He was a full-time freelance translator from 2000 to 2011, specialising in localisation and technical translation. His main field of interest for doctoral research is translation technology, especially the interaction between translators and tools, and the human aspects of technology.

Ricardo Arthur
Ricardo holds a BA in French Studies and Spanish Studies from Concordia University in Montréal, Québec, Canada. He was a full time proofreader in 2008 and 2009, and is currently pursuing a Master's degree at Universitat Rovira i Virgili in Tarragona, Spain.

www.ingramcontent.com/pod-product-compliance
Lightning Source LLC
Chambersburg PA
CBHW021830300426
44114CB00009BA/387